AF361497

WRITING CONSCIENCE AND THE NATION
IN REVOLUTIONARY ENGLAND

Writing Conscience and the Nation in Revolutionary England

Giuseppina Iacono Lobo

UNIVERSITY OF TORONTO PRESS
Toronto Buffalo London

ISBN 978-1-4875-0120-4 (cloth)

Library and Archives Canada Cataloguing in Publication

Iacono Lobo, Giuseppina, 1980–, author
Writing conscience and the nation in revolutionary
England / Giuseppina Iacono Lobo.

Includes bibliographical references and index.
ISBN 978-1-4875-0120-4 (cloth)

1. English literature – Early modern, 1500–1700 – History and criticism.
2. Revolutionary literature, English – History and criticism.
3. Conscience in literature. 4. Great Britain – History – Puritan Revolution,
1642–1660 – Literature and the revolution. I. Title.

PR435.L63 2017   820.9′358   C2017-901749-7

University of Toronto Press acknowledges the financial assistance to its
publishing program of the Canada Council for the Arts and the Ontario Arts
Council, an agency of the Government of Ontario.

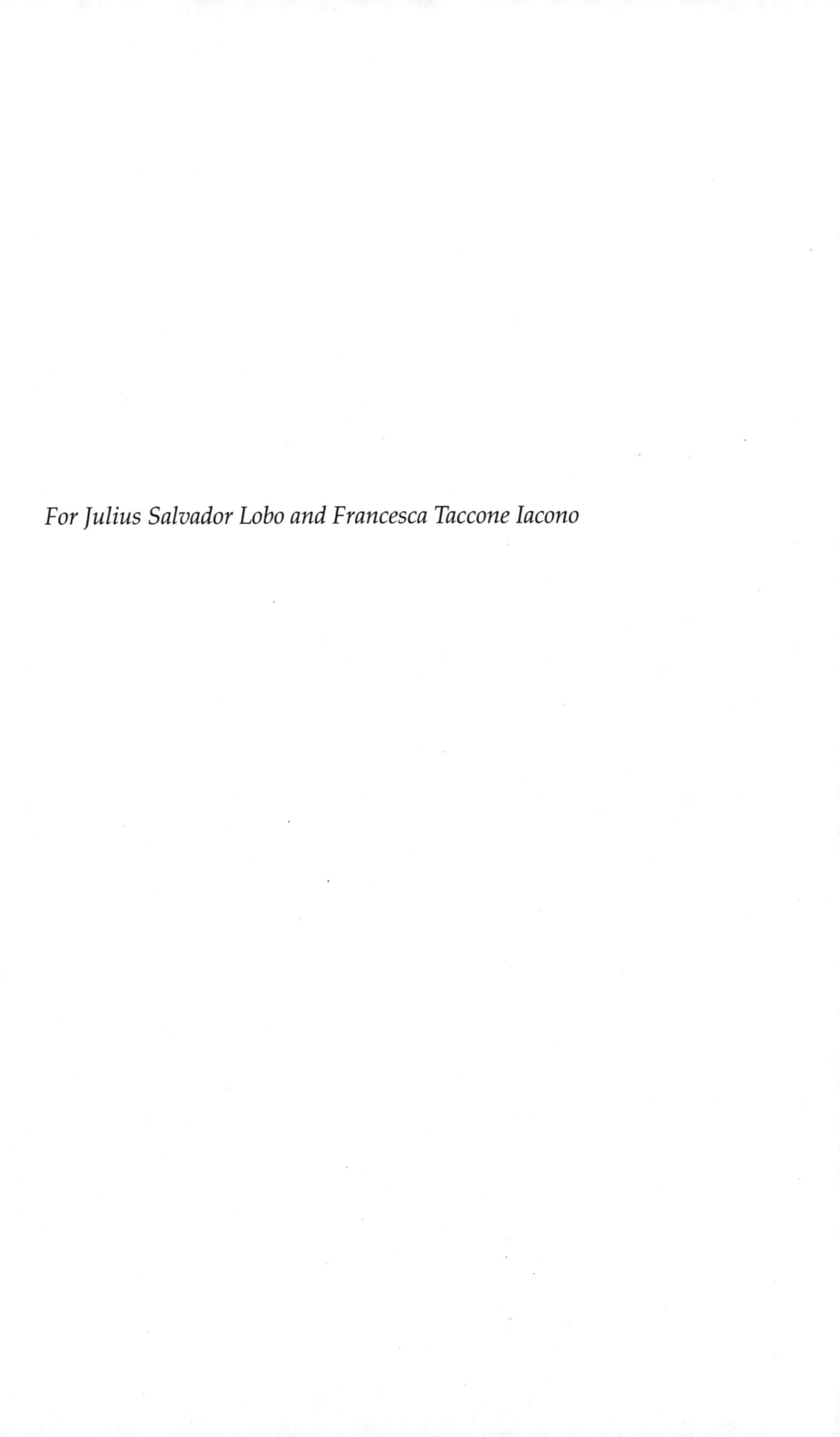

For Julius Salvador Lobo and Francesca Taccone Iacono

What more binding then Conscience?
John Milton, *Of Reformation* (1641)

Contents

Illustrations

Acknowledgments

The debts I accumulated while working on this book over the last eight years are many. I am grateful to Patrick Cheney, Katharine Cleland, Ryan Croft, Clement Hawes, Nicole Jacobs, Anthony Gregg Roeber, Lindsay Simon-Jones, Niamh O'Leary, Chad Schrock, Paul Dustin Stegner, Garrett Sullivan, Jr., Catherine Thomas, and Linda Woodbridge for their guidance, interest, and advice while this project was still in its infancy. And a very special thanks to Ryan Hackenbracht for his insight on Hobbes and Milton and for his enduring friendship.

I cannot even begin to express my gratitude to Laura Lunger Knoppers. She first inspired my passion for the English Revolution and its writers, and has since remained a very model of scholarship, collegiality, and professionalism. I can always count on her for a good laugh too.

Many others offered helpful comments at critical junctures of this book's development. Paul Strohm's Folger Seminar on conscience in 2010 was an invaluable experience, and I am grateful to him and my fellow seminarians. Daniel Shore, Noël Sugimura, and the other participants in the Georgetown Seventeenth-Century English Literature Colloquium offered helpful advice on the Hobbes chapter.

Warm thanks to my colleagues at Loyola University Maryland for their guidance and support, especially Jean Lee Cole, Melissa Girard, Daniel Mangiavellano, Gayla McGlamery, Nicholas Miller, Robert Miola, Brian Norman, and Mark Osteen. I was very fortunate to have a number of talented students in my fall 2015 seminar at Loyola, "Books of Conscience," who gave me a new lens through which to view this topic.

I am also indebted to Gregory Colón Semenza, my undergraduate advisor, who has reminded me time and again why I love this line of work, its rewards and challenges.

I am grateful for funding that I received from Penn State's Rock Ethics Institute and College of the Liberal Arts and from Loyola University Maryland's Center for the Humanities, Office of Research and Sponsored Programs, Summer Research Grant Program, and Dean's Fund. I owe a special thanks to the Folger Institute for grants to support my travel to seminars in 2008–2009 and 2010, both of which were invaluable to the development and conceptualization of this book. Many thanks also to the librarians at the British Library, the Library of the Society of Friends in London, the Nottinghamshire Archives, the Folger Library, and especially the Wren Library at Cambridge for their assistance.

It has truly been a pleasure working with Suzanne Rancourt; I am grateful to her and two very generous readers at the University of Toronto Press for seeing potential in my work and helping to shape the final product.

I would also like to thank my family. My siblings – Mariagrazia, Valentina, Francesco, and Victoria – their spouses and children, and my father, Raffaele, always make visits home a welcome break. Smart, encouraging, and selfless, my mother, Francesca, is my inspiration in many things. My gratitude for her ability always to have the right words to get me back on track knows no bounds. Lorenzo and Lucia, my dear children, were both born while I was still completing this book. I thank them wholeheartedly for showing me every day how marvellous life can truly be. Finally, I owe much to my husband, Julius. He has tirelessly engaged in conversations about conscience over the years, readily offering his support, advice, and insight. Without his companionship and confidence in me, none of this would have been possible. It is to him and my mother – my pillars – that I dedicate this book.

WRITING CONSCIENCE AND THE NATION
IN REVOLUTIONARY ENGLAND

Revolutions of Conscience

In their heated correspondence of 1652, Roger Williams and Anne Sadleir exchange both words and books with the hopes of turning each other's conscience back to the "old way." For Sadleir, daughter of Sir Edward Coke, that "old way" is the "old and best religion" of the bygone Church of England, while Williams, a proponent of toleration and founder of Providence, Rhode Island, proposes a new-old way, "wch is a New Way of Soule Freedome, & yet is ye old Way of Christ Jesus." Along with his first letter to Sadleir, Williams sends a copy of his *Experiments of Spiritual Life & Health* (1652), and he relates how his conscience had been "perswaded ag^st ye Nationall Church" and "beyond ye Conscience of yor deare Father." With her response, Sadleir returns Williams's book unread, confessing that she has "given ouer reading many books" for fear of false prophets. Rather than reading Williams's book or the books of any sectarians, she consults only the scriptures and "the late King's Booke, Hookers Ecclesiastical Politie, Reuerend Bish: Andrews Sermons with his other deuine meditations, Dr Jer. Taylers works, and Dr Tho: Jacksone upon the Creed," all bulwarks of the royally headed Church of England. "These lights," Sadleir avows, "shall be my guide, I wish they may be yours." Williams persists, sending Sadleir copies of his *The Bloody Tenent Yet More Bloody* (1652) and even John Milton's *Eikonoklastes* (1649), both of which she returns unread, calling Williams a "villin" and citing the scriptures in defence of the late King and her conscience.

This fraught exchange captures quite dramatically the contested relationship between conscience, writing, and the nation in revolutionary England. Sadleir's reading list, including *Eikon Basilike* (1649), Jeremy Taylor's casuistries, and even Richard Hooker's *On the Laws of*

Ecclesiastical Politie (1594–97), is composed of books that aim to mitigate the dangerous potential of the individual conscience, suiting it to the demands of a particular national order. Her imagined nation – a nation that could indeed only be *imagined* in 1652 – is one where conscience is instrumental, but only through its obedience to King and Church. Sadleir values these books and the nation they preserve so highly that she returns Williams's volumes unread, for fear that they might pollute her imagination with a recent history she would "fain forget." Yet unable to resist a critique of Williams's books, conscience, and the longed-for nation of free conscience, Sadleir lashes out before retreating back to her own imagination: "I cannot call to mind any blood shed for conscience […] but this I know that since it has bin left to euerie mans conscience to fancie what religion he list, there has more Christian blood been shed then was in the ten persecutians" of the early church. She closes with a warning from Judges 21:25, cautioning Williams that "you know what the scripture saies, that when there was no King in Israell euery man did that which was right in his owne eies but what becam of that the sacred story will tell you." Reducing Williams's conscience to license and consigning his vision of a "holy Nation" to impending destruction, Sadleir signs off, "Your Friend in the Old and Best Way."[1]

Sadleir and Williams are not alone in considering the English Revolution a time when – whether for good or ill – the discourse of conscience radically converged with efforts to reimagine the nation. They are also not alone in their bitter disagreement over the nature, role, and authority of this concept. This book examines how the discourse of conscience emerged as a means of critiquing, discerning, and ultimately reimagining the nation during the English Revolution. Well-known figures such as John Milton, Oliver Cromwell, Margaret Fell Fox, Lucy Hutchinson, and Thomas Hobbes all conceive through conscience radical revisions of the English nation, whether as a republic, an autocracy, the New Israel, or an internalized community of believers. Even the bestselling *Eikon Basilike* (1649), based on Charles I's own writings and published after the regicide, finds in conscience the means to envision a nation loyal to its beheaded king. During this period of unprecedented upheaval, the discourses of conscience and nation converge to inspire revolutionary conceptions of liberty, faith, and national identity.

Literary critics and historians alike have long recognized conscience as central to understanding the religion, politics, and even rhetoric of early modern England.[2] Yet important lacunae remain: in most scholarly studies, the examination of conscience assumes a tangential position in a larger conversation about casuistry, or case-based moral deliberation. While casuistry is an integral part of this complex story, it is only one part. This book thus draws upon the important distinction made by Edward G. Andrew between Hamlet's "cowardly conscience," a conscience focusing on past actions, and Milton's "heroic conscience," an authorizing and forward-looking force.[3] These categories, albeit too simplistic given that even Milton uses both varieties of conscience in *Paradise Lost* and elsewhere, are nevertheless helpful for understanding the complex and often contested nature of conscience. Amid numerous studies on casuistry, these categories also expose the need for critical attention to the heroic, a facet of conscience explored most profoundly in the writing and literature of the English Revolution.

This book thus addresses gaps in literary, political, and religious history by showing how the language of conscience made a significant contribution to the radical ferment of thought and writing in the mid-seventeenth century. Bringing together poetry, polemical pamphlets, manuscript and printed letters, speeches, engravings, biography, political philosophy, and even contemporary marginalia, my study offers a new and historically based narrative of the central role of conscience during this unprecedented moment in English history. Such a study brings little-known materials to scholarly light and offers new readings of more canonical authors. Most importantly, it demonstrates how the conundrums, dictates, and liberties of conscience are a major part of what made this period and the writing it produced so rich, vibrant, and genuinely revolutionary.

The term "conscience" comes from the Latin verb *conscire*, meaning "to know with." This idea of a shared knowledge places conscience in a liminal space between interior and exterior, private and public. It also uniquely equips conscience with the potential to forge dynamic connections between the self and nation, a potential only amplified by the surge in writing on conscience in the mid-seventeenth century. Although scholars have noted the language of conscience in some of the figures examined in this book, such isolated treatments fail to recognize these individuals as participating in a larger cultural discourse at the heart of which is a revolution of conscience itself. More importantly, they also neglect what characterizes that revolution: a distinct and radical connection between conscience and the nation as writers struggle to redefine, reimagine, and even render anew what it means *to know with* as an English people. Despite the enduring differences between figures such as Fell Fox and Hutchinson, or Milton and Hobbes, they all believed conscience to be the bedrock of the nation as they imagined it. And many of those imagined nations were produced over and against one another, whether explicitly or ideologically, making the language of conscience both spirited and contested.

Conscience thus provides a new lens through which to view nationhood and national identity in early modern England. A host of literary critics have long since challenged the modernist view of nationhood, which locates the emergence of a national consciousness in the late eighteenth century.[4] Their important work applies Benedict Anderson's seminal definition of the nation as an "imagined political community" to the world of early modern literature, examining expressions of a national consciousness in Elizabethan and Jacobean writing.[5] More recently, critics have begun to address the dearth of scholarship treating Milton's conceptions of the English nation, a neglect that has occurred not because, as David Loewenstein and Paul Stevens argue, scholars "have denied Milton's imaginative investment in or identification with the nation," but rather "because they tend to take it for granted."[6] This gap still remains regarding the English Revolution more largely, a period whose political, religious, and social upheavals raised urgent questions about England's national identity.

As will be discussed further, the discourse of conscience converged with that of the nation dramatically during the English Reformation, a movement initiated by King Henry VIII's alleged scruple of conscience. From that moment forward, the language of conscience played an influential role in shaping national identity through a bevy of competing discourses: Protestant and Catholic, lay and ecclesiastical, monarchical and dissenting. The execution of Charles I in January 1649 brought about a radical rethinking of the relationship between conscience and the nation. Many supporters of the parliamentary cause saw in this moment the potential for political and ecclesiastical reform, an English nation wrought anew according to conscience and its liberty. In addition, conscience became more than ever an essential component of national identity. Anderson's often-cited definition of the nation includes the idea that such imagined communities are always "conceived as a deep, horizontal comradeship" despite "the actual inequality and exploitation that might prevail in each."[7] Scholars of early modern nationalism have neglected the potential of conscience as an imagined arbiter of this horizontal amity. In *Areopagitica* (1644), Milton imagines a nation united in friendly debate and reform according to free conscience; Hutchinson hopes that her husband's conscience will be a model for her republican readers; and the Quakers maintain that all Englishmen and women are united by the light in their consciences. Such horizontal ties transform conscience – a word whose etymology itself gestures towards community and comradeship – into a national bond, joining believers from within.

Such ties through conscience also transform the meaning of nation. While drawing on Anderson's influential framework, recent scholars have debated precisely how national communities are imagined, what constitutes their core characteristics, and how identity is formed through borders, inclusions, and exclusions.[8] My study will attend throughout, then, to issues of the individual versus the collective conscience as writers navigate how they might come *to know with* others in their imagined communities. Further, how those collectives and communities are imagined will differ from chapter to chapter, ranging from the obedient, to the godly, to the public, to the republic, and even to the disobedient. As such, the link between conscience and the nation revolutionizes not only the former but also the latter, redefining collective identity and constituting one important legacy of the English Revolution.[9]

Finally, this book also sets the English Revolution in a larger historical framework identified as "revolutions of conscience." Since Saint Paul incorporated conscience into the Christian tradition, it has itself endured a series of revolutions – in translation, meaning, usage, authority, and ownership. The revolution treated in this study was still experiencing the aftershocks of a complex history that coincides with critical junctures in the development of Christianity itself. Paul introduced the idea of conscience in order to demarcate the differences between his new faith and Judaism and, more importantly, to "replac[e] ritual observance."[10] In his Letter to the Hebrews, Paul asks, "if the blood of bulls and of goats, and the ashes of an heifer sprinkling the unclean, sanctifieth to the purifying of the flesh: How much more shall the blood of Christ, who through the eternal Spirit offered himself without spot to God, purge your conscience from dead works to serve the living God?" (9:13–14). Martin Luther would later argue that Christ's sacrifice freed conscience from the spiritual burden of Moses's Law so that believers might enjoy the "peace of conscience [...] for indeed peace follows the forgiveness of sins."[11] The word Paul used for conscience, *syneidesis*, was derived from the popular Greek idea of shame or fear in response to one's own past wrongdoings.[12] By incorporating this terminology into Christian belief, Paul transformed this instinctual phenomenon into a response instead to God's wrath, with its chief function being to "*evaluate* actions [...] not to identify and define 'the good' or 'God's will' either concretely or abstractly."[13]

When Jerome translated the Greek New Testament into Latin, he chose the word *conscientia* to express Paul's *syneidesis*, a choice that C.A. Pierce deems "fatal."[14] Whereas the meaning of *syneidesis* was "precise, indeed somewhat narrow," Pierce argues, Jerome's translation changed the idea of conscience into "a conception so broad, vague and form-less as to confuse rather than clarify all ethical discussions from that moment forward."[15] Like conscience, the term *conscientia* is derived from the verb *conscire*. Though the meaning of *conscientia* includes *syn-eidesis*, its definition goes beyond its Greek counterpart, encompassing a much broader and more complex range of use. *Conscientia* can be a joint knowledge, common knowledge, consciousness; it can mean either a good conscience and a sense of right or a feeling of guilt or remorse.[16] What Pierce finds most problematic about this semantic discrepancy is its potential to allow the understanding of conscience to drift from the New Testament's original meaning. Paul's choice of *syneidesis* empha-sized a collective rather than an individual knowledge of God, hence the *syn* in *syneidesis* and the *con* in *conscientia*: "It is as members of the Church and not primarily as individuals that they have a sure knowl-edge of God. This *knowledge* could not have so sufficient a reality as to uphold a man in the face of unjust suffering, were it not fundamentally a *shared knowledge*."[17] This important communal dimension is threat-ened by Jerome's choice of the word *conscientia*, a term that includes even our modern-day conceptions of individual conscience.[18]

Medieval philosophers grappled with this knotty heritage, often treating *conscientia* and *syneidesis* as separate parts of the operation of conscience, a distinction that marks even Protestant casuistries of the sixteenth and seventeenth centuries.[19] While medieval scholastic treat-ments of conscience often disagreed about its nature, origin, and author-ity, they drew from the New Testament's representation of conscience as a shared knowledge rather than individual belief or opinion.[20] Paul Strohm characterizes this period as having a "stabilizing effect" upon conscience because of its union with the Church and its institutional practices and traditions. For this reason, while "medieval conscience retains its capacity to speak within," it "need not in most cases wonder about what to say." Exceptions to this institutionally bound conscience occur in the literature of the period but remain a handful of anomalous references to personal conscience that enter the mainstream discourse only after the Reformation.[21]

Figure 1. Peter Vischer the Younger, "Allegory on the Reformation" (1524). By permission of the Goethe-Nationalmuseum, Klassik Stiftung Weimar.

Martin Luther not only revolutionized the idea of conscience but also brought this concept in all of its complexities to the forefront of the Christian experience. Karl Holl thus calls Luther's religion a "religion of conscience."[22] In his 1524 aquarelle "Allegory on the Reformation," German sculptor and printmaker Peter Vischer the Younger depicts a heroic Luther leading Conscience away from the ruins of the Roman Church and towards Christ (Figure 1). Conscience appears as a young woman whose right wrist is in Luther's grasp, and whose left wrist is manacled to a toddling baby labelled *Jvventvs*, who points towards the artist's signature. Following at her heels is *Plebes*, represented as a man carrying a scythe whose gaze is fixed on Conscience. As he points towards Christ, Luther focuses singularly on Conscience with both his eyes and leading grasp, directing the Commons and the vulnerable Youth through his guidance of Conscience. This dramatic allegory casts

Luther as a hero of Conscience, one whose struggles for her liberty are surpassed only by the work of Christ himself.

This visual depiction also captures with stunning accuracy the crux of Luther's revolution: by leading Conscience away from the Church, a "veritable torture chamber of consciences," Luther displaces this institutional authority with that of the living Word, Conscience's only source of peace and certainty. In Luther's own writings, this supplanting transforms conscience into a theatre in which the drama of Christian salvation is played out in miniature. At times, Luther represents conscience as an accuser, inspiring terror in the sinful; more often, however, conscience itself quakes at the Law, and it is for the freedom of conscience that Christ died. More importantly, it is within conscience that the faithful experience the fruits of Christ's sacrifice while still in the flesh. Though the flesh is still subject to the Law, and thus clings to sin, "conscience remains unmoved; for it has in view Christ the crucified, who abolished all the claims of the Law upon the conscience." And, in order to hearten the conscience against the sinful flesh, Christ replays his first coming daily for the conscience, so that it might "tak[e] hold of Christ more perfectly day by day; and day by day the law of flesh and sin, the fear of death, and whatever other evil the Law brings with it are diminishing." For Luther, conscience becomes the house in which Christ dwells, the kingdom in which He reigns, and even His bride.[23]

Luther's famous declaration at the Diet of Worms in 1521 emblematizes further his revolution of conscience: when asked if he would recant his writings, Luther responded, "my conscience is captive to the Word of God. I cannot and I will not retract anything, since it is neither safe nor right to go against conscience." Johann von Eck, the moderator of the proceedings, implored him, "Lay aside your conscience, Martin; you must lay it aside because it is in error."[24] Strohm argues that, in this moment, Luther was "announcing a new understanding of conscience," a conscience that "may indeed be considered a 'Reformation' conscience."[25] For Luther, this "Reformation conscience" is captive to the Word of God and finds in that Word a shared knowledge reminiscent of the word's etymology. Lodged between conscience and the Word is individual interpretation, a hurdle that Luther believed surmountable because, in his mind, the meaning of scripture was self-evident.[26] Rather than fear subjectivism, he instead held that the faithful embodied this transparent Word, acting as living, breathing manifestations of the gospel.[27] Luther thus inaugurates not only a new understanding of conscience, but also, through that Reformation conscience, a new way of experiencing Christ's sacrifice. More importantly, by replacing the Catholic Church's custody over the individual conscience with the authority of the Bible, he revolutionized both the role and the voice of conscience.

Luther's revolution sent ripples across Europe, not least in England, where his "religion of conscience" inspired yet another revolution. King Henry VIII and his successors found in the Reformation conscience both a new system of faith and a new national identity: one that was distinctly English and fundamentally vexed. They also assumed a national role for the royal conscience, a privileged position that threatened to extend – and in some cases did extend – their jurisdiction into the most private sanctum of their subjects' identities. The struggles over this concept that plagued the Tudor and Stuart reigns laid the foundation for the radical connections between conscience and the nation during the English Revolution.

Henry first publicly raised the matter of his "scrupulous conscience" in 1528, in a speech before the lord mayor, aldermen of London, and members of the nobility. Seeking to remedy "the pangs that trouble my conscience," the King shared his growing concerns that his marriage to Catherine of Aragon, his brother's widow, was a breach of God's law.[28] Like Luther, Henry similarly relied on the Bible to legitimize his scrupulous conscience, yet he also looked first to the counsel of the pope, and then to that of the "greatest clerks in Christendom" for the "discharge of our conscience and saving of our soul."[29] The peace of the King's conscience thus rested upon a shared understanding – or the attempt to carve out a shared understanding – of God's Word upon the matter of his marriage. Writing to Clement VII in 1530, Henry questioned the pope's judgment upon his marriage for lack of consensus: whereas the King "did consult and take the advice of every learned man," the pope depended upon "those few men of yours" to "affirm the prohibition of our marriage."[30] In *The Determinations of the Moste Famous and Mooste Excellent Vniuersities of Italy and Fraunce* (1531), a book amassing support for the King's cause, Henry's supporters similarly created a universal conscience that fell outside of the purview of the Catholic Church, the conscience of Christendom.

Henry's belief that his conscience was authorized by the consensus of Christendom did not go unchallenged. Sir Thomas More made the same claim in his refusal to take the Oath of Supremacy "for the grudge of my conscience," instead casting England as singular.[31] In a letter to his daughter dated 17 April 1533, More related how William Benson, the dean of Westminster, cautioned him that "I had cause to feare that mine owne minde was erronious, when I see the great counsail of the realme determine of my mynde the contrary, and that therefore I ought to chaunge my conscience." He continued,

> To that I answered, that if there were no mo but my self vpon my side, and the whole Parlement vpon tother, I wolde be sore afraide to lene to mine owne mynde only against so many. But on the other side, if it so be, that in some thinges for which I refuse the oth, I haue (as I thinke I haue) vpon my parte as great a counsail and a greater to, I am not than bounden to change my conscience, and conferme it to the counsail of one realme, against the generall counsail of Christendome.[32]

Despite his resistance to the King's headship of the Church of England, More nevertheless found in Henry's revolution of conscience a language of self-defence.[33] When faced with the scruples or grudges of their consciences, both Henry and More grounded their interior surety upon the exterior consensus of what they perceived as Christendom.

While the King's dependence upon authorities other than the Word of God to ground his conscience distinguishes his revolution from Luther's, Henry nevertheless changed forever the relationship between conscience and the English nation with his split from Rome. The Act of Supremacy that was passed in November 1534, declaring Henry and his heirs the supreme head of the Church of England, displaced the pope's authority not only over the Church but also over the consciences of Englishmen and women. Henry had expressed this sentiment in *The King's Proclamation for the Abolishing of the Usurped Power of the Pope*, issued earlier that year, when he presumed to know "right well what great rest, quietness, and tranquillity of conscience" would result if "the clergy of this our realm should set forth, declare, and preach unto [the people] the true and sincere word of God."[34]

The title page of the Great Bible (1539), the first authorized translation into English, similarly casts the King in a custodial role over his subjects' consciences (Figure 2). If the Word of God is the source of peace for conscience, this elaborate woodcut represents Henry as the conduit of that Word. Christ is pictured in the top centre of the woodcut, arms outstretched over the head of an enthroned Henry, with his right hand pointing towards a second image of the King, who kneels with his crown set on the ground before him. On the right banner, Christ declares (from Acts 13:22), "I have found a man after my own

Figure 2. Title page of the Great Bible (1539). By permission of the Rare Books and Manuscript Library of the Ohio State University Libraries.

heart, which shall fulfil all my will," and Henry responds (from Psalms 119:105), "Thy word is a lamp unto my feet." The largest figure in the woodcut is the enthroned Henry, seated just above the title plaque, who declares a modification of Daniel 6:26: "I make a decree, That in every dominion of my kingdom men tremble and fear before the living God." In both of his hands he holds copies of the *verbum dei*, which he passes to Thomas Cranmer on his left and Thomas Cromwell on his right. These two figures then are pictured again below, handing copies of the *verbum dei* to the clergy and laity, while the bottom of the woodcut is populated with numerous subjects, some seated before a preacher, others standing, and still others looking out from within a gaol. Banners are dispersed throughout the crowd, announcing the people's declarations, "Vivat Rex" and "God save the King."[35]

What is perhaps most striking about this woodcut is Henry's absolute authority over the English Bible. The *verbum dei*'s journey down the page ends just before reaching the people, who only receive it through listening. This passive reception is indicated in a draft of the royal proclamation on the reading of the Bible when Henry mandates that his subjects who have questions about the meaning of scripture "not gev[e] to moche to [their] owne mynde," but rather seek the guidance of "suche lerned menne as be or shalbe auctorised to preache and declare" the Word.[36] Individual interpretations should always give way, in other words, to the reading authorized by the King through his clergy. Marking this connection between the King and God's Word, as Lacey Baldwin Smith notes, the subjects below "dutifully sing, not God's praise, but 'Vivat Rex.'"[37] In this way, the English people experience biblically inspired "great rest, quietness, and tranquillity of conscience" only in relation to their sovereign king. Nation and conscience are inextricably intertwined.

Henry VIII's attempt to extend his power over the consciences of his subjects was made most apparent in the Oath of Supremacy (1534), the very bond that proved fatal for More, Bishop John Fisher, and other conscientious dissenters. While oaths of allegiance were enforced during the reigns of both Henry IV and Henry VI, Henry VIII amended the oath to require that his subjects must "utterly testifie and declare in my Conscience" that the King was the "onely Supreame Governour" in spiritual and temporal matters.[38] Jonathan Michael Gray notes that this oath was designed to "invalidate previous bonds of loyalty to a foreign authority and rebind the consciences of English subjects to Henry and his policies."[39] Such language granted conscience an unprecedented place in the national discourse and created out of it (or so the King hoped) a guarantor of royal power.

Queen Mary too furthered her father's revolution of conscience, with her short reign seeing close to 300 Protestants burned at the stake and over 800 exiles to the continent, all for the sake of their consciences. John Foxe's *Acts and Monuments*, the most influential book in early modern England after the Bible and Book of Common Prayer, transformed a phenomenon born out of Henry VIII's Reformation – conscientious dissent – into an act that was not only distinctly Protestant but also English.[40] Throughout the pages of his tome, Foxe catalogues martyr after martyr who could not reconcile their consciences with the spiritual demands of Mary's administration. John Bradford, a popular English reformer executed on 31 January 1555, is recorded as saying that he would "be glad of the Quenes fauour" only if he might also "liue as a subiecte without clogge of conscience." "But otherwyse," Bradford continues, "the Lordes mercie is better to me then lyfe." Similarly, Laurence Saunders, a minister executed a week later, vowed to live as a "most obedient subiec[t]" if only he may keep his conscience "vnclogged." "Otherwise," he maintained, "I will abide the most extremetie that man may do against me, rather than to do against my conscience."[41] This unfulfilled desire to remain obedient becomes formulaic in *Acts and Monuments*, simultaneously reinforcing and transforming the ties made by Henry VIII between conscience and obedience.

Though each of Foxe's martyrs speaks only for his or her own conscience, the repetitive nature of this exhaustive text creates out of their chorus – and presumably within their readers – a unified English conscience. Foxe presents this composite conscience, prizing God's Word over ecclesiastical tradition and urging the reformation of the Church, as foundational to the national identity he hoped would flourish with Elizabeth's accession. First published in 1563, *Acts and Monuments* went through four editions in Foxe's lifetime, with the second, third, and fourth editions having well over 500 references to conscience. The text was considered sacred by many Protestants, and, as John King notes, it was "frequently chained alongside the Bible for reading by ordinary people at many public places including cathedrals, churches, schools, libraries, guildhalls, and at least one inn."[42] Although Foxe expressed deference to Elizabeth's civil authority in his preface and advocated for a unified Church of England, *Acts and Monuments* provided both precedent and a formula for future dissent if the monarch failed to carry out the reforms sought after by evangelical Protestants. Indeed, the woodcuts featuring William Tyndale, whose last words are "Lord open the Kyng of Englands eyes," and Bradford, who, with his hands pressed together in prayer, calls out "Repent England," must have resonated with Puritan readers dissatisfied with the state of the Church of England.[43] It is also no surprise that the eighth edition was published in 1641 against the backdrop of the Bishops' Wars (the Scots' rebellion against Charles I's attempt to impose a new prayer book), and the executions of Archbishop William Laud and Thomas Wentworth, the Earl of Strafford, who lost their heads in 1645 and 1641 respectively.[44]

In 1559, Foxe praises Elizabeth as a "vertuous and long wished for Quene," and thanked God for her "prosperous and luckye coming to the crowne."[45] He and other hopeful Protestants looked to Elizabeth's accession as the end of an era of suffering for the sake of conscience. "For if the Israelites might joy in their Deborah," writes Catharine Bertie, Duchess of Suffolk, to Elizabeth in January 1559, "how much more we English in our Elizabeth, that deliverance of our thralled conscience."[46] Elizabeth encouraged such hopes with immediate open shows of allegiance to the Protestant faith, beginning in 1558 with her defiant departure from a Christmas mass when the host was elevated.[47] Yet expressions of conscientious dissent surged once it became clear that the Queen's settlement of the Church of England would be an impediment to further reformation, the sought-after end of many of Elizabeth's Protestant subjects.[48] More importantly, over the course of her long reign, the Queen and her dissatisfied Protestant subjects both complicated and furthered the revolution of conscience set in motion by her father, continuing the intertwining of nation and conscience.

Edmund Grindal, archbishop of Canterbury, for example, performed one of the most memorable acts of conscientious dissent against Elizabeth with his "book to the queen" in 1576. Elizabeth demanded that he shut down the practice of prophesyings, gatherings of clergy during which several sermons would be delivered on the same passage from the Bible for the edification of all those present. Because he believed these meetings a "necessary institution," Grindal went on to write a lengthy and public rebuke of Elizabeth's efforts.[49] He frames this letter as the discharge of his conscience and as a protection of the Queen's own which would undoubtedly face "heavy burdening" were he to follow her orders. Grindal also cites prophesyings and preaching more generally as the very bedrock of the Queen's rule for their effect upon conscience: "By preaching also due obedience to Christian princes and magistrates is planted in the hearts of subjects: for obedience preceedeth of conscience; conscience is grounded upon the word of God; the word of God worketh its effect by preaching." Grindal concludes, "So as generally, where preaching wanteth obedience faileth." Whereas Elizabeth attached an "anxious importance" to "displays of conscientious assent," Grindal believed conscientious obedience a more organic phenomenon, arising naturally from a well-instructed conscience.[50] The nation Grindal imagined is secured from within, fortified by its clergy's instruction of conscience. Yet his model also set a degree of separation between the Queen and the consciences of her subjects, a space filled by Grindal and his fellow clergy.

In response to threats such as that posed by Grindal, the last decade of Elizabeth's reign was marked by a heightened desire for those "displays of conscientious assent." In a speech before the heads of Oxford on 28 September 1592, the Queen desired that the university's care "be especially to worship God" but "not in the manner of the opinion of all nor according to the over-curious and too-searching wits, but as the divine law commands and our law teaches." She justified this continuity between divine law and her own by assuring her audience that "you do not have a prince who teaches you anything that ought to be contrary to a true Christian conscience." According to this formulation, any conscience whose dictates conflicted with what "our law teaches" was decidedly un-Christian; for this reason, the Queen's edicts should already be in accord with the decrees of her subjects' consciences. This assumption created out of Elizabeth's laws a national conscience, consistent with God's Word and guiding her subjects towards salvation. It also eliminated the possibility of dissent for the sake of conscience, with the consciences of her subjects becoming little more than a reflection of the Queen's law.

King James VI and I continued to cultivate this connection between conscience, obedience, and national identity. More explicitly than his predecessors, James believed in a "'common quality conscience,'" Kevin Sharpe argues, "in which all (himself included) shared, rather than 'distinct individual consciences.'" Yet even in James's own writings, this ideal did not always hold up.[51] Because he believed that the "bond of conscience" was the "only sure bond for tying of men's affections to them whom to they owe a natural duty," James nonetheless sought ways to secure that bond from consciences that might fall outside the purview of his "common quality" construct.[52] This was especially true when considering his Catholic subjects and after the discovery of the Gunpowder Plot of 1605. The Popish Recusants Act, passed soon after this "monstrous, rare, nay neuer heard-of Treacherous attempt," provided a new Oath of Allegiance that was bookended with professions of conscience to the King's civil authority.[53]

In response to King James's attempt to secure "the bond of conscience" from his Catholic subjects, Pope Paul V issued two briefs, the first on 22 September 1606 and the second on 23 August 1607, informing his English followers that they "cannot with safe Conscience take the Oath."[54] James fired back in 1608 with *Triplici nodo, triplex cuneus, or, An Apologie for the Oath of Allegiance*, lambasting the pope for his "prohibition to a Kings Subiects from obedience vnto him in things most lawfull and meere temporall." He assured his Catholic subjects that by issuing the oath, he "intended no persecution against them for conscience cause"; rather, he "onely desired to be secured of them for ciuill obedience, which for conscience cause they were bound to performe." Any Catholics objecting to "so iust a charge" gave him "so great and iust a ground for punishment of them, without touching any matter of conscience."[55] In order to secure the "bond of conscience" from his Catholic subjects, James separated civil acts of conscience from the spiritual. This attempt to bind conscience while not "touching any matter of conscience" shows both the potential and the danger of conscience for the English monarchy.

The King's fear of individual conscience can be seen in his support for a new version of the English Bible, even before he took the crown of England. Writing to his eldest son, Henry, in *Basilicon Doron* (1599), James directs that "yee must onely ground [conscience] vpon the expresse Scripture: for conscience not grounded vpon sure knowledge, is either an ignorant fantasie, or an arrogant vanitie."[56] But the language of conscience found in the current English Bible was, in James's view, dangerous. The Geneva Bible was immensely popular in England since its first complete publication in 1560 because, designed for private study, it was inexpensive and readily available.[57] Yet James thought it "the worst of all" Bible translations, objecting primarily to its annotations that he found to be "very partiall, vntrue, seditious, and sauouring too much of daungerous, and trayterous conceites."[58] When the Hampton Court Conference convened in January 1604, and John Rainolds, president of Corpus Christi College, Oxford, proposed a new translation of the Bible, the newly crowned English King James embraced the idea. One of the rules established early on determined that this authorized version was not to have any "Marginal Notes at all" "but only for the Explanation of the *Hebrew* or *Greek* Words."[59]

More importantly, by excising these annotations, the King James Bible of 1611 had only 54 references to conscience, a far cry from the 182 references in the Geneva Bible of 1587. It seems that the notes James believed contained "daungerous, and trayterous conceites" also housed numerous references to conscience. Over three decades later, William Laud, archbishop of Canterbury, revisited this moment during his trial, recalling James's invective against the Geneva Bible's conscience-laden notes, and insisting that "now of late these notes were more commonly used to ill purposes than formerly."[60] These dangerous annotations often read conscience into verses where the word itself was absent; for example, in the 1560 version, 1 Timothy 2:8 reads, "I wil therefore that the men pray, euerie where lifting vp pure hands without wrath, or douting," and the corresponding note adds, "As testimonies of a pure heart & conscience."

As a result of such notations, then, conscience becomes more present in the text, and a means through which the reader might experience more profoundly the Word of God. Readers missed these notes after 1611: "The people complained that they could not see into the sense of the Scriptures" in the King James version, "so well as formerly they did by the Geneva Bible."[61] Yet by systematically eliminating these extratextual references to the individual conscience, James hoped more easily to fill the role that Henry VIII and Elizabeth assumed: custodian over his subjects' consciences, with his own conscience playing a national role.

With the executioner's fateful stroke on the morning of 30 January 1649, the relationship between conscience and the nation that the Crown had fostered for more than a century underwent yet another revolution. Perhaps even more significant than the execution of King Charles I was the day that he raised his battle standard at Nottingham Castle, 22 August 1642, marking the start of the English Civil Wars. This strife between King and Parliament energized the existing calls for liberty of conscience and inspired talk of a "public conscience," language that Hobbes would further in his *Leviathan*, published nearly a decade later. Though Charles's supporters sought to uphold the connection between conscience and obedience through *Eikon Basilike* (1649), they could not quell the tide of revolutionary reimaginings of the relationship between this still volatile concept and the English nation. Instead, writers and thinkers as different as Hobbes and Milton or Hutchinson and Fell Fox each responded to the upheaval of the civil wars by transforming conscience into an agent of revolution on a national scale.

It is this vibrant, wide, and largely unexplored reimagining of a national conscience that this book will detail and explore. Though organized largely chronologically, the six chapters of this study also at times overlap, revisiting the heady days of the civil wars and moving up to and even beyond the 1660 Restoration of Charles II. The shared timeline of the chapters emphasizes the variable and contested nature of this revolution of conscience. While *Eikon Basilike* encouraged the English nation to recall its conscientious obedience due to the King even in his absence, Milton's *Tenure of Kings and Magistrates* (1649) and *Eikonoklastes* (1649) reimagined the nation on a path towards reformation, guided by free conscience. Similarly, Hobbes's fear-inspired *Leviathan* (1651), a text that at once champions and tries to tame conscience as the linchpin of a peaceful nation, was published as Cromwell defeated Charles II and the Scots at Worcester with the hopes of seeing a godly English people exercising liberty of conscience. And as John Hutchinson recanted his role in the regicide upon Charles II's return, a moment that would fuel his wife's reimagining of the English nation through her husband's republican conscience, the Quakers were reconsidering the borders of the "Holy Nation" that they might finally establish through the light in conscience. Most of these figures, whether Charles I, Milton, Hobbes, Cromwell, or the Quakers, imagined nations not only different from but also in conflict with one another. Even Hutchinson, whose *Memoirs* would remain unpublished during her lifetime, reimagined the English nation over and against what she believed to be Cromwell's betrayal of the Good Old Cause. Yet despite their differences, each of these imagined nations emerge from the same radical ferment: a moment in English history when the questions of nationhood and national identity became most urgent, and a moment when many writers and thinkers found the answers to those questions in conscience.

Chapter 1 of this book focuses on the bestseller *Eikon Basilike* and deepens our understanding of Charles's language of conscience by setting it in the political rather than the private sphere of the mid-seventeenth century. While scholars have examined the language of conscience in *Eikon Basilike*, they have not fully explored the pervasiveness of the language or its crucial work in the political sphere. During the civil war years, the royalist sway over the pulpits waned, depriving the King and his supporters of their most compelling guarantor of the royalist state. The persistent language of conscience in *Eikon Basilike* functioned for the reader as the pulpit would have for the listener: as a call to conscientious obedience. The King's conscience speaks from the grave, ensuring the survival of the royalist cause even in his absence.

While *Eikon Basilike* applies a traditional conception of conscience in a new way, Oliver Cromwell dramatically reconsiders the role conscience might play in buttressing the English nation. Chapter 2 focuses on Cromwell's passionate defence of free conscience in his civil war correspondence, and in his speeches before the Nominated Assembly and First and Second Protectorate Parliaments, while also noting the limits that, in practice, qualified his sense of this liberty. Throughout his public career, Cromwell sought a civil body willing to recognize liberty of conscience as central to the nation's peace and settlement. In this quest, Cromwell defines the free exercise of conscience as a Christian duty incumbent upon each believer rather than a license threatening civil order.

Cromwell's preoccupation with conscience made his own the subject of much scrutiny and even fodder for further revolutions of conscience. Through a focus on Margaret Fell Fox and other Quakers' correspondence with Cromwell, chapter 3 demonstrates how Quakers made (or hoped to make) a more precise political intervention during the Protectorate than scholars have previously recognized. Friends aggressively used the language of conscience to advise, challenge, and reprimand Cromwell in person, in print, and in private correspondence. Bringing new archival materials to an ongoing critical discussion of early Quaker writing, this chapter also shows how Quakers revolutionized the already radical language of conscience by transforming it into a tool through which they expected that Cromwell would shape the nation into the Kingdom of God.

Writing in response to radical sectarian conceptions of conscience, figures such as Thomas Hobbes reconsidered the relationship between conscience and the nation in ways that were both revolutionary and reactionary. Chapter 4 focuses on Hobbes's treatment of a concept set into circulation during the civil wars, the public conscience. Recently, scholars have taken an interest in Hobbes's use of conscience in *Leviathan* (1651), with some focusing on his support of liberty of conscience and others on his construct of the public conscience. The former scholars believe Hobbes a proponent of toleration, the latter a destroyer of subjectivity itself. This chapter puts Hobbes's public and private consciences back into dialogue in order to gain a more holistic sense of the relationship he sets out between conscience and the leviathan. Hobbes imagines public and free forms of conscience that do not compete with one another but rather perform the same function, though in different capacities. Hobbes's conscience, whether public, free, in the condition of war, or in the commonwealth, is a civilizing force, inclining individuals in the state of war towards peace and concord and sustaining the commonwealth from within.

The revolutions of conscience that mark these turbulent years bleed into the Restoration as writers like Lucy Hutchinson use this concept with the hopes of reigniting the nation's desire for political and spiritual liberty. Chapter 5 uses Colonel John Hutchinson's 1660 retraction of his support of the regicide as a lens for reading Lucy Hutchinson's *Memoirs of the Life of Colonel Hutchinson*. More specifically, it focuses on John Hutchinson's use of the word "conscience" in the recantation and on how Lucy Hutchinson uses similar language in the *Memoirs* to recover her husband's reputation as a staunch republican. Drawing on archival materials, this chapter puts Lucy Hutchinson's own source texts over and against her final product in order to demonstrate how she revises her husband's conscience after his death. More importantly, Hutchinson's project is not simply a recovery effort: rather, she sought not only to restore her husband's reputation but also to further the republican cause at a national level through this portrait of his revised conscience.

Chapter 6 glances backward to examine how John Milton revolutionizes conscience and its relationship to free nationhood in response to *Eikon Basilike*, Cromwellian politics, and the republican cause. It also looks forward, capturing how the poet-polemicist's unyielding dedication to conscience and its liberty complicated and, in the post-revolutionary years, even thwarted his sense of national identity. Literary critics have recently taken an interest in Milton's nationalism, yet the role of conscience in this phenomenon remains untreated. This chapter's survey of Milton's wartime, commonwealth, protectoral, and post-revolutionary prose and poetry shows that, as early as 1641, Milton aspired to write an English nation coterminous with his imagined nation of conscience. Milton's revolutionary project begins with the nation he believes to be God's elect and evolves into a nation whose boundaries are determined not by borders but rather by conscientious dissent: a nationhood experienced in and through free conscience itself.

Overall, by moving from Charles I to Cromwell, the Quakers, Hobbes, Lucy Hutchinson, and Milton, and by exploring letters, speeches, works of political theory, and more literary texts, we will see how the English Revolution inspired new ways *to know with*. And, more importantly, we will also see how those new ways *to know with* – with God, with the self, and with others – probed the very potential of conscience, transforming it into a tool for reimagining the English nation.

Their differing views of conscience led Roger Williams and Anne Sadleir, with whose 1652 correspondence we began, on very different paths through the period of the English Revolution. Sadleir continued to use the prayer book during the 1650s despite its proscription, and lived on to see the Cavalier Parliament pass a new Act of Uniformity in 1662.[62] In the meantime, Williams had founded "the most tolerant English society in his time" and continued to advocate for liberty of conscience until his death in 1683.[63] Both figures show the power of conscience and the ways that it impacted and redefined nationhood in revolutionary England: a story that warrants closer examination and to which we now turn.

Chapter One

Charles I, *Eikon Basilike*, and the Pulpit-Work of the King's Conscience

On 29 May 1676, James Duport, dean of Peterborough and college head, delivered a sermon on the anniversary of Charles II's birthday and return to England, asking his congregants, "Is it not strange, that when the Apostle bids us *be subject to the Higher Powers*, and obey lawful Autority *for conscience sake*, any should pretend *conscience* for their disobedience?" Focusing on 1 Peter 2:17, "Fear God. Honour the King," Duport called obedience to the King not merely civil law but also an "act of Religion," rendering it impossible for any man to "truly *fear God*, and not *honour the King*." And, he continued, if any thinks his conscience not in accordance with this due obedience, then his conscience is a "dangerous thing" that must be rectified by "distrust[ing] his own judgment" and accepting the "judgments of so many wise, grave learn'd, and godly men, his Superiors in Church and State." Thus, Duport concluded, "'tis in vain for any to plead or pretend tenderness of conscience for their contempt and disobedience."[1] Though steeped in the Restoration politics of its day, Duport's sermon was typical in its treatment of conscientious obedience towards the King, an idea promoted from the pulpit since the Reformation.

When the royalist sway over the pulpits began to wane during the civil wars, however, the King and his supporters had to turn to another medium in order to preserve this national call to conscientious obedience: print. Such "paper bullets," Jason McElligott points out, exhibited a "vibrant, pugnacious royalism, committed to the need to win public opinion."[2] Despite the steady stream of royalist newsbooks and other illicit royalist publications during this period, no efforts in print rivalled the success of *Eikon Basilike* (1649). *Eikon Basilike* gave the English nation an unprecedented view into its King's conscience. Written in the fashion of Foxe's *Book of Martyrs*, the King's book established the "fixity of the King's conscience," with Charles presented as a figure of "innocence afflicted" and "heroic suffering."[3] This compelling rhetorical strategy was the culmination of both Charles's and his supporters' labours to vindicate the King's actions during the civil wars in terms of his scrupulous conscience.[4] Indeed, the King's attention to his conscience in *Eikon Basilike*, rather than teaching his readers the "arts of holy living and holy dying," taught them the art of civil obedience, for conscience's sake.[5]

Charles's appeal to conscience has long been acknowledged as a cornerstone of the King's book, though the topic has not been explored at length.[6] Viewing *Eikon Basilike* as a casuistical text or as the genuine discharge of the "royal conscience," scholars such as Kevin Sharpe and Andrew Lacey have given due attention to the notion of a "private conscience" and its complex relationship to "public duties." More specifically, they agree that Charles "had great difficulty in separating out the actions of the prince from those of the private individual," and so in "maintaining an unspotted conscience Charles was fulfilling his duty not only as a Christian but also as a virtuous king."[7] Yet the prevalence of this term in *Eikon Basilike*, the very word employed by the King's detractors, suggests that Charles and his supporters sought through their use of conscience more than a picture of Christian and kingly virtue. *Eikon Basilike* recovers this language for the royalist cause against a rebellious and disobedient Parliament, acting as a proxy for the beheaded King's conscience and projecting that conscience onto the nation.

More importantly, this portrait of Charles's beleaguered national conscience functioned for the reader as the pulpit would have for the listener: as a call to England for conscientious obedience to its King. Though Charles was undoubtedly a genuine "man of conscience," he, like his predecessors, believed that his subjects' consciences were the ultimate locus of civil obedience, the "bond of conscience being of all other most straitest."[8] For this reason, *Eikon Basilike* uses Charles's conscience to reach his former subjects' own with the hopes of tightening those bonds. The King's book thus imagines a nation suspended in conscientious obedience to its beheaded monarch as it lies in wait for the royalists' hoped-for restoration of his son. Uniting England in and through conscience, *Eikon Basilike* reminds all that rebellion against Charles – even in death – was rebellion against both God and the self.

Conscience, Obedience, and the Pulpit

Charles was especially attuned to the relationship between the pulpit, the subject's conscience, and his own power.[9] The Reformation had wrested from the Catholic Church guardianship over the individual conscience, offering reformed believers scripture as their consciences' principal guide. Yet mediating between the scriptures and the conscience was the Church of England, and more particularly, its clergy. Preaching thus became more than ever a political act, with sermons negotiating the terms among monarchical power, obedience, and God.[10] For this reason, the only way to forge an enduring connection between obedience to God and obedience to the King was to validate it according to the individual conscience. With secular obedience bound to its divine counterpart and transformed into an act of conscience, the private sphere of conscience was inevitably compromised by its public and political duties.

According to this model, the pulpits would ideally work upon a subject's private conscience in order to compel its public role of obedience. Conscience as a result was thought to be at once permeable *and* unimpeachable: though it could be permeated by a preacher's voice, once an individual accepted the preacher's dictates as true according to the Word of God, that belief became unimpeachable. A sermon delivered to Charles in April 1627 by John Donne, then dean of St Paul's, demonstrated this permeability with its focus on Mark 4:24, "Take heed what ye hear." Donne tells his listeners that "Christ speaks to us in our *Ear*," through which the "Holy Ghost insinuates himselfe into our soules, and works upon us so, by his *private motions*." And Christ's "Ministers are an *Earth-quake*" when they pass on His message; their preaching "batters the soul" and "scatters a cloudy conscience," and "by that breach, the Spirit enters." This violent process of penetrating the conscience confirms the influential nature of the pulpits: it is through preaching that the Holy Spirit enters the soul and the clouds that confuse conscience are dispelled. The flip side of this process, however, also suggests the vulnerability of the ear as an inroad to both the soul and conscience. Later in the sermon the verse "Take heed what ye hear" takes on a foreboding sense: Donne warns his listeners to "Come not so neare evil speaking" because a "man may have a good breath in himself, and yet be deadly infected."[11] The ear could bring one closer to salvation or damnation, depending on what it hears.

If conscience could in fact be permeated in this way, then controlling the information disseminating from the pulpits was especially crucial. Accordingly, Charles's accession marked a striking shift in the content of court sermons and, more importantly, the Paul's Cross sermons. Paul's Cross was the "most public pulpit in the land," and as a result the Church and Crown carefully regulated the sermons preached there.[12] In 1628, Charles forbade preachers to discuss the Calvinist doctrine of predestination, a declaration catalysing a dramatic change in the content of the Paul's Cross sermons (or at least those being printed) beginning that same year. Replacing the orthodox Calvinist sermons relatively common during Elizabeth and James's reigns were those betraying Arminian sympathies.[13] These sermons promulgated not only the doctrine of universal grace but also unconditional obedience to the sovereign and conformity to the Church of England.[14] Millar MacLure characterizes the Paul's Cross sermons of this era as but "an echo, sometimes fuzzy, always monotonous, of the administration."[15]

Because of this belief in the connection between monarchical power and the pulpit, Charles feared that if his influence over the pulpit waned, so would his national support. As early as 1642, Charles was anxious about an idea "vented in some Pulpits (by those desperate turbulent Preachers, who are the great Promoters of the Distempers of this time) *That humane Laws do not bind the Conscience.*"[16] Similarly, in "His Majesties Declaration to all His Loving Subjects" issued later that year, Charles lamented that "licence even to Treason is admitted (that is, not punished) in Pulpits," with "Persons ignorant in Learning and Vnderstanding, turbulent and seditious in disposition, scandalous in life, and unconformable in Opinion to the Laws of the Land [...] imposed upon Parishes to infect and poyson the mindes of Our People."[17] Later in the "Declaration," he asked "by what measure and rule the Reformation they so much talk of, is to be made" when

> the blessed means of advancing Religion, the preaching of the Word of God, is turned into a Licence of libelling, and reviling both Church and State, and venting such seditious positions, as by the Laws of the Land are no lesse then Treason, and scarce a man in reputation and credit with these Grand Reformers, who is not notoriously guilty of this; whilest those learned, reverend, painfull, and pious Preachers, who have been and are the most eminent and able assertours of the Protestant Religion, are (to the unspeakable joy of the Adversaries to Our Religion) disregarded and oppressed.[18]

Charles's concerns regarding what he saw as a hijacking of the national pulpit were not completely unfounded. William Haller confirms that "by the time fighting began," Parliament made "certain that the Word should be preached and that the Puritan brotherhood should be free to preach it as they saw fit."[19] Similarly, Edward Hyde, the Earl of Clarendon, claimed that the "strange wild-fire among the people" in 1642 "was not so much and so furiously kindled by the breath of the Parliament as of the clergy, who both administered fuel and blowed the coals in the Houses too." These preachers, Clarendon continues, having "driven all learned and orthodox men from the pulpits [...] under the notion of reformation and extirpating of Popery, infused seditious inclinations into the hearts of men against the present government of the Church, with many libellous invectives against the State too" and "the person of the King."[20]

In reality, between 1640 and 1660, about 3,000 of England's 8,600 parish clergy lost their positions, were pressured to resign, were imprisoned, or were even fined. In 1642, Parliament created a Committee for Plundered Ministers, which would replace royalist clergy with Parliamentarian supporters. In 1643, local officials were also given the permission to expel royalist clergy. Despite these efforts, however, many of the pre-war clergy maintained their positions in the Church, and Independent and Presbyterian clergy most likely remained in the minority throughout the republic.[21] Charles's perception of Parliament's ability to reconfigure the Church of England was exaggerated, yet his anxieties regarding this matter of the pulpits fed into his correspondence during the civil war, and most pervasively into *Eikon Basilike*.

The King's Irresistible Conscience

In a copy of the twenty-fifth edition of *Eikon Basilike*, an eighteenth-century collector and reader has left telling notes in the front and back covers of the book. Those written in the front cover indicate that the book's owner was an antiquarian: he has recorded what seems to be a shelf mark as well as the pedigree of his edition.[22] The notes in the back cover, written in the same hand, show that his interests went beyond those of a collector. There, the owner began indexing moments in *Eikon Basilike*, particularly those related to the King's policies in the English and Scottish Churches: "yᵉ bill of putt[in]g yᵉ B[isho]ps out of yᵉ house of Peers.55," "yᵉ abolishing of Episcopacy in <u>Scotland</u>.153.256," "Whence yᵉ dislike to yᵉ <u>Lord's Prayer</u>?.131." Because the handwriting is small and starts in the right-hand corner, we can assume that the owner intended to record more entries. Tucked to the right of the first two entries, he squeezed in a third: "v. Clar[endon] State Pap[er] s ii.296." This reference leads to a letter written by Charles to Henrietta Maria in November 1646 wherein Charles tells his wife (not for the first time) that he cannot consent to the Scots' request to establish a Presbyterian church government in England for his conscience's sake. This impulse to key *Eikon Basilike* to Charles's letters during this pivotal year of failed negotiations was undoubtedly connected to the reader's interest in Charles's church policies. Whatever the owner's motivation, setting *Eikon Basilike* alongside the King's letters helps to clarify the complexity of *Eikon Basilike*'s discussions of episcopacy, Presbyterianism, and conscience, as this eighteenth-century reader-antiquarian seemed to understand.[23]

Charles's correspondence of 1646 reveals how he used the language of conscience for both political leverage and to secure his subjects' obedience. Parliament's New Model Army defeated the royalist forces in 1645–6, concluding the First Civil War. Charles's next step after this devastating loss was questionable. David Scott identifies two warring factions among Charles's advisors: the "foreign-alliance faction" were grandees in favour of Charles's appeal to foreign powers, primarily Scotland, for assistance, while the "pro-accommodation camp" encouraged Charles to negotiate a settlement with his opponents.[24] Seeming to side with the pro-accommodation faction, Charles initially wanted to make for London, as he wrote to Lord Digby in March 1646, where he hoped that he could "draw either the Presbyterians or Independents to side with me, for extirpating one or the other," resulting in him being "really King again."[25] A set of letters sent to Sir Henry Vane the Younger at the same time similarly betrays Charles's hopes of re-entering England.[26] Charles soon abandoned this manoeuvre and was persuaded by the foreign-alliance faction to flee from Oxford in April 1646 so that he might surrender to the Scottish army at Newark the following month.

While imprisoned by the Scots at Newcastle in July of that year, Charles received Parliament's peace terms. The nineteen clauses of these "Newcastle Propositions" demanded that episcopacy be abolished and a Presbyterian system of church government be established in England and Ireland; that Charles sign the Solemn League and Covenant, thereby endorsing the reformation of the Churches of England and Ireland, and imposing the Covenant on all of his subjects; and that he acknowledge that Parliament took up arms in its just defence against him and his supporters. A large section of the propositions names royalists who would not be pardoned for their actions against Parliament. Not surprisingly, Charles found these terms unacceptable and a threat to his monarchical power.

It is during this period of negotiations that Charles received the letter from Henrietta Maria that interested the eighteenth-century reader of *Eikon Basilike*. This exchange between the King and Queen was part of a larger correspondence that Charles had with his most trusted advisors of the foreign-alliance faction, John Ashburnham, John Culpepper, and Sir Henry Jermyn. Like the Queen, these advisors implored the King to take the Covenant and approve the Presbyterian Church settlement so that he might form an alliance with the Scots against the English Parliament. Such an alliance, they believed, would instigate a second civil war through which Charles could hope to regain his power with the help of both the Scottish and French forces.[27] The one casualty in this plan would be episcopacy; but, for Jermyn, Culpepper, Ashburnham, and the Queen, episcopacy could be sacrificed in order to ensure the survival of monarchy itself.

Responding to his advisors on 22 July 1646, Charles takes issue with this plan, contending, "It is not the change of Church government which is chiefly aimed at [by the Scots] (though that were too much); but it is by that pretext to take away the dependency of the Church from the Crown, which, let me tell you, I hold to be of equal consequence to that of the Militia." "For people," he insists, "are governed by the pulpit more than the sword in times of peace" (*The Letters*, 200–1). In a letter dated 19 August 1646, Charles makes a similar argument, reminding his advisors to "belive it, religion is the only firm foundation of all power; that cast loose, or depraved, no government can be stable." "For where was there ever obedience," he asks, "where religion did not teach it?" (*The Letters*, 203–4). While his advisors deem episcopacy the one roadblock between the King and victory against the English Parliament, Charles instead regarded royal influence over the pulpit as the only guarantee of maintaining monarchical power. Fearing this loss of power over the pulpits, Charles tells his advisors that with such an alliance, "all our orthodox devines will be expelled or silenced, and theirs introduced" along with their "doctrine, which is antimonarchicall." Again in a letter dated 7 September 1646, Charles claimed that if Scottish Presbyterianism prevails in England, "then the Clergie will depend upon none" and "the King will have more cause to sew to them then they to the King"; and if English Presbyterianism, then "the two houses (without the King) will have the dependancy upon them [the clergy]" (*State Papers* 2:247, 260). As a result, it would be "in the power of the pulpits (without transgressing the law) to dethrone me at their pleasure, at least to keep me in subjection" (*The Letters* 207).

Charles did not rely upon this argument alone; instead, he characterized his unwillingness to treat with the Scots as a matter of conscience. In response to his advisors' repeated requests for him to accept the Scots' terms, Charles revealed the desperate and victimized condition that his conscience had been brought to as a result of their persistence. "Albeit my condition be sufficiently sad," Charles tells them,

> yet it is made so strangely worse by your misunderstanding the point of Church government, whereby I am made the scourge of my kingdom and family, that rather than I will undergo that burden, I will (laying all other considerations aside) hazard to go to France, to clear my reputation to the Queen, and all the world, that I stick not upon scruples, but undoubted realities, both in relation to conscience and policy. (*The Letters* 207)

Throughout this correspondence, Charles increasingly refers to his conscience as the cause of his seeming wilfulness. He uses this language, moreover, with the hopes of persuading his advisors to agree with his policy, asserting that their disagreement with him was a result of their own misunderstanding. In a letter dated 31 August, Charles similarly describes his condition as made more desperate by pity for his over-precise conscience:

> For when those few from whom I can only expect encouradgement in my constancy, shall condemn me of willfulness, and by it make me the distroyer of my Crowne and Family, how can you think it possible for me to joy in any thing after this? It is such a greefe, that must sinke any honest hart, and I am sure would soone doe myne, if I did not hope, (and that shortly) to make you see and confess your error.

"Nor will it satisfie me," he continues, "that you pitty my misled or too strict conscience." Rather than unfounded pity, Charles instead "must make you acknowledge that the giving such way to Presbiteriall government as will content the Scots, is the absolut distruction of Monarchy" (*State Papers* 2:255–6). This desire to shape their judgment and make them confess their supposed error becomes more persistent as the correspondence progresses. For the King, outward obedience to his dictates was not enough. When he fears that his letters might have "silenced you by way of obedience," Charles confirms that he will not be satisfied "unless your reasons be likewise convinced" and he is able to "make your judgement concur with mine" (*The Letters* 204). Citing his own conscience, the King hoped to satisfy his advisors' judgment and convince them of their error. He seems not to have considered – or to have been unwilling to accept – the possibility of their consciences differing from his own.

Charles concludes his letter of 7 September 1646 confident in the fact that his advisors would be satisfied with both his conscience and his policy, with them "heerafter assist[ing] (but no more trobl[ing])" him "in matters of Religion" (*State Papers* 2:260–1). By asking for more than their silent obedience, however, Charles unknowingly invited opposition from his advisors. Jermyn and Culpepper respond by presuming the "liberty to reply fully and plainly to what you are pleased to urge against our opinion."[28] In their letter dated 12 and 28 September 1646, not only did they challenge Charles's use of conscience in his previous letters, but also they undercut the political expediency of Charles's preserving episcopacy for fear of losing his power as a King. Because Charles mixed the discourse of conscience with a discourse of "civill enforcements," Jermyn and Culpepper conclude that the King does not "center only upon this foundation [conscience]" and thereby leaves his position regarding episcopacy open to debate. Treading tenuous ground, they deduce that if "by conscience is intended to assert that Episcopacy is *jure divino* exclusive, whereby no Protestant (or rather Christian) Church can be acknowledged for such without a Bishop, we must therin crave leave wholly to differ" (*State Papers* 2:262–3). Jermyn and Culpepper's strategy here is to divorce Charles's policy from his conscience in order to reveal the weaknesses in both. First, they suggest that his language of conscience has been used incorrectly: episcopacy is not backed by divine law, and therefore he is not obliged in conscience to defend it at the risk of losing his kingdom.

Second, Jermyn and Culpepper attack his connection between royal power and the pulpits. They acknowledge the King's argument as "solid and strong," but only "so far as it reacheth." If Charles does not treat with the Scots, they threaten, "Presbitery, or somthing worse, will be forced upon you, whether you will or no." "Com," they continue, "the question in short is, whether you will chuse to be a King of Presbitery, or no King; and yet Presbitery or perfect Independancy to be." They assure him that "a disease," like the Presbyterianism demanded by the Scots, "is to be preferred before dissolution" of the monarchy altogether (*State Papers* 2:261). In this brazen letter, the King's supporters turn his connection between the pulpit and monarchical power on its head, thus questioning Charles's own judgment and conscience. To refuse the Scots' terms in order to preserve episcopacy at this moment would, according to Jermyn and Culpepper, have the opposite effect: rather than strengthening the King's power, it would be his downfall.

Though Jermyn and Culpepper initially abstain from using the word "conscience" in these letters, Charles nonetheless insists on reading their disobedience as a matter of conscience. Responding once again, Charles no longer poses as the martyr-King victimized for his conscience's sake. He claims that the "chyding part" of this letter refers only to Culpepper and Jermyn since Ashburnham did not endorse the letter of 12/28 September. And, Charles claims, he expects that Culpepper and Jermyn will not "beare less the frendship to him, because his conscience discents not from myne." Charles believes that Ashburnham acted in good conscience because he agrees with Charles's own; yet he also implies that Culpepper and Jermyn are not acting out of conscience since they dissent "from myne." In the face of such disagreement, Charles asks,

> must I be caled single, because some ar frigted out of, others dares not avow, there opinions? And who causes me to be condemned, but those who either takes courage and morall honesty for conscience, or those who were never rightly grounded in Religion according to the Church of England.

Condemning Culpepper and Jermyn further, the King groups them with either those who are too frightened to declare their opinions, those who fail to realize what conscience is, or, worst of all, those who were never true members of the Church. He concludes this fit by advising them to "instruct yourselfes better, recant, and undeceave those whom ye have misinformed." Though Charles closes by claiming "nether anger nor greefe shall make me forgett my frendship to you," his anger towards their "discent" still rings loudly, as does his command that they "instruct" themselves better according to the dictates of his conscience (*State Papers* 2:270).

Sharpe argues convincingly that Charles "thought his first responsibility was to do according to God's dictates, as his reason and conscience discerned them, rather than act 'politically,'" yet this correspondence

tells a more complex story.[29] Undoubtedly there is some genuine sentiment when Charles writes to his advisors regarding the preservation
of episcopacy and his conscience. As Sharpe and others have aptly
pointed out, Charles was a man of conscience. His attention to conscience, however, did not compromise his ability to be a good politician.
At the same time that he appeared inflexible in this correspondence,
Charles was making plans to compromise with the Scots: he was willing to allow Presbyterianism in England for a period of three years, an
agreement that the Scots finally consent to in December 1646. In a letter
to the bishop of London on 30 September of that same year, Charles
asked Bishop Juxon if, in "compliance to the iniquity of the times"
he may agree to terms with "a safe conscience" that "at another time
were unlawful" (*The Letters* 208). Charles, however, did not wait for his
response and instead sent his old companion Will Murry to London to
offer the proposition to the Scots' commissioners.[30] That Charles would
agree to such an accommodation without receiving the bishop's reply
demonstrated that, with an advantage over Parliament in his sights,
Charles found a way to reconcile his conscience with political expediency.[31] Charles's tie between conscience and policy, then, did not inhibit
his ability to act "politically." Instead, it seemed that, in some circum-
stances, not only could conscience be used to validate the King's politics, but also that his politics could be used to validate his conscience.

In the face of these negotiations with the Scots' commissioners,
Charles's rigidity for his conscience's sake in his correspondence with
Jermyn and Culpepper seems entirely misleading.[32] While Charles
decides that he could allow Presbyterianism in England for a set period
of time and not violate his conscience, he chooses to withhold this information from his advisors temporarily. Once this initial offer to the Scots
fails, Charles is again pressed by his advisors to yield to the Scots on
their terms. This time, he exasperatedly writes, "God God, what things
are thease to try my patience!" In his past letters, Charles argues, he
gave "reasons (which to me are unanswerable) why I cannot yeald unto
it" and made it "my verry earnest desyre ye would hartely joyne with
me in my way" – a desire that remains unfulfilled (*State Papers* 2:314).

Culpepper and Jermyn were similarly attuned to the rhetorical power
of the word "conscience" and the King's use of it. Having repeatedly
accused Charles of being wilful (as opposed to conscientious), they
respond by telling him that they "have done with the argument" since
"it is your pleasure" – *not* his conscience. More importantly, Culpepper
and Jermyn insist that they cannot change their advice or judgment

upon the matter for *their* conscience's sake: "if we should give you any other advice we should dispairely (against our consciences) [...] betray you, your posterity, and all your party to utter ruin" (*State Papers*, 2:269). Though Charles had earlier accused his advisors of not acting in conscience, here Culpepper and Jermyn assert the dictates of their consciences against the King's. They couch their disagreement in terms of their obedience to him; yet they simultaneously emphasize the independence of their consciences from his own – a possibility that the King had repeatedly resisted by accusing them of error and misunderstanding. What is worse, this show of obedience seeks to prove above all else that it is the King's conscience, not their own, which is wrong.

As this correspondence demonstrates, Charles does not allow for anyone's conscience – even those of his closest advisors – in cases where they disagree with him. He attributes Culpepper and Jermyn's dissent from his conscience to their judgment, or their opinions, rather than their consciences, while he grants that Ashburnham acts according to his conscience solely because of his agreement with the King's own. In this way, Charles envisions his conscience as representative of the nation, with his subjects' individual consciences dependent upon the King's for validation.

Eikon Basilike presents a similar view of conscience. Unlike this correspondence, however, the King's book leaves little room for opposition like Culpepper and Jermyn's. Once the mode of writing shifts from that of a private correspondence with political advisors to one with God Himself, the King's conscience becomes truly unassailable. More importantly, it is this representation of the King's unimpeachable conscience that grants *Eikon Basilike* its rhetorical punch: establishing the privilege of the royal conscience, the King's book seeks to compel national obedience by securing anew the consciences of Charles's subjects. This state of conscientious obedience to its beheaded King is meant to captivate England, priming the nation for the royalists' hoped-for restoration of his son.

Securing the Bond of Conscience: *Eikon Basilike*

Eikon Basilike's extensive use of conscience was anticipated not only by Charles's correspondence with his advisors but also by royalist newsbooks. In such publications, the King's conscience was similarly presented as the basis of his unwillingness to compromise with Parliament. *Mercurius Elencticus*, October 1648, claims "here you have a *King* proffering all things imagineable to satisfie them in matters of *Religion*; or conduceing to their own *security*: Refusing nothing but what he cannot yield to, without *violence* to his *Conscience*." Also in 1648, *Mercurius Elencticus* and *Mercurius Pragmaticus* drew increasingly dire pictures of Charles's prison conditions. A January issue of *Mercurius Pragmaticus* portrayed Charles as the "most unfortunate (though the most rationall, Pious, Gracious and Conscientious) of all men living; being shut up as a close prisoner; deprived of Wife, Children, Friends, Servants, and all but a good conscience."[33]

These newsbook exposés of Charles as a man and King suffering for his conscience's sake, however, did not rival the rhetorical power of *Eikon Basilike*, nor could they produce its effect. The King's book was made available on the very day of Charles's execution, 30 January 1649, and it quickly became "the most popular and influential tract of the English Revolution."[34] In 1649 alone, the book went through thirty-five editions, and over the next decade it was translated into Latin, French, German, Dutch, and Danish. Unlike the periodicals, *Eikon Basilike* was not written as a public vindication of the King's actions.[35] Rather, the King's book is presented as a private meditation, Charles searching his conscience before God, as its full title – *Eikon Basilike, The Povrtraictvre of His Sacred Maiestie in His Solitvdes and Svfferings* – indicates. Despite the seemingly private and meditative nature of *Eikon Basilike*, the anonymous author of *Eikon Alethine, The Povrtraitvre of Truths most sacred Majesty truly suffering, though not solely* (26 August 1649) and John Milton in *Eikonoklastes* (6 October 1649) nevertheless tried to refute the irrefutable book.

Richard Helgerson called *Eikon Basilike* "unbookish – indeed antibookish," a book that "turned print against itself" in its iconic affront to print-based Protestantism.[36] Yet it seems that the King's book actually embraced print culture as essential to its success: *Eikon Basilike* played upon certain print norms, dictating how it should be read and regarded by its audience. For instance, it was printed as an octavo for the first three editions, and subsequently as a duodecimo.[37] While the duodecimo format was undoubtedly more economical for both printer and buyer, it was also the format increasingly used for devotional literature and Bibles.[38] That *Eikon Basilike* was made to look and function like a devotional book was bolstered by the fact that later printed versions separated out the prayers that were appended to early editions of *Eikon Basilike* as a stand-alone book and printed them as *His Majesties Prayers Which He used in time of Sufferings* (1649).[39] Also, in the twenty-fifth edition, the lines throughout the text were marked in five-line intervals so that they might be keyed to the apophthegmata printed at the back of the book. Compiled by Edward Hooker, the apophthegmata separated out from the main text Charles's theological, political, and moral adages, and provided the page and line number for each.[40] Such a supplement made Charles at once a politician, moral philosopher, and theologian, and mirrored the contemporary impulse to condense scripture into a set of helpful aphorisms, like those in *The Souldiers Pocket Bible* (1643).[41] And, just like *His Majesties Prayers*, the apophthegmata was subsequently printed as a separate book. This continuous modification of the text speaks not only to its enduring popularity but also to its intended devotional qualities and how its reader might use the text.

Also important is how *Eikon Basilike* could be treated as a result of its being printed in this small format. Its size was more conducive to keeping it by one's side or carrying it in one's pocket at all times for consultation or private reading. Many surviving duodecimo copies of the book are well worn, suggesting such treatment by the owners.[42] And this format could not help but draw attention to the fact that owning this book was dangerous in post-regicide England: Richard Royston, the first publisher of *Eikon Basilike*, had to move his press outside of London after having had his printed copies twice destroyed by parliamentary censors.[43] As Henri-Jean Martin points out, clandestine publications often appeared in octavo and duodecimo formats because small books "could be transported more discreetly and hidden more easily, and perhaps their reduced size was a more enticing wrapping for the attractions of forbidden fruit."[44]

Also attractive was *Eikon Basilike*'s striking frontispiece (Figure 3). Certainly the book's devotional function was tied intricately to its iconic function, duly produced by William Marshall's fold-out engraving. The picture displays a weary Charles kneeling, one hand on his chest, the other holding a crown of thorns above which is the tag *Asperam et Levem*, or "Bitter and Light," and within which is the key to salvation, *Gratia*. Below him on the ground is his earthly crown, over which is inscribed the words *Splendidam et Gravem* ("Splendid and Heavy") and within which is the motto *Vanitas* or "Vanity," and above is the heavenly crown labelled both *Beatam* and *Æternam* ("Blessed" and "Eternal"). To Charles's back is a landscape representing the steadfastness of his conscience through extreme duress. Interestingly, Charles's enemies are consumed by this metaphorical landscape, represented as winds, waves, and weights. This strategy allowed the focus to be

Figure 3. Frontispiece of *Eikon Basilike* (1649). By permission of the British Museum.

on the King and God, once again appearing to drain the book of any polemical agenda. Also, the structure of the engraving, with the left-hand page representing the landscape and the right the King himself, encourages the reader's eye to make the progressive movement from the metaphorical representation of the King's internal struggles to the King himself. Charles's concentration, however, is not on that suffering but rather on the crown of glory awaiting him in heaven as a reward for his commitment to conscience and ultimately to God.

In many editions, the frontispiece is the first item to greet the reader, immediately opposite the title page. Its presence there is especially striking in the duodecimo editions where, once unfolded, the engraving is four times the size of the book itself. Significantly, this engraving is the only prefatory material other than the title page, table of contents, and list of errata, before chapter 1, *"Upon His Majesty's calling this last Parliament."* As Elizabeth Skerpan-Wheeler points out, "there was at the outset a decision not to allow any material beyond the basic design of the book and the chapter heading to intervene between king and readers."[45] This unmediated stream between the King's private meditations and his subjects emphasizes the idea of the book as a "portrait" of Charles, as the title appropriately suggests. In reality, after all, the book is just that, a representation of the King, though not composed by the King alone and, more importantly, composed with a purpose other than its form might suggest.

Although the size and content of *Eikon Basilike* make the text seem sacred and private, with the reader positioned as a voyeur to Charles's relationship with God, it was meant to perform a public function. Francis F. Madan recounts that as early as 1642, the King "declared his intention of writing his own defence." According to Sir John Brattle, "In the year 47 King Charles, having drawn up the most considerable part of this book, and having writ it in some loose papers, at different times, desired Bishop Juxon to get some friend of his (whom he could comment as a trusty person) to look it over, and to put it into an exact method."[46] These "loose papers" made it into the hands of John Gauden, bishop of Exeter and later of Worcester, who shaped the material and most likely added the chapter headings (they are all notably in the third person). Though we cannot be sure how much of *Eikon Basilike* can be attributed to Charles and how much to Gauden, we do know that the King approved the enterprise and "'sometimes corrected and heightened'" Gauden's work.[47] Royston also testifies that "his late Ma[jesty] of blessed memory King Charles the first did sent to him about Mich[ael]mas before his Martirdome to provide a Presse for hee had a Book of his owne for him to Print."[48] Thus, despite the private appearance of *Eikon Basilike*, Charles and his supporters clearly intended the book to be a "spectacular propaganda coup" – spectacular enough to outdo all of their previous efforts.[49]

Eikon Basilike, however, was more than mere propaganda. It was so popular precisely because it was not designed to look like propaganda; instead it was designed to look like and, as I argue, serve the function of a devotional book. But if *Eikon Basilike* was supposed to function like a form of prayer or worship, *what* exactly did it teach readers? Lacey, focusing on the extensive use of the word "conscience" in *Eikon Basilike*, suggests that the King's book provided readers with "a pattern and example for their own discernment of right action and the achieving of a quiet conscience," thereby deeming *Eikon Basilike* and the King "casuistical texts" or "teachers of holy living and holy dying."[50] Skerpan-Wheeler similarly argues that the "emphasis on conscience" along with "the insistence on the depth of sorrow at his suffering" finally "present a vision of Charles the man, rather than Charles the king."[51] While such arguments assume that the reader could see himself in Charles, the text itself seems to suggest the exact opposite: *Eikon Basilike* never lets its readers forget that they are in fact reading about a king. Though the author flirts with Charles's humanity repeatedly, the structure, form, and function of the text all work to turn those moments into reminders of his royal privilege and the obedience due to him as a monarch. The frontispiece itself acts as proof of this reminder: though at the height of his humility, the Charles pictured in the engraving is significantly still dressed like a king. He did not trade in his royal robes for those of a penitent, a martyr, or an everyman. This image is so striking because he is clearly a martyr-*king*: he has traded in his earthly crown for a crown of thorns with the promise of the crown of glory. Charles was a king in life, a king in his suffering, and he will be a king in death: his readers could hardly replicate this trajectory.

Rather, *Eikon Basilike* uses Charles's conscience as a reminder of the King's power and the subject's obedience. The King's book not only "literally took the place of the king" but also took the place of the bishops, who helped to shape and edit the text, and, by extension, the pulpits.[52] In his letters to Culpepper, Jermyn, and Ashburnham, Charles believed the pulpits the very source of obedience in his subjects: without this venue, he feared, his power was null and void. To replace them, Charles and his book's compilers turn to the space where divine and civil power meet: the conscience, and more specifically, Charles's conscience. Certainly most infuriating for his detractors was the fact that Charles mobilized the very source of power used by Presbyterians, Independents, and other sectarians when their influence over the pulpits had been nearly non-existent.

Yet Charles's allies had a strong advantage on their side: in metaphorical terms, the King's conscience, like the King's body, played a national role.[53] *Eikon Basilike* blurs the lines between Charles's conscience and his subjects', with the King's conscience acting as the conscience of the nation. This unifying force urges readers to affirm their conscientious obedience to Charles, performing the work of the pulpits and imagining the then kingless nation as nonetheless loyal to its late monarch. It also played the role of intermediary between Charles's subjects and God, transforming the act of reading into a devotional act of obedience to both God and King. In this way, *Eikon Basilike* compels readers to find in the King's conscience and their obedience to it the only national identity sanctioned by the divine.

To transform the King's conscience into such an effective rhetorical tool, *Eikon Basilike*'s authors first fashion Charles as a martyr suffering for conscience's sake. In an England now controlled by Parliament, Charles's triumphant enemies are presented as denying him *his* freedom of conscience. In chapter 2, *"Upon the Earl of* Strafford's *death,"* Charles identifies his sole blunder during the wars as his signature on Strafford's death warrant. Thomas Wentworth, president of the Council of the North, Privy Counsellor, and Lord-Lieutenant of Ireland, was tried by Parliament as one of Charles's "evil counselors" and finally condemned by a bill of attainder. Charles hesitantly consented to the bill, and Strafford was beheaded on 12 May 1641. In *Eikon Basilike*, this incident is introduced early on as a confession to God for choosing "rather what was safe, than what seemed just."[54] Having learned his lesson after once going against what "My Conscience suggested to Me," Charles uses this incident as a precedent for following his conscience in all subsequent matters of state (55). The King affirms that after this one error he now prefers "the inward peace of My Conscience, before any outward tranquility," including his own "liberty" and "life," it being "dearer to me than a thousand Kingdoms" (81, 167, and 194).

Having established the necessity of conscience's supremacy, the King's book next characterizes Charles's enemies as attacking his freedom to use that conscience. Chapter 2 already laid out the dangers of separating policy from conscience, a mistake that Charles vows not to replicate. Yet, according to *Eikon Basilike*, the King's enemies in Parliament tried to make him do just that. Charles assures God, however, that "They have no great cause to triumph [...] since my Soul is still my own: nor shall they ever gain my Consent against my Conscience" (166). The King's language repeatedly casts the civil wars as a battle between Parliament and his afflicted (though steadfast) conscience: a battle, in other words, between good and evil with the stakes being his eternal soul. In this way, though Charles has lost the physical battle, he emerges as victorious before God within *Eikon Basilike* and before the book's readers. Looking to God to buttress his own accusations against Parliament, in the prayer appended to chapter 11, "*Upon the* 19 *Propositions first sent to the* KING; *and more afterwards,*" Charles implores God to "*confirm My will and resolution to adhere to* [*Truth, Reason, and Justice*], *that no terrors, injuries, or oppressions of my Enemies may ever enforce me against those rules, which thou by them hast implanted in My Conscience*" (100). This prayer assumes not only that God is on Charles's side, but also that the King is working in harmony with God's will because he chooses his conscience even at the expense of England's tranquillity. Those reading such a prayer, then, must accept the deaths and chaos of the 1640s as both necessary and divinely sanctioned since Charles's will dovetails with God's.

Also striking in this prayer is Charles's characterization of the attack upon his freedom of conscience as an attack on his fundamental rights as a man and Christian. He tells God that He did not make him king so that he might be "*less than a Man,*" denied the power to say "*Yea, or Nay*" as he saw fit, a freedom "*not denied to the meanest creature*" (100). Charles repeatedly calls the divestment of his negative voice in Parliament an attack on his liberty of conscience and thus "against the very natural and essential liberty of our souls" (144). The "blind obedience" that Parliament required of him was "never expected from any Freeman" (94); and, what is worse, Parliament attempted to deny him a right that "all the Commons of *England* enjoy" and "demand for their own Consciences" (70 and 180). These isolated moments speak to the message of *Eikon Basilike* as a whole: embedded in the text is the idea that Charles died to preserve both the peace and the liberty of his conscience, like many of the martyrs in Foxe's foundational Protestant martyrology.

This sustained argument for the "natural and essential" liberty of conscience belonging to everyone makes Charles seem like an advocate of this fundamental liberty for all Christians. Yet when contextualized within *Eikon Basilike*, it is clear that he is martyred to defend his liberty of conscience, a liberty different in quality and degree from that enjoyed by his subjects. Had the text advocated an equal liberty of conscience for everyone, not only would Charles sound dangerously like his enemies, but also *Eikon Basilike* would fall short of its message of obedience. The only way to advocate both liberty and obedience was to allow readers to participate in Charles's liberty of conscience, a participation that is featured as their only inroad to enjoying the liberty of conscience promised them in the gospels. The King's conscience is thus fashioned as exceptional in its closeness to and understanding of divine law. Charles claims that his conscience, whose freedom belongs to him "as a King [...], as a Man, and a Christian," owns the "dictates of none, but God, to be above me, as obliging Me to consent." "Better to die," he continues, "enjoying this Empire of My Soul, which subjects me *only to God* [...] than live with the Title of a King, if it should carry such vassalage with it" (70). This same freedom is qualified, however, when Charles turns to his subjects and their duties to him as their King. Just as natural as his right to liberty of conscience are the "bonds of nature and Conscience" that his subjects "have to Mee" (113).

It is these "bonds of nature and Conscience" that determine the difference between a King's conscience and a subject's. This distinction becomes especially apparent in chapter 14, *"Upon the Covenant."* The Solemn League and Covenant, signed on 25 September 1643, made official the alliance between the English and Scottish Parliaments. Its terms were both military and religious: in exchange for Scottish military aid, Parliament agreed to move towards the Scottish goal of uniting the Churches of England and Scotland under a Presbyterian church government. For Charles, such "after-Contracts" as the Solemn League and Covenant, administered without "My consent, and without any like power or precedent from God's or man's laws," cannot "absolve or slacken those moral and eternal bonds of duty which lie upon all My Subjects' consciences to both God and Me" (115). Without regal, and thus divine, approval (as the adage "God and Me" suggests), the "cords and withes" of the "later Vows" to Parliament cannot "hold men's Consciences" as their previous vows to the King do. After all, they lack the "commands of God's word, or the Laws of the Land" (116). Several times in this chapter and elsewhere in the text, Charles uses the maxim "God and Me" or "God and My self." Such repetition continuously links Charles's will, law, and word with that of God Himself. He defines the "bounds of a good Conscience" as "fixed and certain" in both God's laws and the "Laws of the State and Kingdom" (117). In the closing prayer to this chapter, Charles once again emphasizes this inextricable link between God's law and his, asking God to remind his subjects of those *"just, moral, and indispensable bonds, which thy Word, and the Laws of this Kingdom have laid upon their Consciences"* (120). Whether composed by Charles, Gauden, or another editorial hand, this prayer has the effect, once again, of enacting obedience in the subject for conscience's sake.

In the next chapter, "*Upon the many Jealousies raised, and Scandals cast upon the* KING, *to stir upon the People against Him,*" Charles humbly states that he did not seek this bond of conscience between subject and monarch, but rather that God put it in place. "In point of *true conscientious* tendernous," attended, Charles maintains, "by humility and meekness" rather than "proud and arrogant activity," he "oft declared, how little I desire My Laws and Scepter should intrench on God's Sovereignty, which is the only King of men's Consciences." Instead, it was God Himself who "hath laid such restraints upon men," commanding that they be "subject for Conscience sake" (128). As Charles's reference to Romans 13:5 suggests, though God may be the only king of men's consciences, subjects are conscientiously bound to "God and Me" rather than just God, a privilege reserved only for the King. This moment in the text is pivotal, marking a clear rhetorical shift: the liberty of conscience employed by Charles throughout *Eikon Basilike* is here qualified for the reader in terms of obedience.

Though in chapter 24, "*Upon their denying His Majesty the Attendance of His Chaplains,*" Charles admits that in the deepest recesses of the soul, "every private believer is a King and Priest," he at the same time reflects that if the "outward polity of the Church" were left up to such governance, "confusion in Religion" would ensue, with every man "turning Priest and Preacher" (173). As the King of England, Charles rightly deems himself the "*Defender of the Church, both in its true Faith, and its just fruitions*" (119). Disagreement among Charles's enemies did not stem necessarily from his office as such, but rather from what level of involvement in the church such an office permitted. In the Independent treatise *The Ancient Bounds* (1645), the writer affirms that the King, as defender of the church, rules "*for* the Church, not *in* the Church and *over* it" (264). Charles, however, believed that this office necessitated his defence of the church from "*Sacrilege and Apostasy*" (119). Accordingly, he deems episcopacy the "Ancient" and "most Universal way of Church-government," whereas Presbyterianism would leave the Church of England vulnerable to any such "Sects, Schisms, or Heresies" that would be able to get "but numbers, strength and opportunity" (111). Significantly, Charles does not here speak of the connection between episcopacy and civil obedience. Rather, he positions his defence of episcopacy as part of his duty to God, and his subjects' acceptance of this form of church government as part of their duty to King and God.

For this reason, not only are those who do not accept episcopacy schismatics, but more importantly they have ignored their consciences and its duties. His enemies, Charles tells God, merely use the name of religion to mask their political agenda – an accusation that Milton will recycle in *Eikonoklastes* against the King himself. More than that, while Charles adheres to his conscience even in the face of adversity, Parliament's supporters "stop [conscience's] mouth with the name and noise of religion" when it accuses them "for Sedition and Faction" (186). He cannot believe, after all, that their "own consciences are so stupid, as not to inflict upon them some secret impressions of that shame and dishonour" that follows upon losing the "respect and Honour, which they owe to their KING" (161). Though valiant in the field, Charles argues, his enemies are "more afraid to encounter those many pregnant Reasons, both from Law, Allegiance, and all true Christian grounds" that "accuse them *in* their own thoughts" (151). Charles is confident of his enemies' guilt "before God and man" and "in their own consciences too," and he implies that to war against the King is to wage war against God Himself (197–8). Parliament has gone against its natural and divinely ordained duty to the monarch, as its lost battle with conscience indicates. Indeed, Charles maintains that his enemies should remember "at best they sit in Parliament, as my Subjects, not my Superiors": they can only provide counsel, "recommend[ing] their advice" not "command[ing] my Duty" (96). In the prayer capping off chapter 26, Charles recounts Parliament's violation of these boundaries directly to God: they have fought *"against thee and the clear convictions of their own consciences,"* and so they also *"fight more against themselves, than ever they did against Me"* (183). With this argument, Charles transforms his own military failures into Parliament's spiritual self-destruction.

Eikon Basilike thus affirms civil obedience to the King as an act of conscience. More importantly, it does so by charting out what Charles argues is the natural and divinely ordained relationship between the King's conscience and the consciences of his subjects. Through Charles's conversation with God, readers learn of the King's exceptional liberty of conscience, a liberty that, ironically, must limit their own in order to exist. For this reason, Charles's subjects can only experience a full sense of this freedom through their own conscientious obedience to the King. His liberty of conscience limits their own, and their experience of that same liberty should be coterminous with civil obedience. Written amid numerous calls for liberty of conscience on behalf of Charles's enemies, *Eikon Basilike* not only reclaims this language for the King but also redefines its terms and reach. Moreover, Charles is merely a vehicle for these limitations on the individual conscience as he heroically struggles to uphold God's law.

Beginning with the twenty-third edition, supplementary materials were added to the end of the official text of *Eikon Basilike*, including additional prayers used by the King, his reasons against the jurisdiction of the High Court, a letter from Prince Charles dated 23 January 1649, the King's last words to Princess Elizabeth and the Duke of Gloucester, and an epitaph attributed to James Howell.[55] These supplemental materials transformed the book into a documentary history of the King's final days, heightening the reader's sense of both pathos and reverence towards Charles. The last text available to the reader in most subsequent editions was the epitaph beginning "So falls that stately Cedar," often attributed to Howell and John Hewett. Characterizing Charles as an "earthly God" and "Celestial Man," the poem situates the King somewhere between an everyman and God. Moreover, the King's "heavenly Virtues" are a "theam to high for humane Verse." "He that would know Thee right," the epitaph advises, "let him look / Upon Thy rare-incomparable Book" and "read it o'er and o'er."

This process of continuous reading and rereading would result both in the reader "find[ing] thee *King*, and *Priest*, and *Prophet* too" and in his "fruitless wishes to call Thee back again." Like the voice of *Eikon Basilike* that speaks to God, the reader here is positioned on the outside of this text in that the poet speaks not to him but rather to Charles. The poet's voice thus establishes the book's absolute accomplishment: after all, he tells Charles how the reader and rereader will undoubtedly react to the King's book. Having read the book, then, the reader will feel compelled to "call Thee back again," and once he rereads the book, he will again call the King back again, and so on in a continuous exchange between reader, text, and martyr-King. Instructing the reader indirectly, the epitaph thus attributes to *Eikon Basilike* the creation and renewal of a fruitless desire for the King, and in doing so it incites conscientious obedience to his legacy – again and again with each reading. In this way, it keeps its readers in a state of mental fixity while the nation remains kingless, awaiting the restoration of Charles's son.

Not surprisingly, in some editions, this epitaph bookended *Eikon Basilike*, appearing both on the verso of the title page and at the back of the text.[56] In the absence of a pulpit dedicated to the King's cause, then, the reader's rereading, as encouraged by this epitaph, could fill that void.

The King's Portraiture and the Subject's Conscience

Milton hopes to undo the work of this masterful piece of royalist propaganda in *Eikonoklastes* by attacking *Eikon Basilike*'s representation of Charles's conscience. While he is confident that the King's book falls short of its ultimate goal, "to stirr the constancie and solid firmness of any wise Man, or to unsettle the conscience of any knowing Christian," Milton's assault on Charles's conscience throughout tries to realize this conclusion.[57] As Sharon Achinstein notes, Milton casts the King as a hypocrite with an erroneous conscience.[58] If Charles's claims to conscience in *Eikon Basilike* are in fact genuine, Milton contends, then his conscience must be "defil'd," "variable and fleeting," "facil," "perverse and prevaricating," "self-will'd," and even "cruel" (*CPW* 3:368, 371, 375, 418, 460).

However, Milton also strives to counteract what he considers Charles's most egregious misstep: projecting his conscience as "a universal conscience, the whole Kingdoms conscience" (*CPW* 3:459). In order to resist the nationalization of the King's conscience, Milton emphasizes instead its very singularity. He highlights the peculiarity of Charles's conscience most vividly in his response to *Eikon Basilike*'s chapter on the Earl of Strafford: Milton is exasperated that the King "repents heer of giving his consent, though most unwillingly, to the most seasonable and solemn piece of Justice, that had bin done of many yeares in the Land." His conscience judging against what Milton deems the "unanimous demand of three populous Nations" reveals it as not only "sole" but also "one mans opinionated conscience" (*CPW* 3:368). Whereas Charles constructed himself as a victim for his singularity in this case, Milton casts him – and his conscience – as unfit. "If his conscience," Milton concludes, "were so narrow and peculiar to it self, it was not fitt his Authority should be so ample and Universall over others. For certainly a privat conscience sorts not with a public Calling" (*CPW* 3:369).

Milton's language in this episode, and his repetition of words such as "sole," "one," "narrow," "peculiar," and "private," paint a rather different portrait of the King than that presented by *Eikon Basilike*'s striking frontispiece. *Eikon Basilike*'s compilers designed the King's book around what Skerpan-Wheeler calls Charles's celebrity status, assuming that its appeal would be nearly universal. Yet Milton compromises this portrait of Charles-as-martyr for his conscience's sake and at once aims to expose and depose *Eikon Basilike*'s goal of aligning subjects' consciences with that of their King. By accusing Charles's conscience of being "so narrow and peculiar to it self," Milton objects to the nature of his conscience and is appalled that such a man with such a conscience would possess "so ample and Universall" a power over others. While Milton certainly objected to the nationalization of the King's conscience over his subjects', his attack here is not based on principle, but rather it is personal: the King's conscience is a public enemy because of its dissent from the righteous desires of Charles's three kingdoms. Had the King's conscience been less "narrow" and "peculiar to it self," would it have been more worthy of a "public Calling"?

Although several scholars deem *Eikonoklastes* a rhetorical failure, it seems that its more poignant failure might be its inability finally to "catch the conscience of the King."[59] *Eikon Basilike*'s portrait of the King was so successful, in fact, that some writers even began to replicate its promotion of Charles's conscience to national status. The anonymous author of a poem recounting the "memorable Modell of King Charles" that was "throwne from the West end of Paules, by the mallicious Souldiers" which then "did light uppon itts feete, and stood upright, to the admiration of ye Beholders," supposed the soldiers' violence against the statue a result not of their own riotousness but rather their guilty consciences. "But, alas!," he insists, "'twas not so much insultinge Glorie, as / corrodinge Guilte, that made them undertake / this lesser mischief: injur'd Statues speake / terrour to tyrants; who could neuer see / the awefull shape of murtherd Majestie wthout tormentinge horror. Consciences / are Executioners, and witnesses." This poet envisions the soldiers' consciences as assailants seeking retribution for the executed King. The statue itself seems an extension of this conscience-as-executioner and conscience-as-witness, it too inspiring a "tormentinge horror" in the guilty. In an attempt to stifle this overwhelming sense of remorse for betraying their King, the soldiers try to dash the statue, and, effectively, the sensibility awakened by their consciences, to the ground just as Milton tries to smash the image of Charles in *Eikonoklastes*.

Yet once they commit this act of violence to soothe their guilty consciences, those same consciences only torment them further: after the statue miraculously lands on its feet, the poet asks, "But why (stout-rude-ones) doe yee trembling stand? / few minutes since, each thrust his forward hand / to this strange worke, as if the pow're yee had / were uncontrolable? Why, now, so sad? / Oh! the sharpe stinge of conscience! how itt cowes / the boldest Rebells, shames their brazen browes!" While they had hoped to staunch conscience's sting by destroying its outward manifestation in the statue of Charles, they instead exacerbated their own terror when the image survived their assault. Once again collapsing the fear produced by conscience and the fear produced by the statue, the poet taunts, "how will yee looke uppon / our livinge Charles (dead Charles His angry Sonne) / leading a num'rous Armie to requite / His owne and others wronges? if the bare sight / of His Renowned Fathers Portraicture / strike yee with such affrightment, when secure?"[60] In words reminiscent of the full title of *Eikon Basilike*, the poet similarly deems the statue Charles's "Portraicture," and one also capable of affecting his subjects' consciences. Just as Charles was confident of the "horrid guilt" that his enemies' "convicted Consciences do pursue them" with, so this poet is confident of the "sharpe stinge of conscience" plaguing the statue's assailants – a sting, he is sure, that will only be worsened when faced by "our livinge Charles" (152).

While Milton repudiates Charles's presumptions regarding his subjects' consciences, this poet assumes a similar knowledge because of their disobedience towards the King and his representation. In this way, he reproduces the effect of *Eikon Basilike* by strengthening the exchange between conscience, obedience, and the posthumous King. Just as Charles concludes in one of his prayers, since his enemies fight against *"the clear convictions of their own consciences,"* they also *"fight more against themselves, than ever they did against Me"* (183). The soldiers' assault on the statue is yet another iteration of this self-battle, with the statue's survival representing their inability to destroy Charles or the power he exercises over their consciences – even in death.

As *Eikon Basilike*, and by extension this poem, would suggest, the King's execution did not disrupt the bond between conscience and obedience. Rather, manifestations of Charles's portraiture – whether book, poem, statue, or frontispiece – reinforce that bond in the King's stead as the nation awaits his son's return.

Published with Duport's sermon celebrating Charles II's return and birthday was his sermon delivered on the anniversary of Charles I's execution. Directing his congregation to *Eikon Basilike*, Duport implores them, as *"Pilat* did of him whose example this our Royal Martyr follow'd,"* to look to the King's book in order to *"Behold your King*, and again, *Behold the man*: Look upon him as a *King*, and look upon him as a *Man*, he was a Mirror of both, the best of *Kings*, and the best of *Men*." As in *Eikon Basilike*, Duport reminds his audience of Charles's privileged status as both man and king. More importantly, with Charles acting as a mirror for both the best of men and the best of kings, his readership is meant to treat his book and the cornerstone of that book – the King's conscience – as a reflection for their own lives. Rather than a lesson in casuistry, this reflection of the King's conscience was a lesson in obedience: obedience towards the throne that would translate into obedience towards conscience and God.

Once again reproducing Charles's own connection between the state of his subjects' consciences and their obedience to him, Duport tells his audience that *Eikon Basilike* proved that, whatever the King's enemies "pretended, to palliate so foul a cause" "their Conscience told 'um, they cu'd find not fault in him."[61] Charles's detractors could only accuse him through pretence, all the while their consciences declaring him spotless. Even after the Restoration, Duport imagines through *Eikon Basilike* a nation bound to and by Charles's royal conscience, an identity that becomes compulsory if his listeners were to turn inward. Reinforcing from the pulpit *Eikon Basilike*'s message, Duport reminds his congregants that they must obey the King not only for his sake but also – and more importantly – for their consciences' sake.

Chapter Two

Oliver Cromwell and the Duties of Conscience

Oliver Cromwell's pervasive language of conscience made him and his conscience a target for supporters and critics alike. Some contemporaries feared his conscience morally inept, believing that he might "dispense with any Oath or Protestation without troubling his conscience." A wartime writer similarly thought it both "perjured and seared," and replaced by Cromwell for his own "Covetousnesse."[1] Even after his death, Cromwell's detractors continued to imagine his conscience in writing, often revivified and exacting its sting upon Cromwell in the afterlife.[2] Perhaps most imaginative is Cromwell's response to King Charles I's query about his death in *A New Conference between the Ghosts of King Charles and Oliver Cromwell* (1659). Charles asks, "Didst thou not come out of the World by the Rope or the Ax or by the hand of some *Felton* or other?" and Cromwell assures him, "No; but I came by the Immediate hand of God, who never suffered the worm of Conscience to die within me, but it still lay Gnawing and Tormenting of me, brought an unusual Feaver upon me, that dryed up all my blood, that at my departure not one drop almost was left within me."[3] For this author, Cromwell's conscience was neither inept nor seared; instead, it was the very agent of his death. Cromwell's demise sets him up as Charles's foil: the King, after all, did "come out of the World" by human agents, leaving behind his *Eikon Basilike* as a testament to both his innocence and his clear conscience. Cromwell's death, however, was exacted by the "Immediate hand of God," a divine intervention meant to rid the world of his hypocrisy.

In its focus on his gnawing conscience, this posthumous dialogue foists upon Cromwell the very thing he sought to avoid throughout his public career, for himself and the godly: an encumbered conscience. It also gets at a central aspect of Cromwell's rhetoric that has not received adequate critical attention. Christopher Hill's conservative reactionary still contends with a more religious and radical figure in contemporary Cromwell scholarship.[4] If there is any consistency amid such criticism, it is for an inconsistent Cromwell, marked by an "ideological schizophrenia," or even a Cromwell of "paradoxes."[5] It is difficult, after all, to reconcile the Cromwell who successfully led the New Model Army against Charles I's forces with the Cromwell who dissolved the Rump Parliament on 20 April 1653; or the Cromwell who valued religious conviction over class hierarchy during the civil war years with the Cromwell who was installed as Lord Protector on 16 December 1653; or the Cromwell who supported regicide with the Cromwell who was offered the crown on 23 February 1657.

Yet when viewed in light of the relationship he set out between free conscience and godly nationhood, Cromwell's behaviour seems less erratic. In this chapter, I will examine the central and ongoing language of liberty of conscience in Cromwell's letters and correspondence from the civil war years and in his speeches before the Nominated Assembly and First and Second Protectorate Parliaments, while also noting the limitations that, in practice, qualified his sense of this freedom. From the very start of his military career, Cromwell championed liberty of conscience. His defence of this freedom would become only more forceful during the years of the commonwealth and protectorate as Cromwell sought a civil body willing to promote liberty of conscience in its constituents. More importantly, he increasingly comes to recognize in the free exercise of conscience the potential for a more profound experience of nationhood, one that would unite the nation from within.

As he continued to refine this connection, Cromwell revolutionized the relationship between conscience and the nation. Whereas Charles I, even posthumously, relied upon the bond of conscience between monarch and subject as a guarantor of civil obedience, Cromwell instead envisioned liberty of conscience both as an exercise of obedience of the highest order – to God – and as a bridge to peace and settlement. For Cromwell, the job of the magistrate was simply to lead his subjects towards that liberty and to allow them to enjoy it, his and their ultimate duty to Christ. He thus reimagines obedience – civil and spiritual – as a product of the dutiful enjoyment of liberty of conscience, rather than a limitation of it.

For much of his public career, Cromwell believed the nation at the threshold of "the door to usher-in the things that God has promised."[6]

In his unyielding quest for a parliament "pliable to his purposes," Cromwell also sought the means to cross that threshold so that England might realize its status as the nation of God – a nationhood fully experienced only through the free exercise of conscience.[7]

Liberty of Conscience and the "Real Unity": The Civil War Years

When the First Civil War broke out in August 1642, the Commons made immediate use of Cromwell's natural military acumen. He rose rapidly through the ranks of the parliamentary forces, and by 1650 he would become commander-in-chief of the army. Throughout the civil war period, Cromwell used the language of liberty of conscience to overturn deeply entrenched class values in the parliamentary forces. His defence of sectarians caused friction between Cromwell and his military and parliamentary colleagues, and gained him a reputation as a guardian of religious liberty.

As early as 1643, Cromwell recruited only "godly honest men" to fill his ranks, and he encouraged his colleagues to do the same (1:154). Writing to Sir William Spring and Maurice Barrowe, two members of the Suffolk Committee of the Eastern Association, in September, Cromwell maintains that "it much concerns your good to have conscientious men" fighting for Parliament's cause. In this famous letter, Cromwell defends Captain Raphe Margery, a Suffolk farmer who had raised a cavalry troop of 112 men and whose services had been rejected by the committee possibly because of his social standing and religious enthusiasm.[8] Believing Margery one of those conscientious men that he sought, Cromwell assures Spring and Barrowe that "a few honest men are better than numbers" since "honest men will follow them." This troop of honest men would not only follow one another loyally but also would exhibit a higher loyalty to Parliament's cause: indeed, Cromwell makes a direct link between Margery and his followers being "conscientious" and "what much concerns your good," that of Spring and Barrowe and, by extension, the cause. He signs off by imploring them to "let him not want your favour in whatsoever is needful for promoting this work" (1:154–5).

Cromwell would defend this position over a decade later before the Second Protectorate Parliament, recalling how he "raised such men as had the fear of God before them, and made some conscience of what they did." This army of conscience, he continued, was "never beaten" by the enemy but rather "beat continually" (3:66). In seeking men of conscience, Cromwell insisted that those volunteering to serve not be subjected to religious tests.[9] His tolerance in this matter drew criticism from his Presbyterian colleagues, one of whom accused him of choosing "common men, pore and of meane parentage" for officers, "onely he would give them the title of godly pretious men."[10] In 1644, Cromwell twice had to persuade Lieutenant Colonel William Dodson, who objected to serving with sectarians, not to resign. And on 10 March of that same year, Cromwell wrote an irate letter to Major-General William Crawford for his dismissal of Crawford's own lieutenant colonel, Henry Warner, on the grounds, Cromwell suspects, of intolerance. "Ay, but the man is an Anabaptist," Cromwell asks, "admit he be, shall that render him incapable to serve the Public"? Cromwell protests Crawford's dismissal of "one so faithful to the Cause, and so able to serve you." He continues, "Sir, the State, in choosing men to serve them, takes no notice of their opinions, if they be willing faithfully to serve them, that satisfies" (1:170–1).

While on the surface Cromwell's quarrel with Crawford was a practical one – Cromwell needed men to fill his ranks, after all – his reproach towards Crawford's intolerance revealed the nature and cause of his own acceptance of religious radicals.[11] Cromwell makes an important separation between his men's religious opinions and their ability to serve Parliament: the latter is not contingent upon the former. Yet at times he suggests that the former may make men more capable of the latter. In a second letter to Spring and Barrowe in September 1643, Cromwell writes again of his choice of honest men,

> Gentlemen, it may be it provokes some spirits to see such plain men made Captains of Horse. It had been well that men of honour and birth had entered into these employments, but why do they not appear? Who would have hindered them? But seeing it was necessary the work must go on, better plain men than none, but best to have men patient of wants, faithful and conscientious in the employment, and such, I hope, these will approve themselves to be. (1:161)

Setting class aside, Cromwell thinks it best to choose men based on their faithfulness to the cause and their being conscientious. And, in this case, it just so happens to be "plain men" rather than noblemen who fit the bill. Moreover, in his letter to Crawford, Cromwell tells his opponent that if he only had men such as Warner in his ranks, "you would find as good a fence to you as any you have yet chosen" (1:171).

In the case of Warner, not only is he at once an Anabaptist, "one so faithful to the Cause," and "so able to serve" Crawford, but also he and those like him are Crawford's best defence against the royalist forces.

Cromwell's "godly pretious men," those who "made some conscience of what they did," it seems, were most faithful to the cause. Rather than their godliness being a detriment to their obedience, Cromwell tries to convince his colleagues that the qualities of such men – honesty, faithfulness, and conscientiousness – were actually an asset. Cromwell's staunch defence of his men was not confined to army correspondence during the civil war years, however. In fact, it seems that it was in response to these encounters with intolerance among his military colleagues that Cromwell began to develop and deepen his rhetoric of conscience. While in his correspondence with Crawford, Cromwell uses the language of toleration, hoping that his opponent will "bear with men of different minds from yourself," when addressing Parliament the following year, Cromwell writes regarding his men's "liberty of conscience," a much more active language of acceptance (1:171).

After his decisive victory at Naseby in June 1645, Cromwell writes to William Lenthall, Speaker of the House, that "honest men served you faithfully": "I beseech you in the name of God, not to discourage them." Rather, he continues, "I wish this action may beget thankfulness and humility in all that are concerned in it. He that ventures his life for the liberty of his country, I wish he trust God for the liberty of his conscience, and you for the liberty he fights for" (1:205). Cromwell uses this recent victory as a platform for his own appeal to Parliament. The "honest men" he defends in this case are those soldiers who have not taken the Solemn League and Covenant (1643), which was required of all Englishmen over the age of eighteen by 1644. Under the terms of the Covenant, the Scots joined the parliamentary army against the royalist forces with the expectation that the Scottish and English Churches might be united under a Presbyterian Church system of government.[12]

In order to prove these soldiers "honest men" who "served you faithfully," despite their refusal to take the Covenant, Cromwell bifurcates liberty along religious and national lines. The "liberty of his [the soldier's] conscience," according to Cromwell, is God-given, not granted by the state. Rather than look to Parliament for matters of conscience, the men instead look to them as protectors of the nation's liberty. It is the nation's liberty that is under siege, after all, and their nation's liberty for which they venture their lives, their liberty of conscience persisting in a realm unreachable by parliaments, civil wars, and beleaguered monarchs. By exercising this freedom in the matter of the Covenant, then, these men do not compromise their faithfulness to Parliament's authority: liberty of conscience and obedience to the cause of the nation's liberty can coexist. Not sharing in Cromwell's sentiment, the Commons excised this final paragraph regarding the soldiers' free consciences from his letter before sending it to press. His supporters in Parliament, however, printed the conclusion of this letter, "Whereby the World may know, how both Truth itselfe, and that worthy Gentleman are wronged (as well as other men)," and scattered copies of it in the streets on the night of 21 September.[13]

Unrelenting in the pressure he put on Parliament in this matter, Cromwell writes to Lenthall once again after the surrender of Bristol in September 1645. Returning to the topic of liberty of conscience, Cromwell this time addresses Parliament's fear of the disorder that would arise if a variety of religious opinions were permitted. He points to the liberty of conscience enjoyed among his own ranks as a successful model for both Parliament and the nation: "Presbyterians, Independents, all had here the same spirit of faith and prayer; the same pretence and answer; they agree here, know no names of difference: pity it is it should be otherwise anywhere" (1:218). Cromwell's language of sameness overrides any doctrinal differences held by the Presbyterian and Independent soldiers: in the safe space created by the New Model Army – "here" Cromwell repeats again and again – spirit and prayer prevailed over formal divisions.

Hoping to redirect Parliament's energies in the spiritual realm, he argues, "All that believe, have the real unity, which is most glorious, because inward and spiritual, in the Body, and to the Head. As for being united in forms, commonly called Uniformity, every Christian will for peace-sake study and do, as far as conscience will permit; and from brethren, in things of the mind we look for no compulsion, but that of light and reason" (1:218). Cromwell borrows the language of Ephesians 4:3 in order to distinguish carefully between unity and uniformity.[14] By prizing the former over the latter, Cromwell hopes to revolutionize Parliament's sense of reformation. Moreover, he presents liberty of conscience not as a divisive force, but only as a check upon an imposed uniformity. For this reason, the differences – not divisions – created by the exercise of this liberty were not disruptive, heterodox, or blasphemous but rather Christian, being created only out of a sense of duty towards God (1:353). And it was this universal duty, rather than doctrine, that would create the "real unity" that Cromwell, and, he hoped, Parliament, sought.

The responsibility that Cromwell places upon Parliament in this let-ter is more global than in the last. In June, he had reached out to Parlia-ment as a political body protecting its soldiers; in September, he calls on Parliament as a national Protestant entity. He refers to MPs as the army's "brethren," from whom "we look for no compulsion" as fellow Christians but only "light and reason" towards those who may err. The Christian authority that he grants his forces heightens their credibility in the spiritual realm, while making Parliament's contingent upon their similar embrace of the liberty necessary to allow for that unity.

Cromwell's increasing defence of liberty of conscience during the civil war period extended beyond his forces. In July 1646, Cromwell solicited Thomas Knyvett on behalf of Knyvett's "honest poor neigh-bors of Hapton." One of Knyvett's tenants, Robert Browne, "seeks their disquiet all he may" because he is "not well pleased with the way of those men." Cromwell writes passionately for the cause of these ten-ants, informing Knyvett that "nothing moves me to desire this, more than the pity I bear them in respect of their honesties, and the trouble I hear they are like to suffer for their consciences." More importantly, he writes both in their defence and defensively: "and however the world interprets it," Cromwell continues, "I am not ashamed to solicit for such as are anywhere under a pressure of this kind; doing herein as I would be done by." As he sees it, liberty of conscience is subject to the golden rule, and so by petitioning for others' consciences, he is in a way petitioning for his own.

While these early years of Cromwell's public career are often con-sidered his most radical, they are in fact only the beginning of his campaign for free conscience. In his correspondences with military colleagues, Parliament, and even noblemen, Cromwell continued to sharpen his thinking about the relationship between free conscience and godly nationhood.

The Parliament of Saints and the "Good of the Whole Flock"

On the morning of 20 April 1653, Cromwell entered Westminster Hall with a company of twenty to thirty musketeers and forcibly dissolved the Rump Parliament. Since members of the Rump and its support-ers believed this body to be the legitimate Parliament of the Com-monwealth of England, they regarded this violent dismissal a betrayal of the nascent republic. Yet Cromwell doubted that they could be "a Parliament for God's people," accusing them of having "sat too long for any good you have been doing lately" (2:265, 264). He would also justify his unprecedented actions according to the role he believed conscience should play on the national stage.

After the Rump's dismissal, the Council of State convened the Nominated Assembly, a body of 140 "saints" nominated by radical congregations in London and the army and modelled on the Sanhedrin from the Hebrew Bible.[15] Its members were meant to represent "the various forms of godliness in this nation." On 4 July, Cromwell delivered an optimistic keynote address to this hand-picked assembly. Before looking forward, however, he wanted to divulge the army's reasons for dissolving the Rump, an action that he deemed an "unavoidable necessity, nay even [a] duty that was incumbent upon us." Leading up to that fateful morning, Cromwell characterizes himself and his men as "very tender" towards both the cause and the Rump's reputation, and they tried petitioning and "humbly begging and beseeching of them" to "bring forth those good things that had been promised and expected." Moreover, they found "the people dissatisfied" with the Rump "in every corner of the nation, and all men laying at our doors the non-performance of these things, which had been promised, and were of duty to be performed" (2:277, 279, 278). Rather than act out of a selfish grasp for power against the Rump, the army, according to Cromwell, *re*acted out of a selfless response to duty.

More importantly, he recounts this narrative because it "hath been in our own hearts and consciences, justifying us, and hath never been yet thoroughly imparted to any" (2:281). Their consciences had judged within the "compass of our own certain knowledge," and Cromwell now invited the delegates before him to participate retroactively in the conscience-driven expulsion of the Rump. Believing that the Rump's spirit had no longer been "according to God" because of its refusal to support liberty of conscience and its desire to perpetuate itself, Cromwell and his men felt that it was no longer a valid representation of the nation as a whole (2:280–1). Instead of a betrayal of the revolution, as it was perceived by many, the expulsion of the Rump became, in Cromwell's words, a very act of conscience, and by extension, an exercise of faithful service towards God and the state.

As he turns from the past to the future, Cromwell deems the remainder of his speech yet another duty and another discharge of "our own conscience" (2:289). He advises them regarding the power he is about to lay into their hands and how they might employ it well. Cromwell asks first that they "be as just towards an unbeliever as towards a believer"; second, he desires that they "be faithful with the Saints," a feat only accomplished if they are "pitiful and tender towards all, though of different judgments"; and finally, he feels confident that they will "endeavour the Promoting of the Gospel" and "encourage the Ministry," as Paul writes in Romans, to be "humble and sober-minded, and not stretch themselves beyond their line" (2:292–4). Their ultimate duty is to "win the people to the interest of Jesus Christ, to the love of godliness," victories that he considers the "likeliest way to bring them to their liberties." Cromwell intends for the Nominated Assembly to guide the people towards accepting the liberties that have been earned for them: liberty from regal power and liberty of conscience. For Cromwell, these two liberties – civil and spiritual – were now one and the same, and needed only to be recognized by the people. In this way, the Nominated Assembly was meant as a temporary body, a guardian of the people's liberty until they were able to take up this responsibility themselves.[16]

This task of guidance lay upon them as both a civil and a Christian duty. Whereas earlier Cromwell had sought the approval of their consciences in his and the army's civil duty, he now hoped to transfer to their consciences an irresistible sense of their own. He repeatedly reminds them that they were "called by God [...] to rule with Him, and for Him." Laying the charge of their vocation to their consciences, Cromwell insists, "If a man should tender a Book to you to swear upon, I dare appeal to all your consciences, neither directly nor indirectly did you seek for your coming hither." Since even in conscience they know that they did not call but were called to their positions of power, Cromwell obliges them to "own your call!" (2:291, 296). His language makes them both passive and active at once: by stressing time and again that they were called, he amplifies the sense of duty that lay upon their future endeavours as a civil body. Even in their activity, then, they would still be operating as passive instruments of God's power, helping to forge a nation of people as "fit to be called" into God's service as they had been (2:296).

Believing it to be "the day of the power of Christ," Cromwell asks, "And why should we be afraid to say or think that *this* [assembly] may be the door to usher-in the things that God has promised"? Believing them "at the threshold" of what the Rump would never have accomplished, Cromwell ends his speech with hope and expectation (2:298). Less than two months after this optimistic speech, however, Cromwell lamented to Lieutenant General Fleetwood that "being of different judgments, and of each sort most seeking to propagate their own," the delegates did not possess "that spirit of kindness" that he felt towards them. Their failure to embrace the duty upon their consciences only strengthened Cromwell's resolve to find a body that would.

"Is Not Liberty of Conscience in Religion a Fundamental?": The First Protectorate Parliament

In a move that some still regard as sheer ambition, or, at the very least, social conservatism, Cromwell and the Council of Officers established the Protectorate on 16 December 1653. Ironically, this decision was made in response to the Nominated Assembly's unwillingness to adhere to Cromwell's program of spiritual radicalism. If the creation of the Protectorate was in fact a socially conservative manoeuvre, Cromwell chose this path purposefully, and with the hopes of pursuing his radical agenda of liberty of conscience, the duty that, he believed, lay upon his own conscience. Cromwell sought to establish this liberty within limits, or what J.C. Davis deems "red lines," "points beyond which there was no compromising."[17] For example, the Instrument of Government, the constitution adopted by the Council of Officers the day before Cromwell's installation as Lord Protector, exempted those practicing either "Popery or Prelacy," those committing "licentiousness" in the name of God, and disturbers of the public peace from its guarantee of liberty to all who "profess faith in God by Jesus Christ."[18] Despite these red lines, the Cromwellian Protectorate launched a period of unprecedented religious freedom in England whose impact would resonate into the Restoration.[19]

During the nine months before the First Protectorate Parliament would meet, the Protector and his council catalysed what they hoped would be the beginning of a full-scale reformation in England.[20] In Cromwell's inaugural speech before this parliament on 4 September 1654, he puts upon them the "interest of all the Christian people in the world." Turning to England itself, he marvels at the "door of hope opened by God to us," comparing their nation to "Israel's bringing-out of Egypt through a wilderness, by many signs and wonders, towards a place of rest." Hoping that his and the council's work towards reformation would continue under this first parliament,[21] Cromwell boasted of their accomplishments, and mostly their dispelling of the "heap of confusions [which] were upon these poor nations!" (2:339, 340–1, 352). He describes the nation's deplorable condition when the Protectorate was established, a state troubled by civil unrest and prodigious blasphemies. Cries for "liberty of conscience, and liberty of the subjects" were "abused for the patronising of villanies," and their enemies at home and abroad took advantage of this confusion. In response, the Protectorate set the nation on the path towards reformation; but Cromwell believes it "my duty to let you know" that "these are but entrances and doors of hope, wherein, through the blessing of God, you may enter into rest and peace." But, he reminds the delegates, "you are not yet entered!" (2:345, 350, 358).

He tasks the MPs before him with the end of "Healing and Settling." Casting them as passive recipients of God's will, Cromwell trusts that it is in their minds to heal the nation because it is in God's mind, and God has been "pleased to put it into yours." Cromwell once again draws on the language of duty towards God, his own as well as theirs. He also reminds them throughout of the privileged status that he grants to conscience: "in our old system," he laments, there was "too much of an imposing spirit in matter of conscience; a spirit Unchristian enough in any times, most unfit for these." By eliminating such impositions upon conscience, he expects, it will play an instrumental role in the healing and settling of the nation. Indeed, in speaking of the Commission of Triers appointed to vet new clergy, Cromwell believes that "they have laboured to approve themselves to Christ, the nation and their own consciences" in their work (2:341, 346, 354). This sought-after harmony between Christ, nation, and conscience is but a microcosm of what Cromwell hopes for from Parliament itself: their liberty as a free Parliament and as Christians not only allows them to seek a similar harmony but also obligates them to.

In exercising their Christian liberty, then, they will also be fulfilling their duties in "the interest of these great affairs, and of the people of these nations." He closes this speech persuading them to "a sweet, gracious, and holy understanding of one another and of your business" (2:359). The French ambassador Antoine de Bordeaux, taking note of the Commons' relationship to the Protector, recorded that "it was observed that as often as [Cromwell] spoke in his speech of liberty and religion, that the members did seem to rejoice with acclamations of joy." Bordeaux's account confirms that the Commons too held religious liberty a priority, yet, when considering MPs' subsequent debate over choosing a speaker, he also concludes, "By this beginning one may judge, what the authority of the lord protector will be in this parliament."[22]

The ambassador's musings proved true but one week later, when Cromwell delivered a second and more impassioned speech before the same body, hoping to mitigate their growing hostility for the Protectoral regime and redirect their attention towards his program of reform.[23]

Cromwell aggressively defended his position before Parliament as unsought and providential, sharing his former desire to be "quit of the Power God had most clearly by His Providence put into my hand." "I called not myself to this place," he insists. "I say again, I called not myself to this place!" (2:372, 367). In language reminiscent of that he used when speaking before the Nominated Assembly, Cromwell talks of himself as God's passive agent: he had not called for, but rather he had been called to this position of power. In his role as Protector, then, he is fulfilling his duty towards God and conscience.

More importantly, he lays claim to three types of witnesses who might corroborate this fact, those "within, – without, – and above!" Confirming his own conscience, the people of England, and God Himself as his witnesses, Cromwell turns to the delegates before him, determined to "make *you* my last witnesses" by "approving myself to every one of your consciences in the sight of God." He believed that by validating himself to their consciences, he might also invalidate their current disapproval of the Instrument of Government and his position as Lord Protector. Cromwell trusts that the delegates before him "know God, and know what conscience is, and what it is to 'lie before the Lord!'" (2:376, 379, 380, 371). He felt confident in the fact that while their politics might deem the Protectorate unjust, their consciences "in the sight of God" could not. By drawing on what he believed to be an irresistible call to duty, Cromwell hoped to secure Parliament's obedience.

In seeking their compliance, Cromwell responds to the delegates' challenge of the Instrument of Government. He details for them which provisions within the settlement were circumstantial, and so up for debate, and those that were fundamental, and so fixed. Among the fundamentals, Cromwell lists liberty of conscience, asking, "Is not liberty of conscience in religion a fundamental?" He considered it not only fundamental to the Instrument of Government but also a "natural right" and "a thing [that] ought to be very reciprocal." If the magistrate might exercise his liberty of conscience in establishing the church government, Cromwell asks, "Why should he not give it, the like liberty, to others?" According to this reasoning, the magistrate is essentially bound to extend that same liberty to his people. Liberty of conscience, he insists, cannot be exclusive.

Looking back to the wars, Cromwell gives himself permission to push his idea of reciprocity to its very limits: "I may say it to you, I can say it: All the money of this nation would not have tempted men to fight upon such an account as they have here been engaged in, if they had not had hopes of liberty of conscience better than they had from Episcopacy, or than would have been afforded them from a Scottish Presbytery, – or an English either." The driving force behind his men was their hope for this fundamental. The wars were not just fought for liberty but specifically for liberty of conscience. Their successes on the battlefield legitimated this war of conscience, and Parliament now owed them the fruits of their hard-won victory. "This, I say, is a fundamental," Cromwell repeats. "It ought to be so." Cromwell's language – "It *ought* to be so" – seeks to inspire in Parliament a moral imperative. He implores them to consider not only the men who fought in the present but also generations past who, "for the enjoyment of their liberty, were necessitated to go into a waste howling wilderness in New England," and the "generations to come" who would also reap the benefits of Parliament's bolstering of this liberty. "You have been called hither together," he cautions them, "to save a nation, – nations" – nations that could only be saved through the free exercise of conscience (2:383, 387).

While Cromwell spent much energy defending conscience and articulating the terms of its liberty, liberty of conscience was not one of the topics discussed at length by Parliament during the turbulent days of 5–11 September.[24] Also interesting is the fact that the indenture he forced delegates to sign after this speech if they wished to remain MPs did not include a stipulation for liberty of conscience.[25] Perhaps he expected that his words would make them a parliament for conscience: in exercising the liberty of their own, they would inevitably protect the liberty of others' consciences. When speaking of the indenture to Parliament, Cromwell tells the delegates before him that when they were first called, he had a "just confidence" in their "owning of your call and of the authority bringing you hither" (2:389). Though he now felt that they had necessitated the indenture in order for them to acknowledge his authority as Protector, Cromwell still seemed to place in them a "just confidence" with the cause closest to his heart.

Or he might have feared that, had a stipulation been included in the indenture regarding this liberty, he would have lost more than the fifty to eighty MPs who ultimately decided not to sign the agreement. Either way, his confidence that this body could rule with and for conscience on the terms that he established would soon be dashed.

Despite the indenture and the departure of Cromwell's greatest detractors, debates continued over the next five months. Parliament failed to pass any of Cromwell's eighty-two ordinances, and religious liberty became a hotly contested topic. Samuel Rawson Gardiner notes that "whilst his [Cromwell's] mind was fixed on including as many as possible within the limits of toleration, they [the parliamentary majority] were thinking of making the exemptions as numerous as possible."[26] In November, tensions were so high that Cromwell refused to advise the committee appointed by the Commons regarding articles of indemnity and toleration.[27] These debates continued on into December, with some MPs pushing for an "enumeration of heresies," an inventory, which others feared might "expose the godly party, and people hereafter, to some danger of suffering under those laws," while others tried to take away Cromwell's veto power in matters of religion (neither of which passed).[28] David L. Smith and Patrick Little argue that not only was liberty of conscience low on this Parliament's list of priorities, they also actively tried "to obstruct Cromwell's promotion" of that same freedom.[29] The draft of the constitutional bill that Parliament prepared before its dissolution reveals that the majority of MPs desired to limit both the Protector's power and his program for liberty of conscience.[30]

For their seeming inaction and desire to alter the present government, Cromwell dissolved this body on 22 January 1655, the earliest opportunity allowed him under the Instrument of Government.[31] Rather than "peace and settlement," "mercy and truth," and "righteousness and peace," Cromwell accuses, Parliament sowed "dissettlement and division" and "discontent and dissatisfaction" over the five months of its sitting. Most neglected, however, was "that slighted Cause" of God, liberty of conscience. God Himself, Cromwell believed, had restored to His people "a liberty to worship, with the freedom of their consciences, and freedom in their estates and persons when they do so." Thus they have finally "found the Cause of God by the works of God" (2:409, 411, 412). Cromwell casts liberty of conscience as the cause of God as well as a foundational liberty for the nation itself: only when God's people have exercised their restored liberty of conscience might they similarly enjoy "freedom in their estates and persons." Without liberty of conscience, civil liberty itself could not exist.

For this reason, Parliament's failure to establish this liberty upon his parameters also indicated their failure as a political body. Had they bolstered liberty of conscience, they might also have rendered "these nations both secure, happy and well satisfied." Instead, there is "yet upon the spirits of men a strange itch": "Nothing will satisfy them unless they can put their finger upon their brethren's consciences, to pinch them there." Just as the wars had revealed to them the cause of God, so it had also proved that liberty of conscience was "that which was most dear to us," a cause for which Parliament has "done just nothing!" (4:17–18).

With Cromwell positioning his voice as the voice of the people, he strips Parliament of its authority as a representative body. For the remainder of the speech, he turns within to his own conscience and the duty upon him as Protector. He tells Parliament that he does not desire to keep his position an hour longer once he has "preserve[d] England in its just rights" and "protect[ed] the people of God in such a just liberty of their consciences." Believing this protection the nature of his office, Cromwell next "consulted what might be my duty in such a day as this." While maintaining that he acts in conscience, Cromwell finally declares that "I think myself bound, – in my duty to God and the people of these nations, to their safety and good in every respect, – I think it my duty to tell you that it is not for the profit of these nations, nor fit for the common and public good, for you to continue here any longer." He had earlier warned Parliament that those who come up against the cause of God shall "suffer shipwreck," and he now positions himself as that rock upon which the First Protectorate Parliament would split (2:419, 423, 430, 412).

Fulfilling the "Debt Due to God and Christ": The Rule of the Major-Generals and the Second Protectorate Parliament

The First Protectorate Parliament's failure to attend to what he perceived to be God's cause, as well as their efforts to weaken his regime, encouraged Cromwell to seek further political support from the army. His disillusionment was only magnified by Penruddock's uprising in the spring of 1655 and the failure of the Western Design in the summer of that same year.[32] Also troubling Cromwell that summer was the vexed case of John Biddle, a moment that challenged him to consider his duty to liberty of conscience and where he must draw what Davis calls his red lines. A religious controversialist and antitrinitarian, Biddle penned an appeal to Cromwell from Newgate, insisting that he possessed a "conscience void of offence towards God and men," and demanding that the Protector "make good what you have published unto the world [...] and restore me to my liberty."[33] Biddle's case was a difficult one for Cromwell: while he considered Biddle's denial of the divinity of Christ an intolerable heresy, he also baulked, it seemed, at the threat of Biddle's persecution. On 5 October, the Protector intervened in the legal proceedings against Biddle and banished him to St Mary's Castle on the Isles of Scilly. This way, Cromwell rid London of a tireless blasphemer while also sparing Biddle's life.[34]

These disappointments to the Protector's vision abroad and at home made him fear God's displeasure. In November 1655, Cromwell invites the nation to observe a day of solemn fasting and humiliation, fearing the "Tares of Division that have been sown" throughout the nation as well as the "abhominable blasphemies vented & spreading of late, through the Apostacy of, and the abuse of liberty by, many professing Religion." Believing their prayers unanswered, the Protector calls for another fast day in March 1656, lamenting among other national failures that "the People of God continue still in their animosities, and improve not such strokes unto Love and Union." He prays that God will "unite us in love [...] and thereby exalt his own great name, make our Land glorious."[35]

Cromwell's certainty that the nation's persisting spiritual iniquities were the cause of God's displeasure only made his desire for a reformation more urgent. The path of least resistance seemed to be establishing the Rule of the Major-Generals and tasking them with this grand undertaking on a local level.[36] Speaking to the Second Protectorate Parliament in September 1656, Cromwell lauds the Major-Generals as having been "more effectual towards the discountenancing of Vice and settling of Religion, than anything done these fifty years" (2:543). His trust in the success of this godly government was also expressed in *A Proclamation Prohibiting the Disturbing of Ministers and other Christians in their Assemblies and Meetings*, published on 15 February 1655. Cromwell opens by celebrating that God has "crown[ed] Us with this," the "free and uninterrupted passage of the Gospel running through the midst of Us, and Liberty for all to hold forth and profess with sobriety, their Light and Knowledge therein." Moreover, the nation enjoys this liberty of conscience "without any Interruption from the powers God hath set over this Commonwealth, nay with all just and due Encouragement thereto, and protections in so doing by the same," a "Mercy that is the price of much Blood."[37]

Several critics read this edict negatively for its purpose of curtailing some sectarian behaviours, believing it "a proclamation to restrict religious liberty."[38] Yet Cromwell only denounces those who, "instead of a suitable return to the Lord our God for this Liberty," "do openly and avowedly, by rude and unchristian practices, disturb both the publique and private meetings for preaching the Word, and other Religious Exercises, and vilifie, oppose, and interrupt the publique preachers in their Ministry, whereby the Liberty of the Gospel, and profession of Religion, and the Name of God, is much dishonoured and abused, and the Spirits of all good men much grieved." Singling out Quakers and Ranters as those responsible for such activities, he condemns neither their convictions nor ways of worship; he asks only that they "forbear henceforth all such irregular and disorderly practices" that might disturb the worship of others. Rather than restrict religious liberty, this proclamation, Cromwell maintains, is meant to ensure its survival. In the edict, he also declares that "he reckons it a Duty incumbent upon him, and shall take all possible Care to preserve and Continue this Freedom and Liberty to all persons in this Commonwealth fearing God, though of differing Judgements, by protecting them in the sober and quiet exercise and profession of Religion" against "all such who shall, by imposing upon the Consciences of their Brethren," "seek to hinder them therein." And it is his duty not only to protect liberty of conscience but also to "Declare his dislike of all such practices" that are "contrary to the just Freedome and Liberties of the people."

Despite Cromwell's professed optimism in the Rule of the Major-Generals, the Protectorate's financial struggles hit a breaking point by the summer of 1656. England had declared war with Spain in October 1655, which required adequate funding along with the military government at home.[39] The major-generals convinced Cromwell to call the Second Protectorate Parliament, confident that they might influence the elections in their favour. In reality, the elections doubled as a referendum on the major-generals' governance, and the Second Protectorate Parliament would soon vote for the end of their rule.[40]

In his opening speech on 17 September 1656, Cromwell reflects on Spain's long-standing enmity with England and Charles Stuart's dangerous alliance with this opponent. He also cautions Parliament about the dangers at home, particularly the threat from the republicans, Levellers, and Fifth Monarchists that could throw the nation once again into civil war. Cromwell considered each of the obstacles "complications" of God's interest, an interest that he expected this parliament would first "be convinced" of and then "prosecute it" (2:518). In order to encourage their convincing, Cromwell speaks to them from his own conscience of their duties to God and nation: "in my conscience, if I were put to show it, this hour, Where the security of these Nations will lie … I would say in my very conscience, and as before Almighty God I speak it: I think your Reformation, if it be honest and thorough and just, *it* will be your best security!" (2:533). He speaks not only to the MPs before him but also "as before Almighty God" Himself. Through this language, Cromwell invites Parliament to participate in the certainty of his conscience, encouraging their trust in him and confidence in his program.

More importantly, he asks that they too use their consciences when considering the duties upon them as a political body. Cromwell asks, "Do I come to tell you that I would *tie* you to this War?" (2:533). Answering his own question with an emphatic "no," Cromwell includes himself among their ranks, believing that they should "let you and me join in the prosecution of that War, – according as we are satisfied, and as the cause will appear to our consciences in the sight of the Lord" (2:533–4). Cromwell once again expresses a "just confidence" in the judgment of the delegates' consciences, believing that if only he might appeal to that most trustworthy of witnesses within each MP, he might also see God's interest realized.

Transitioning quickly from talk of war to religious liberty, Cromwell speaks to Parliament's duty in the realm of conscience. He details the current policy of toleration, telling MPs that "whatever pretensions to Religion would continue quiet, peaceable, they should enjoy conscience and liberty to themselves; – and *not* make Religion a pretense for arms and blood, truly we have suffered them, and that cheerfully, so to enjoy their own liberties" (2:535). Cromwell implores Parliament "in the name of God" to continue to encourage the faithful irrespective of forms, so long as they "continue to be thankful to God, and to make use of the liberty given them to enjoy their own consciences!" (2:536). In this way, Parliament's favour would only cease were an individual not to make use of his liberty of conscience. This dynamic created two duties at once: the first was upon the believer to exercise his liberty of conscience, and the second upon Parliament to support his ability to do so. Cromwell cautions Parliament that not only is liberty of conscience "the peculiar Interest all this while contested for," but also "it is a debt due to God and Christ" (2:536). "He will require" that debt, Cromwell threatens, were Parliament to deny liberty of conscience to any of the faithful.

Once again, Cromwell characterizes religious freedom as a negative liberty: rather than view liberty of conscience as a license being afforded the individual, he instead casts it as a freedom from obstacles for the believer. More importantly, the faithful are required to enjoy this liberty as Christians, and to deny it them would be a crime against God Himself. Cromwell closes by identifying the type of men who will be able to carry on this work of reformation: not "Doubting, hesitating men," but rather "men of honest hearts" who are "engaged to God; strengthened by his Providence; enlightened in His words, to know His Word" (2:548). And they cannot accomplish this work alone; instead, they must unite with their Protector "in faith and love to Jesus Christ, and to His peculiar Interest in the world" (2:549). Guaranteeing Parliament that when he speaks, "I speak my heart before God," Cromwell hopes to earn their confidence in him. Discoursing at once with the delegates before him and the Almighty, Cromwell hopes that this parliament will finally usher in an era of "Comfort and blessing" (2:552).

"Nothing Must Make a Man's Conscience a Servant": The Offer of the Crown and a Crisis of Duty

Like its predecessors, the Second Protectorate Parliament too had difficulties embracing Cromwell's program of liberty of conscience. Their most notorious flouting of toleration came in 1656 with the case of James Naylor. On 24 October, Naylor rode into Bristol accompanied by four men and three women singing "Holy, holy, holy, Lord God of Sabbaoth," in imitation of Christ's entry into Jerusalem on Palm Sunday. The group was arrested and charged with blasphemy. Parliament examined Naylor, during which he denied repeatedly that he thought himself Christ, and he narrowly escaped a death sentence with a vote of 96 to 82. Instead, he would be whipped through the streets and exposed in the pillory, his tongue would be bored through with a red-hot iron, and he would be branded with the letter "B" on his forehead to mark him out as a blasphemer.[41]

Prior to his sentencing, Parliament debated Naylor's fate in secret for ten days. Many MPs shared concerns that Cromwell's policy of liberty of conscience was allowing for the growth of groups they considered dangerous, like the Quakers. Major-General Philip Skippon, a Presbyterian representing King's Lynn in Norfolk, remarked, "It has been always my opinion, that the growth of these things is more dangerous than the most intestine or foreign enemies. I have often been troubled in my thoughts to think of this toleration; I think I may call it so. Their great growth and increase is too notorious, both in England and Ireland." Appropriating Cromwell's own language of conscience,

Skippon continues, "My conscience would fly in my face, if I should be silent … I am as tender as any man, to lay impositions upon, men's consciences, but in these horrid things."[42] Other MPs similarly believed Cromwell's toleration too liberal, fearing for the safety of the commonwealth were it to be extended to groups like the Quakers.

On 26 December and after the first part of Naylor's punishment had been carried out, the Speaker read aloud a letter from the Protector in which he questioned both the punishment levied against Naylor and Parliament's authority to carry out such a judgment. Cromwell requests that "the House will let Us know the grounds and reasons whereupon they have proceeded" against Naylor, their judgments in the matter having taken place "wholly without Us" (3:20). Like the Biddle case, Naylor's offence butted against Cromwell's red lines, pushing the limits of his promise of liberty of conscience. Throughout the proceedings, the Protector desired that his allies in Parliament work for leniency in sentencing, yet he chose to abstain from interfering personally on Naylor's behalf.[43] It is likely that Cromwell believed Naylor guilty of blasphemy, but he nevertheless feared the constitutional precedent that such a sentence might set.[44] In a speech before the major-generals the following month, Cromwell still lamented Parliament's cruel treatment of Naylor. He believes Parliament in need of a "check or balancing power" because of their "arbitrary proceedings," threatening his listeners that the "Case of James Naylor might happen to be your own case" (3:488).

Yet it was Cromwell who next found his conscience imposed upon by Parliament. On 23 February 1657, Sir Christopher Packe, a former lord mayor of London, brought before Parliament a constitutional document known as the Humble Address and Remonstrance, which would later become the Humble Petition and Advice. Among proposals that would establish a second House of Parliament and a national church, the document also asked that Cromwell assume the title of king. Those in defence of this motion, primarily civilian MPs, argued that the office of king, unlike that of Protector, was an ancient one and well defined according to English law. A king's powers were known and limited accordingly, whereas the Instrument of Government left the Protector's power undefined.

For years, scholars have speculated as to why Cromwell ultimately turned down the offer of the crown. C.H. Firth argued over a century ago that Cromwell would have "waived his scruples and accepted" had it not been for the many letters that he received from godly congregations and for his own knowledge of the army's opposition to the offer.[45] More recently, historians have recognized the possibility of religious motives behind his decision, yet many continue to identify other reasons as prime catalysts behind his refusal of the crown.[46] While undoubtedly the advice of "good and godly friends"[47] held sway with Cromwell, as well as his standing with the army, his several responses to Parliament regarding this crisis played out in miniature the disagreement between Cromwell's vision of godly nationhood and Parliament's.

In his first official response to what Cromwell calls this "Frame of Government," he asks for "some short time to ask counsel of God and of my own heart" (3:25, 28). Three days later, Cromwell asks that a committee attend him so that he might give an answer to the Humble Petition and Advice. He begins by praising Parliament for having "done that which never was done before!": "they have been zealous of the two greatest Concernments that God hath in the world," religious and civil liberty. "If I were to give an account before a greater Tribunal than any earthly one," Cromwell continues, "and if I were asked, Why I have engaged all along in the late War, I could give no answer but it would be a wicked one if it did not comprehend these Two ends!" (3:30–1). Yet when he turns to the matter of the crown, Cromwell informs Parliament that "I am not able for such a trust and charge." Citing his search for spiritual counsel in this matter, he says that he was unable "to find it my duty to God and you to undertake this charge under that Title." "Nothing must make a man's conscience a servant," Cromwell goes on, "And really and sincerely it is my conscience that guides me to this answer" (3:32–3). Exercising his own liberty of conscience in this matter, he cannot accept the crown for his conscience's sake. Were he to do so, he would compromise his conscience's liberty – the very thing he seeks for his compatriots. Cromwell, to his dismay, ends this declination speech on Parliament's terms: "if the Parliament be so resolved, 'for the whole Paper or none of it,' it will not be fit for me to use any inducement to you to alter their resolution" (3:33).

Despite Cromwell's decisive and conscientious response, Parliament considered the matter unresolved. On 4 April, they voted on whether or not the House still adhered to the Humble Petition and Advice, with an outcome of 65 nays and 78 yeas. On 6 April, Parliament resolved to acquaint Cromwell with the results of their vote, along with the following reasons for their continued support of the document:

> That the Parliament having lately presented their humble Petition and Advice to your Highness, whereunto they have not as yet received satisfaction; and the matters contained in that Petition and Advice, being agreed upon by the great council and representative of the three nations; and which, in their judgments, are most conducive to the good of the people thereof, both in their spiritual and civil concernments, they have therefore thought fit to adhere to this advice; and to put your Highness in mind of the great obligation which rests upon you, in respect of this advice; and again to desire you to give your assent thereunto.[48]

Countering Cromwell's dutiful claim to conscience, Parliament reminds him of his "great obligation" to its recommendation as the "great council and representative of three nations." Parliament's reasoning raised for the Protector a crisis of duties. He begins his speech on 8 April assuring MPs that "no man can put a greater value than I hope I do, and shall do, upon the desires and advices of Parliament" (3:34). Yet he is also bound to "measure your Advice and my own Infirmities together." "And truly," he continues, "these will have some influence upon conscience!" Cromwell reminds Parliament of the great burden that comes with authority, a burden that nothing less than "Assistance from Above" will "enable him to the discharge of it." More importantly, that divine support is only available to him who is "convinced in his conscience" regarding the legitimacy of his authority (3:36). "If I undertake anything *not* in Faith," he cautions, "I shall serve you in my own Unbelief; – and I shall then be the most unprofitablest Servant that ever People or Nation had!" (3:36–7).

Whereas in chapter 2 of *Eikon Basilike* Charles had come to count his inward peace of conscience "dearer to me than a thousand Kingdoms," Cromwell here strives to reconcile his inner promptings to his national duties. His obedience to conscience is what sustains, determines, and finally authorizes his service to the nation. To violate that bond between conscience and the nation would compromise Cromwell's ability to fulfil his role as Protector. In charting out this formula for Parliament, Cromwell models what he believed to be the central role conscience might play in the experience of godly nationhood. If his conscience disagrees with Parliament's counsel, then the former's judgment must trump the latter's. Cromwell assures MPs that "before and then and since" he gave his answer to them, he has been "lifting up my heart to God, To know *what* might be my duty at such a time as this" (3:36). Though Parliament would "mind me of the duty that is incumbent upon me," he reminds them that "in such cases as these are, the world hath judged that a man's conscience ought to know no scruples; yet surely mine doth, and I dare not dissemble." Because of his duty to conscience, he is not persuaded "by a call of duty" to Parliament's judgment, "as I know you intend I should be" (3:37). In order to resolve this crisis, Cromwell invites Parliament to share with him their reasoning, as he hopes to do for them in turn. He closes with his hope that, with greater understanding, they might "find out those things that may answer our duty. Mine, and all our duties, to those whom we serve" (3:38).

When discussing the matter with MPs once again on 11 April, Cromwell is willing to hear Parliament's reasoning but also reminds them that "I did not indeed in vain allege conscience in the first answer I gave you." And though he asks for a time to consider their conversation, Cromwell laments that "things did stick upon my conscience" initially, and "I must still say they do!" (3:51). He replies on 13 April, arguing that while Parliament's reasons for wanting him to accept the crown were "strong and rational," they were not "necessarily conclusive" (3:52, 55). He announces that his "present answer" still "sways with my conscience." Reminding his audience that he has the Word of God "for the rule of my conscience," he points out that "the Providence of God hath laid aside this Title of King providentially *de facto*" (3:69–70). "I will not seek to set up that, that Providence hath destroyed," he continued. "And this is somewhat to me, and to my judgment and my conscience. That it is true, it is that that hath an awe upon my spirit" (3:71). Cromwell concludes with the hope that God will "direct you [Parliament] to do what is according to His will" (3:73).

On 20 April, Cromwell revisits Parliament's language of duty, language that "doth a little pinch upon me." "I think it can be no man's duty nor obligation," he continues, "but between God and himself, if he be conscious of his own infirmities, disabilities and weaknesses; and conscious that he is not able perhaps to encounter with it" (3:81). Moreover, not only was Parliament's reasoning unable to "convince my judgment of what was of my duty," but also he is no longer sure how taking this title can be "laid upon me as a duty" (3:82, 81). According to Cromwell, Parliament was unable to reconcile their language of duty with his conscience and consciousness of his duty to God.

In his final speech on this "great matter" on 8 May, Cromwell tries again to justify his disagreement with Parliament on the matter of duty. While "no private judgment is to lie in the balance with the judgment of Parliament," in matters "that respect particular persons, – every man is to give an account to God of his actions, he must in some measure be able to prove his own work, and to have an approbation in his own conscience of that that he is to do or to forebear." He implores Parliament not to "deny *me* this" freedom of conscience "whilst you are granting others Liberties." As he had insisted on behalf of the godly time and again over the last decade, Cromwell now declares for himself that this same liberty is in fact a duty, "and such a Duty as I cannot without sinning forbear, – to examine my own heart and thoughts and judgment, in every work which I am to set my hand to, or to appear in or for" (3:127). In exercising his liberty of conscience, Cromwell also exercises an irresistible duty towards God and his eternal soul. Parliament finally appeased him when, in June 1657, the Humble Petition and Advice was adopted with Cromwell maintaining his position as Protector.

Yet Cromwell's conflict with this body did not end with this compromise. Parliament reconvened on 20 January 1658, and acting upon the terms of the new constitution, the "Other House" of Parliament was appointed, and the ninety-three MPs excluded by Cromwell in 1656 were readmitted. Cromwell ushers in this parliamentary session with a cautious optimism nonetheless, declaring that "we hope we may say we have arrived at what we aimed at … the maintaining of the Liberty of these Nations; our Civil Liberties as Men, our Spiritual Liberties as Christians" (3:151). Involving Parliament more directly in this aim, Cromwell anticipates MPs' uncertainty: "If, therefore, you would know upon what foundation you stand, own your foundation to be from God. He hath set you where you are: He hath set you in the enjoyment of your Civil and your Spiritual Liberties" (3:157). In a second speech only five days later, Cromwell pleads with Parliament to turn its attention to "these evils that are upon us" both at home and abroad rather than debate the legitimacy of the current government and Other House (3:164). He ends on a determined note, proclaiming,

> I shall, – I must! – see it done [that] liberty of conscience may be secured for honest people, that they may serve God without fear; that every just Interest may be preserved; that a Godly Ministry may be upheld, and not affronted by seducing and seduced spirits; that all men may be preserved in their just rights, whether civil or spiritual.

It was, he argued, "Upon this acount" that "I took my oath" (3:184).

At the start of this speech, Cromwell had hoped that once he had spoken, he would leave his words "to such an operation on your hearts as it shall please God Almighty to work upon you" (3:163). Two weeks later, however, he would stand once again before this body, to deliver his final speech to Parliament. Cromwell condemns MPs for having "not only disjointed yourselves but the whole Nation" in the "fifteen or sixteen days that you have sat" (3:191). He dissolves Parliament passionately, declaring, "Let God be judge between you and me!" This was the final parliament that Cromwell would contend with: on 3 September of that same year, Cromwell died, leaving his son Richard to take his place as Lord Protector.

Ironically, by rejecting the crown for his conscience's sake, Cromwell ultimately made the Protectoral government weaker, precipitating the return of Charles II in 1660. Richard, after all, would not hold the sway that his father did, and without the crown he could not sustain his power as Protector. Rather than retreating from the revolution, then, it was instead Cromwell's refusal to retreat from the revolution that ultimately sounded the death knell of the commonwealth and the godly nation he hoped it would become. And while he often believed England at the very threshold of the door "to usher-in the things that God has promised" – this connection between civil and religious liberty – for Cromwell, that threshold was never crossed.

As in *A New Conference* discussed earlier, *The English Devil: Or, Cromwell and his Monstrous Witch* (1660) similarly appropriates Cromwell's own language of conscience as the foundation for its attack on his character. The author, calling him a "Hellish Monster," a "damnable Machiavilian," and an "audacious Rebel," believed Cromwell a lawless scourge upon the nation whose program of liberty of conscience only advanced his villainous rule. "No Liberty was granted to the Subjects," he laments, "unless it were that of the Conscience; and that too was denied the more Orthodox and Loyal Party." Whereas Cromwell promoted liberty of conscience as a gateway liberty that would lead to others, this author finds the former Protector's singular focus both stifling and partial. Cromwell only "granted a toleration for all Religions" because, the author contends, "his own was to choose; and that he might not offend the Tender Consciences of his pretended Zealots and Favorites, who were true Vassels to the Lust and Villainy of such an Imperious Usurper."[49] Rather than transform England into the nation of God, Cromwell's focus on this liberty instead allowed for "a Chaos of confusion" to "bespread the whole Nation," during which "Honesty was so much out of fashion, that he that was Vertuous was a Malefactor, and deserved Death"; "An honest loyal Subject was as much hooted and pointed at, and judged as ridiculous an Object, as a *Spanish Don* in his Country Garb at *Paris*"; and "An honest man was as strange a sight in *England*, as a Horse in *Venice*, or a Beggar in *Holland*." This topsy-turvy existence was only righted when "Providence divine" finally "cut him off, to the general benefit and rejoycing of the Nation."[50]

The national chaos prompted by Cromwell's support of liberty of conscience was only rivalled by that produced within his own conscience. The author wryly adds, "But since he is in his Grave, We will not take up his Ashes any further: if he can find any rest there now dead, who living I am sure had little or none in his Conscience (for he ever carried a Civil War in his Breast, of Fears, Suspicions, and Jealousies) he shall lye secure, for *we* intend to disturb him no farther." Like the author of *A New Conference*, this writer imagines a Cromwell tormented by his conscience. He also exacts against Cromwell a national justice of sorts, transforming the former Protector's conscience into a microcosm of England's recent ills, including the civil wars that thrust Cromwell and his conscience onto the public stage. Even the *"English* ground groaned with the burthen of his inhumane Tyrant" upon his burial, a traitor both to the English people and to the very land itself.[51]

The revolutionary relationship that Cromwell imagined between free conscience and the nation would remain what Little and Smith call a "minority agenda" for the duration of his public career.[52] Though his critique is at times amusing and at others absurd, the author of *The English Devil* accurately captures Cromwell's marginal status. The Protector hoped to lead England towards its God-given liberty, yet, in pursuing his program of liberty of conscience, he alienated not only much of Parliament but also much of the nation. However, his preoccupation with conscience also set into circulation new questions about the nature of conscience, its liberty, and its role on the national stage. Both his supporters and, as demonstrated by the authors of *A New Discourse* and *The English Devil*, his detractors participated in this revolutionary discourse of conscience, inspired in part and fuelled by the Protector. As the next chapter will demonstrate, the Quakers even try to influence Cromwell's perception of his own conscience, addressing letter after letter to the light they believed dwelled within his and their consciences alike.

Chapter Three

Early Quaker Writing and the Unifying Light of Conscience

"I stood still & gaue him not a word," Anthony Pearson writes to George Fox regarding his first meeting with Oliver Cromwell in 1654, "but waited a pretty while my eyes being fixed on him wch putt him into a maze." Once Cromwell was transfixed, Pearson continues, "the Lord opened my mouth & I declared unto him y^t I was moued of ye Lord to come to him." Pearson, a Quaker administrator and later defector, was but one of a number of Friends who visited Cromwell during his term as Lord Protector to caution him that "ye Lord [was] comeing to establish his own law" in England "& to sett upp righteousnesse." His message, like that of his fellow Friends, was specifically addressed to Cromwell's conscience: having put the Protector "into a maze," or state of amazement, Pearson believed that "[I] spoke plainly to y^t [of God] in his conscience & was made manifest to it." Though he later confesses to Fox that "my words to [Cromwell] were other then I looked for," and that "it was shewed to me since y^t there is nothing left in him of God," Pearson's attempt was neither the Quakers' first nor last effort to shape the nation at large through the conscience of its Lord Protector.[1]

Scholars have long shown an interest in the early (and most radical) years of the Quaker movement,[2] and more recently, literary historians in particular have taken an interest in early Quaker writings.[3] Despite this rich body of scholarship, however, the prevalent language of conscience in early Quaker writing has not been explored at length.[4] Often taken for granted, such language was central to the Quakers' radical discourse of the "light within" and their revolutionary belief in that light as an alternative site of authority to both church and state. And, as this vignette suggests, the language of conscience was also vital to their relationship with Cromwell. The Protector's conversations with

George Fox, the founder of the movement, have been well noted; yet Cromwell's equally important – and persistent – contact with other prominent Quaker leaders has received little attention.[5] In addition, scholarly discussions of Cromwell's interactions with Friends have been more concerned with the dramatic case of James Naylor or the degree of liberty of conscience granted individuals than with how Quakers deployed the language of conscience during these formative years.[6]

Letters to Cromwell from the Library of the Society of Friends in London and "private" letters that were printed for public viewing show that Quakers used conscience to make a precise intervention in the politics of the 1650s. Indeed, though the idea that "politically the Quakers were unimportant" was debunked over half a century ago,[7] little has been done since to flesh out the complexities of the Quakers' relationship to Cromwell, and through him, to the nation. Quakers aggressively used the language of conscience to advise, challenge, and reprimand Cromwell in person, in print, and in private correspondence. In doing so, they revolutionized the already radical language of conscience, giving it new meaning and purpose. More specifically, they transformed this language into a tool through which they expected – and demanded – that Cromwell would shape England into the Kingdom of God.

Conscience, Conversion, and Community in Early Quaker Writings

In *To all the Professors of the World* (1655), Margaret Fell, known as the "nursing mother" of Quakerism, proclaims to her readers, "To the Light in all your Consciences do I speak, that to it ye may turn, to see what ye know of the living God." "There [in your conscience] he is," she continues, "unknown to you yet [...] though he be not far from every one of you."[8] During the early years of the Quaker movement, Friends' distinctive notion of "conscience" was central both to their theology of the "light within" and to their project of national conversion. Addresses such as this one – written directly to the "light" in the reader's conscience" – were a Quaker commonplace by 1655. Fell writes to inspire spiritual awareness in her readers, who, unbeknownst to them, already possess an intimate knowledge of the living God. By speaking directly to the light in their consciences, she asks that they turn to it, confident in the power of her words to pierce that inner sanctum. Friends understood conscience to be the vehicle of the "light of Christ," also referred to as the "light within" or "that of God within." Though not itself divine, conscience was where this divine light was "loved, and the voice [of God] heard."[9] This understanding of conscience's spiritual role within the individual made it a key component of Quaker evangelism, and the only means through which "*we, and what we declare,* [shall] *be approved.*"[10]

Friends often confirmed the importance of conscience when recollecting their own moment of convincement or spiritual conversion.[11] Hearing Fox preach in 1654, Richard Hubberthorne, a former soldier in Cromwell's army and later an active Quaker minister and polemicist, describes that it was then that God's "Power was made manifest and his Word spoke within me [...] my Conscience being awakened by the Light of God." In a private correspondence with Fox that same year, Hubberthorne similarly recalled that his "conscience opened" after hearing Fox preach, and "thy words found there are my life, and I live in thee in measure."[12] These accounts detail what happens when one, as Fell implored, turned to the light in his conscience. Hubberthorne's conscience awakens and opens at Fox's call, making it not only aware of that light but also receptive to it.

Quakers privileged this moment of "awakening" the conscience over the historical moment of Christ's death as the actual instant of atonement. They believed Christ "an everlasting Priest" who "for ever stands offered up to the Father, with his bloud in the everlasting Covenant an atonement making, and besprinkling the hearts and consciences of every one of his."[13] Christ's eternal offer to God can only be accepted if the believer actively turned to the light in his conscience, making the process of atonement both active and passive. For this reason, while "the end of that blood" which He shed was to "purge every Conscience from dead works," those who "den[y] the light Shall never know what a Cleane conScience is."[14] Christ's sacrifice was thus ongoing, offered up to each believer once his conscience became aware of God's presence within. It was only through "his pure light" in the conscience, after all, that Christ could "revea[l] the man of sin" to believers and "by his power cas[t] [the man of sin] out." This process of purgation transformed the "bodies of the Saints" into "a fit Temple for the pure God to dwell in," reconciling "*God* and man."[15]

The result of this reconciliation was a more profound union with God and also with each other. Hubberthorne's accounts of his awakening reveal that this experience connected him just as much to God as to Fox himself. In his published narrative, Hubberthorne writes that God's Word had been made "manifest within me" as a result of Fox's preaching, while in his private correspondence, he finds Fox's words within his conscience, words that "are my life." This conflation of God's word and Fox's seems no accident. For Hubberthorne, whose conscience was opened during Fox's sermon, he and Fox were now united through their shared experience of the light of Christ within. Preaching from the light in his own conscience, Fox spoke to Hubberthorne's conscience in words that already dwelled in its recesses. Edward Burrough, a Quaker leader and pamphleteer, further explored the possibilities of this conscience-based union:

> The only chief and perfect Rule of the *right Exercise of Conscience*, both to *God* and *all men*, is, *The SPIRIT of CHRIST* […] and all, whose Consciences are guided and exercised by it, are in *Unity* and *Peace* in their *Worship*, *Doctrine*, and *Religion*; for the *Spirit of CHRIST* is but *one* in it self, and guideth the *Conscience* into the *exercise* of *one Truth* and *Faith*; and in this same Spirit is the *true Union* and *Communion of Saints* in *Religion* and *Worship*.[16]

This understanding of the one light of Christ inhabiting all consciences divested the Quaker conscience of any sense of privacy or individualism, granting it a radically new collective dimension.[17] As a consequence, it also became an essential proponent of the Christian community. When guided by this *"Spirit of CHRIST,"* the individual conscience joined a larger network of the divine, connecting it to the consciences of others who had similarly submitted to this "light within." Emphasizing this sense of interconnectedness, Fell wrote in 1657 to her fellow Friends William Caton and John Stubbs as they prepared to sail for Holland on a mission, "yee are present with mee, you in mee, and I in you" (224).

This network doubled as a surveillance mechanism. Writing in 1653 to Friends who "have not been faithful" to the light, William Dewsbury, a charismatic Quaker activist, warned them that "the all seeing eye, that light in your consciences," is "the eye with which I see you." "For I am with you," he threatens, "though absent in body, and see you with the invisible and eternal eye which nothing can be hid from."[18] Just as Fox's words converge with God's, so Dewsbury believed he could know the consciences of his brethren through their shared experience of the light. Fell presumes a similarly privileged view into Jeffrey Elletson's conscience when writing to him in 1654: arguing that his worship of the gospels lacked the "Substance & the life that Spoke it," Fell assures him, "that in thy Conscience which is of God, will answeare mee, that this is truth" (58). If he wanted to test the veracity of her words, Elletson need look no further than his own conscience.

Quakers' presumed knowledge of others' consciences met with much opposition from those outside the movement. In *The Worlds Wonder, Or the Quakers Blazing Starr* (1654), Edmund Skipp, a clergyman from Herefordshire, marvels at how Quakers "charge and accuse me for acting against my own conscience, meaning my living, dwelling and preaching constantly unto a particular people in a publick meeting place, this they say is against my own light and convictions of heart, as though they knew my conscience better than my self." "Hereby," he concludes, "do I see again they are acted through delusion and mistake [...] Now let any sober man observe by what power these creatures are acted while they charge me with doing this against my conscience."[19] Humphrey Smith, a Quaker preacher also from Herefordshire, is unmoved by Skipp's charges and responds in *Something in reply to Edmund Skipps Book* (1655), hoping that he might yet awaken Skipp's conscience:

> Return, return, unto the light of Christ in thy own conscience, which will let thee see the deceit of thy own sinful heart, out of the abundant deceit thereof, thy pen hath run so largely in confusion: now I charge thee in the presence of the living God, (in as much love to thy soul as ever) that thou return to the light of Christ in thy own conscience and mind, that which checks thee in secret. I tell thee man in love, there is something yet in thee, which will witness me to be true.[20]

Smith imagines Skipp's own "sinful heart" as guilty of deception, blinding him to "that which checks thee in secret." He affectionately bids Skipp turn to the light in his conscience, believing him still capable of conversion. Several years later, Fox revisits Skipp's argument to challenge him once again on this point of conscience: "the apostles knew the state and condition of Jews, and Gentiles, and people, better than they did themselves, and so do the Quakers that are in their spirit; and this is not delusion."[21]

Despite such opposition, Friends used this language of conscience with the hope of reaching as many people across England – and eventually the world – as quickly as possible. In *To all the Professors of the World* (1656), Fell asks her readers to "call [the living God] while he is near, and seek him while he may be found."[22] This sense of urgency indicated that the "living God" would not be available indefinitely if her readers failed to turn to him. In order to make readers and listeners recognize England's fleeting "day of visitation," Friends systematically took advantage of the lack of censorship after the civil wars more than any other sect.[23] Over 100 Quaker writers authored or co-authored about 300 tracts between 1652 and 1656 alone, a publication frenzy that continued into the second half of the 1650s and even into the Restoration.[24] In 1660, John Gaskin, a bitter opponent of the Quakers, accused them of "writing and printing so many Books, to spread abrode their Errors": "*some of them have affirmed in my hearing*, That there is a thousand of their erronious Books printed every week, *and most of them given away on purpose to delude ignorant people*."[25] Similarly, in 1656, William Thomas notes the dangers of Quaker publications. Calling their books "Corrupt and corrupting," he believed them specially designed to disseminate their damaging messages swiftly: such books, he claims, were "purposely made little, that they may be made nimble, and passe with more speed, and at an easy rate, to infect the Nation." Thomas feared Quaker books a contagion threatening the whole of England. "May we not fear," he finally asks, "a flying roule will go forth over the face of this *God-neglecting* Nation, because the wings of such Books are not clipt"?[26] Because the rapid flight of Quaker books had not been quelled, Thomas worries that God will send his own "flying roule," reminiscent of the divine curse envisioned by Zechariah.

Though exaggerated, Gaskin's and Thomas's fears were not entirely unfounded. Friends had an acute awareness of the power of the written word and the effect it could have upon the reader, and accounts in contemporary journals and elsewhere confirm that reading Quaker literature often prompted conversion.[27] Similarly, Thomas's concern that Friends hoped to reach the entire nation was also based in truth. Addressing England directly in 1655, Dewsbury asks the nation to turn to God "who waits on thee" so that He might "make thee the glory of all the Nations of the world." He calls on "every particular Inhabiter of *England*" to "examine your hearts, and mind the light in your Consciences," while he expects the "Rulers of *England*" to "obey the light in your Consciences to rule in the power of the spirit."[28] Unlike private individuals, whose only task was to "mind the light," Dewsbury compels the "Rulers of *England*" to imagine their very power derived from and exercised through the light in their consciences. Recalling the fortunes of rulers past, he warns that God would "*overturn, overturn, overturn until I have given it* [the nation] *unto him whose right it is*, and he will give it to me," as he had with "the Bishops, and the King, the Lords, and the late Parliament, who all professed the name of the Christ, but they would not obey his Counsel, the light in their Consciences."[29] Dewsbury sees providence at work in the toppling not only of the monarchy but also of the Rump Parliament, recently dissolved by Cromwell. If the unnamed rulers he addressed also fail to govern the nation according to conscience, he threatens, they too would be overturned.

While Dewsbury's message was already radical in its presumption to advise the "Rulers of *England*" regarding the nature of their authority, he also envisioned for them just what such a rule would look like. If the light in their consciences "alone guide you in all your Counsel," they would remove "the Judges that judg for rewards, and the Lawyers that plead for mony, and the Priests that teach for hire." And in place of these corrupt judges, lawyers, and priests, they would set "men *fearing God, and hating Covetousness*" so that "the people may be taught freely, without mony or price, by the free Spirit of Christ."[30] This simple program would allow England to be a nation whose citizens are guided by the light within their consciences. Yet establishing this nationwide uninterrupted flow of spirit depended upon the rulers Dewsbury addresses: if only they would listen to the light in their consciences, then the rest of the nation would do the same. Writing to the Protector and Parliament as late as 1657, Fox supposes that if they would "stand in his [God's] counsel," they could "come to reach that of God in every one, under all your Dominions."[31] During the years of the Protectorate, then, reaching the consciences of the "Rulers of *England*" was essential to the success of the Quakers' national vision. In other words, England's spiritual fate depended upon their convincement.

Dewsbury and Fox were not alone in their efforts to link the fate of the nation to the consciences of its rulers: early Friends strove to create a nationwide, and eventually worldwide, communion of saints by calling upon Cromwell in particular to heed the light in his conscience. Their goals were far-reaching but, they believed, attainable.

"Thou Wilt Come to Witnesse a Tender Conscience": The Conscience of the Lord Protector

While groups like the Fifth Monarchists felt betrayed when Cromwell was appointed Lord Protector, the Quakers regarded his new position as an opportunity for national reform. Cromwell's overwhelming success during the civil wars convinced Friends that he was (or had been) an instrument of God. Between his installation in December 1653 and up until days before his death in 1658, the Protector was bombarded with letters, pamphlets, and visits from Quakers intent on reaching his conscience and, through his conscience, the nation.

In 1653, Fell was "moved of the Lord to write" her first of five letters to Cromwell, "A warning to thee from the Lord God of heaven & Earth that thou harken to the light of god in thy Conscience." Written very soon after Cromwell's installation as Lord Protector, this letter was bold in both its timing and tone.[32] Fell begins by informing him that England has entered a new era in its relationship with God, a time "wherein he is teaching his people himselfe, by his owne Imediate light and power" in their consciences. Her refrain throughout the opening passages of this letter is "now": "now is the time come & comeing, wherein the Lord is fullfilling his promisse," "now is he fullfilling his promisse," "now is the spirit of the Living god made manifest," "now is the Lord seperateing betwixt the pretious & the vile." This divine immediacy eliminates the need for intercessors between God and his people, and Fell invites Cromwell to partake in this great moment of God's imminence (36–7).

Indeed, she concludes her litany of "nows" by turning directly to Cromwell's conscience: "Therefore to the Light of Christ in thy conscience I Speak, which is pure and tender, which if thou harken to it & come downe and be low, it will lead thee into obedience of the Lord." Having established that God is present, Fell asks not only that Cromwell acknowledge the light within him but, more importantly, that he subject himself to that light. He must "come downe and be low" if he ever wishes truly to obey the Lord. While Cromwell's salvation is dependent upon his being led by the light, Fell also writes with the hope that, through his subjection, he will also come to a fuller and more mature understanding of God and conscience. Indeed, Fell informs the Protector that "by the obedience of the leading of it, thou wilt come to wittnesse A tender Conscience, and then thou wilt know what it is to offend that in the Conscience which is of god, which is pure & tender, & is not to be offended in Jew nor in Gentile, nor to be Limitted by the will of man, nor any Carnall Law." Only by subjecting himself to the light in his conscience will Cromwell finally know how to protect the consciences of his subjects so that they too might obey the living God. After all, it was only through the conscience that God is "served&obeyed," and finally "knowne," making its liberty all the more urgent. Fell warns him not to "stan[d] against the mighty dreadfull god that is now made manifest" by creating laws that would hinder God's immediacy or by "harkening to evill Councellers." If he should try to inhibit the light from working freely in his subjects' consciences, she threatens, he would "partake of the woe & plagues" suffered by the enemies of God (37–8).

Fell concludes more boldly still, first dismissing and then donning his newly acquired title, "Protector." "Not for any favour or protection from thee as thou art A governour outwardly doe I write this," she assures him, but rather "for the good of thy soull which is dear unto mee, have I written these lines unto thee." Fell writes not seeking his protection, since she stands "in the eternall power of the living God." Instead, she writes for his protection, assuming the role of protector over his soul, "which is dear unto mee." Finally, and most importantly, she also writes for the sake of the light "in thee with which I have unitie." Fell imagines herself linked to the Protector through this light of Christ and implores him to turn to it so that he too might recognize their divine connection. She closes confident that "to that of god in thee have I cleared my Conscience," the same God in him that will "Condemne thee if thou disobey." Her duty fulfilled, Fell signs off with one last expression of hope that "thou may be guided by that of god in thee which cannot erre" (38–9).

"Thou Canst Not Deny Us": Duelling Liberties of Conscience

Despite Fell's threats, Cromwell's legislation during his first year as Lord Protector often clashed with the program envisioned by the Quakers. Friends sought a swift disestablishment of the national church and the abolition of tithes; yet Cromwell's church settlement of 1654 not only guaranteed the continuance of tithes but also established a system of "Triers" and "Ejectors" as a centralized check on the suitability of ministers.[33] While he hoped this settlement would reconcile many of the Protestant sects, Cromwell's decision to maintain a national church met with opposition from the Quakers. More importantly, the Protector's notion of "liberty of conscience" differed from the freedoms that Friends demanded of Cromwell, particularly the liberty to disrupt church services and to preach openly in all public spaces. As a result, Quakers were often prosecuted under the Blasphemy Act of 1650, the Vagrancy Act of 1597, and even by Cromwell's own proclamation of 1654 aimed at Quakers who were considered disturbers of the peace, *A Proclamation prohibiting the Disturbing of Ministers and other Christians in their Assemblies and Meetings.*[34]

In response, many Friends were careful to record what they saw as injustices against their evangelism in manuscripts like "Great Book of

Sufferings" (ca. 1650–1856), or tracts like the anonymous *The Cry of the Oppressed from under their Oppressions* (1656).[35] The former is housed in forty-four volumes in the Library of the Society of Friends and, organized chronologically by county, catalogues meticulously accounts of imprisonment, fines, seizures of property, and other penalties levied against Quakers for their failure to pay tithes, take oaths, or attend church. The latter lists Friend after Friend who was similarly punished, often "because for conscience sake they cannot swear, and transgresse the plain Command of Christ, though any service for the good of the Country they are willing to perform, and will be faithful without an oath." Yet, "for the keeping of their consciences clear," the author continues, "with joy they can suffer the spoyling of their Goods, and give their backs to the Smiter."[36] Quakers not only desired to present these injustices to the *"Publick view,"* as *The Cry of the Oppressed* announced on its cover page, but they also sought to confront the Protector himself with similar grievances. Elizabeth Hooten, presumably the first person to be convinced by Fox in 1647, wrote to Cromwell in 1653, attacking him for not fulfilling promises she believed he had made: "did you not promise this nation should bee made free from oppression, & that tythes should be taken away"?[37] Similarly, Thomas Aldam, a Quaker preacher and writer who was imprisoned in York Castle for two and a half years for his opposition to a Warmsworth priest, wrote to Cromwell from prison on multiple occasions to question the justice of his imprisonment.[38]

Despite this mistreatment, many Friends still believed they could awaken Cromwell to the light of God that dwelled within him. Writing to the light in Cromwell's conscience in 1654, Aldam calls himself a "prisoner of ye Lord," held "in outward Bonds of Yorke Castle" for "witnesseinge ye truth wch I haue receiued from God."[39] That same year, Aldam also sends a letter to Fox regarding his efforts to reach the Protector: "I am often in spirit waiting at London at the doors of Oliver Cromwell's house without, as if clothed in sackcloth, standing in sackcloth in body, and weeping over a seed [of God] which is in bonds in that creature [...] Oliver Cromwell, with which I suffer."[40] Unlike Pearson, who, that same year, feared that "there is nothing left in him of God," Aldam still believed that seed or light existed, though "in bonds." He imagines himself dressed in sackcloth, mourning over and suffering with that imprisoned light of God as he writes letter after letter, hoping to reach its jailor, the only one capable of setting that seed free.

Fell's second letter, also sent in 1654, similarly reveals both her disappointment in Cromwell and her belief that he could still be reached.[41] Casting his position as Lord Protector as a test of faith, Fell urges Cromwell to recognize that "the Lord putt an opportunity into thy hand, and he is trying of thee whether thou wilt stand for him or against him," and she cautions him throughout to "mind what it is thou dost protect." Fell writes partly on behalf of Dorothy Benson (the wife of Gervase Benson, one of the founders of the Quaker movement), who was imprisoned at York for speaking against "the deceite of the priest" at the "great steeplehouse." "Being great with child," Benson was, according to Fell's account, not only "abussed by the rude multitude, and throne downe under their Feet" while the magistrate looked on, but also she "hath bene imprisoned this quarter of A year, and is delivered of the child in the prison, contrary to all humanitye or any appearance of god in the least measure" (116). Outraged by Benson's ill treatment and that of Friends across England, Fell calls repeatedly upon the light in Cromwell's conscience so that he might "see all the Lawes of this nation to be corrupt, And all the priests of this nation to be changeable," as opposed to Christ who is "unchangeable, eternall and forever." His clergy, she warns, build the church upon a sandy foundation rather than "the rocke Chr[ist] which is the light within every mans conscience." Critiquing his church settlement and vetted clergy, Fell instead asks Cromwell to replace the national church with a spiritual one, established upon and through the light of Christ within all consciences, the only sure basis for the "Kingdome of heaven" (115, 114). She is confident, moreover, that if only he would harken to the light in his conscience, he too will see his clergy to be "blind guides, leaders of the blind, and wittnesse the same against them as we have declared" (117). His heeding this light would put him in agreement with the Quakers and, more importantly, Cromwell could then reconcile the nation to the light in his and all consciences.

Fell assures him once again that it "is for no protection from thee" that she and others write because "our protector is the liveing god." Instead, she writes both for the sake of his soul and to redefine his conception of "liberty of conscience." "As thou hast often declared for the libertie of conscience, and the propigateing of the Gospell," she cautions, "mind what Libertie that in the conscience hath, which is limitted by A Carnall Law, which is of god, which cannot be limitted, but limitts" (117). Since Cromwell's calls for liberty of conscience were so frequent, Fell seeks to correct his understanding of this crucial spiritual freedom. "Cruell oppression" and "tyranny" now "rul[e] in the Land," a godless reign that, she accuses, Cromwell protects. His laws regarding tithes, church attendance, and oaths threaten to limit the freedom he so passionately defends in words. Fell asks that he not only turn to the light in his conscience but also that Quaker pamphlets that "declar[e] for the truth" be allowed to enter the marketplace of ideas and be "published to open view" without interception. In order for Cromwell truly to protect liberty of conscience, he must cease to protect those laws and persons that try to limit the unlimitable, God Himself.

Fell closes once again with the hope that Cromwell will "waite in the Light" in his conscience, allowing Christ to illuminate his path moving forward. She also closes with a threat: if he should continue to "Act contrary to that in thy Conscience," "the light of christ in all consciences will cry against thee for vengance from God, so faretheewell." Fell moves swiftly from mention of "*thy* conscience" to the depersonalization of this inner sanctum, warning Cromwell that he is under spiritual surveillance. According to her vivid construction, it is not the thousand tongues of his conscience alone that will condemn him, but also the thousands of tongues of others' consciences, all calling out to God through the light of Christ. Cromwell's continued disobedience would prompt a national and conscience-driven outrage.

Fell sent Francis Howgill, Quaker activist, and John Camm, Quaker preacher, to deliver her letter personally to the Protector. On 27 March, they write her an account of their meeting, lamenting that Cromwell "gathered the substance of all the words we spake unto him […] and went about to question whether they were the word of the Lord or not, by his carnal reason." They feared him "in great danger to be lost." What most troubled them, however, was his toleration of sectarians: Howgill and Camm report that the Protector "pleads for every man's liberty [of worship] and none to disturb another" and "holds that all the worships of this nation is the worship of God." Cromwell's brand of liberty of conscience was too liberal for Friends, and it differed dramatically from the freedom Fell and others asked Cromwell to protect, a liberty that would promote conformity to Quaker doctrine. While the Protector hoped to provide as much liberty as believers needed to seek out truth, whatever that truth might be, Friends believed such liberty should move individuals to discover the truth that was already within them. As long as Cromwell believed that different worships were all the "worship of god," Howgill and Camm relay, "sin must be upholden by law."[42] This aversion to Cromwell's program reveals the striking difference between their understanding of conscience and the Protector's own, as well as how integral conscience was to their hope for spiritual unification at a national level.

Camm and Howgill were inspired by this meeting to write their own letters to the Protector. Camm claims their visit was meant to compel him to take up a role he occupied in the past: to be "an Instrument in the Lords hand," "to take off oppression from off the necks of the people, and to remove their Yoke which hath been promised long." He must fulfil this office "for the righteous seeds sake," which "lyes in bondage every where." Yet Camm fears that Cromwell might have misunderstood their earlier requests that he become an instrument of God. "Wherein thou apprehendedst us that should be established by an outward Law," Camm corrects, they actually desired "that there should be no Law upon Religion, for it need no Law to defend it." To be an instrument of God in this case was not to act but rather to abstain from acting in the realm of religion. More importantly, Camm believes his exhortation irresistible if Cromwell is to heed his conscience: "therefore friend, to thy conscience I speak, and witness this to be true in the presence of God: that as thou art guided by this pure light in thy conscience [...] thou canst not deny us." To deny them, Camm maintains, would be to deny his own conscience.[43]

Assuming the voice of God, Howgill takes a more aggressive approach in his letter to Cromwell. "I chose thee out of all the Nation," he writes, yet now "thou art establishing peace, and not by me; and thou art setting up Laws, and not by me; and my Name is not feared, nor I am not sought after: but thy own wisdom thou establishest." His anger mounting, Howgill, still writing as God, asks, "Have I thrown down all the oppressors, and broken their Laws, and art thou now going about to establish them again? and art going to build again, that which I have destroyed? [...] wilt thou limit me, and set bounds to me, when, and where, and how, and by whom I shall declare my self, and publish my name?"[44] Outraged that Cromwell tries to limit God's power and to rule the nation through human rather than divine agency, Howgill ends his letter threatening that Cromwell "shalt know that I am the Lord" if he should continue along this ungodly path. Interestingly, Camm and Howgill publish these letters to Cromwell, publicizing this seemingly private correspondence, imagining their audience as both the Lord Protector and England itself. Perhaps they thought their words most effective if shared with the nation they still hoped Cromwell would help shape into the Kingdom of God.

Writing from York Castle, where he was imprisoned in 1645, Dewsbury adds his voice to the chorus of Friends repudiating the Protector for neglecting his conscience. Like Howgill, Dewsbury too boldly assumes the voice of God, prefacing his lengthy letter with meticulous detail regarding this divine message's delivery: presenting himself as God's instrument, Dewsbury writes that God's Word "came to me about ye time of ye first hour in ye morning on ye twelft day of ye fourth month, saying, Arise, & write, to Oliver Cromwell, what I make knowne unto y^e by my Spirit concerning him." This voice begins by looking back to the civil wars, recalling how "I chused ye out of ye nations of the earth [...] to stand against ye heathenish council of oppressing Tyrants" who "cast my law behind their backes in not regarding the light in their consciences."[45] Worse than simply ignoring the light in their own consciences, these "oppressing Tyrants" also threatened the liberty of all consciences, including Cromwell's own. For this reason, Dewsbury continues, Cromwell "promised to me before my children many times, & in tenderness of heart wth teares y^t if I would hear y^e & answer thy desires, in delivering these oppressing Tyrants in thy hands [...] y^t no outward law should command the consciences of my people." Responding to this vow, Dewsbury, still assuming the voice the God, reminds Cromwell that "I heard y^e & appeared thy Lord Protector who preserved ye out of their power" so that he and God's people might "mayest have fre[e] liberty to worshipp me in spirit & in truth according to my law in thy conscience."[46]

According to Dewsbury's dramatic historical narrative, Cromwell entered the civil wars to fight for liberty of conscience, his own and that of God's people. More importantly, his pledge to God reveals that he wanted to be a divinely appointed deliverer of conscience from the hands of oppressing tyrants. Dewsbury's construction places an obligation upon Cromwell: since God had satisfied his duty as Cromwell's Lord Protector, he must now perform the same office for God's people, fulfilling the terms of his passionate pledge. Up until this moment, "contrary to all thy faire words & promises," Cromwell had "dep[ar]ted from my counsel, ye light in thy conscience" and, as a result, had become for Friends the very tyrant over their consciences that he had earlier overthrown through God's power. Dewsbury, still ventriloquizing God, finally threatens to "arise in power like a Gyant refreshed wth wine & manifest myselfe Lord Protector of my people" once again. If Cromwell would not fulfil his promise, God would take back his title and perform it himself.[47]

Though ominous, Dewsbury's message is also tinged at moments with a sense of desperation. He pleads, "Oliver Cromwell, turne turne [to your conscience] [.] why wilt thou dye? what hast thou against me y^t thou wilt not stand in my counsell but dep[ar]ts from me who hath been thy protector & preserver"? While Fell, Camm, and other Friends continually tell the Protector that they do not need his help or protection, Dewbury's tone and the Quakers' steady stream of letters, public and private, suggest that they certainly wanted it – for his sake and for their own. Writing to Aldam some time later, Dewsbury inquired after his letter: "I would have thee to let me know as way is made what is done in the delivering of the word of the Lord I sent to O. Cromwell." "It lies on me untill it be delivered to his hands," he persists, "& that he it read to know the mind of God concerning him."[48]

As did his fellow Friends, Dewsbury sought to heal the rift between Cromwell and God, between Cromwell and the Quakers, and, he believed, between Cromwell and his own conscience. He also shared with them the belief that the Protector was still capable of shaping a nation suitable for God's children, if only he would turn to the light in his conscience.

"The *Presence* of the *Lord* Is Departed from *Thee*": Failures of State, Failures of Conscience

These messages unheeded, Quakers deemed their sustained persecution an outward manifestation of Cromwell's private failures of conscience. Writing in 1655, John Stubbs, a former soldier in the New Model Army and prolific Quaker minister who had been attacked at Coldbeck by enemies of the movement, compounds Dewbury's passing moment of desperation with pathos and a call for reflection. He begins by asking explicitly for Cromwell "to protect my harmless person from ye violence & cruelty of wicked & unreasonable men." "Y^e Lord," he maintains, "requires it of thee." Though Cromwell possesses the power to free the innocent from such violence, he "sits silent." "Is y^s ye end of ^thy^ protection?" he asks despairingly.[49] Hoping to strike a personal chord, Stubbs recalls their time together on the battlefields in England and Scotland: "Oh remember, remember the dayes of old [...] how through much co[l]d, misery, perils, straits, extremities, & several other exegences I & many more have followed thee." "[H]ast thou forgotten them?" he asks; "I have not."

Now that Friends are trying to enjoy that liberty won on the battle-field, they find themselves engaged in a new war against magistrates and priests who accuse them of disturbing the peace and people who follow Quakers as they declare the Word of God, "punching, buffitting, [and] knocking" them in the streets. What is worse, these violent incidents often result in the imprisonment of Quakers while the "stone[r]s & buffeters" go free. Repeating that he writes only "to claime protection from thee," Stubbs cites Cromwell's open declaration for "liberty to tender consciences." If the Protector seeks to protect this Christian liberty, Stubbs insists, he must first "look to it [...] who are Christians": "magistrates, ministers, & people that persecute & imprison" or "they that declare against sin in tenderness of conscience," albeit in public places. Imploring Cromwell finally to "let that in thy conscience speake, & be singlehearted, & judge," Stubbs wants him to recognize his grave failures: because of the Protector's misrule of himself and the nation, Stubbs concludes, "tender consciences are embondaged, & the wicked set free."

In addition to this sustained violence against Quakers, Fell also read Cromwell's failures into one of the many plots against his life, exposed in May 1655. A group of royalist exiles allegedly planned to assassinate Cromwell with a "stone-bow made after a very extraordinary manner," a discovery that led to a series of arrests throughout the summer.[50] Fell prefaces her message with a nod to previous attempts against his life, perhaps even thinking back to John Gerard's failed assassination plot the year before. She tells him what she believes the light in his conscience would tell him too if only he would listen: God put him in a place of power so that he might "performe FaithFully the End [...] for which end thou was reserved marrucullously many A time[,] which end was liberty of Conscience." While God waits on Cromwell to use his power for liberty, he has in the meantime "preserved thee from many cruell plots, and bloody designes, which hath beene against thee, by murderous spirits." Yet Cromwell has failed God time and again. More importantly, she continues, his failures are jeopardizing his own life. Indeed, this last assassination plot was discovered "by his owne true wittnesse in the Conscience, which wittnesse would not suffer it to bee hid, but forced the man to discover it." The man she refers to here is presumably Richard Hannam, who informed John Thurloe, the director of the Protectorate's spying and intelligence network, of the conspiracy.[51] Yet "this [message] mighit have reached that in thy Conscience," Fell insists, "if that thou had stoden in the feare of god."

Cromwell might have spared his own life had he only heeded the light in his conscience, the light that "reveales the secrets of all hearts," including those of potential assassins (141–2).

Despite this failure, God had spared him once again, but only to give him "space to repent," a space, Fell urges, that was limited. She implores him to use this space to consider "what thou hast done for god, sinse hee put thee in power and Authority," and to take this opportunity finally to create laws "as were According to liberty of Conscience" (142–3). God and his people are waiting upon Cromwell to "performe FaithFully" that end, transforming England into a nation coterminous with the light within all consciences. If he should continue to fail God and England, then "woe unto the oppressor."

Finally, Friends and even Cromwell himself regarded England's failed military campaign in Hispaniola, the "Great Western Design," in April 1655 as a sign of God's displeasure towards the nation. Cromwell "shut himself up in his room" for an entire day, "brooding over the disaster," and held a national day of solemn fasting and humiliation in November 1655, and again in March 1656, fearing their prayers unanswered.[52] Yet Quakers such as George Bishop, a prolific leader of the movement and former New Model Army captain, blamed Cromwell and his failings in the realm of conscience for this perceived shift in England's martial successes. Writing to the Protector a year after this blow, Bishop asks, "Perceivest *thou* not that the *presence* of the *Lord* is departed from *thee* [...] and the Magificence and *State* of *England*, which whilst the *Lord* was with *it*, stood with *dread* & *terror* over the *Kingdoms* roundabout, *sinking* down, and *falling, languishing*, and *crumbling* in the *Dust*?" Moreover, the English soldiers abroad, once regarded as the "*Mightiest* Powers of the *world* at *Sea*" were now "*dead at the heart, lumps of flesh*, and *averse to War*," taunted by their captors in Hispaniola, who asked, "*Of what Nation are ye? Ye are not English men.*"[53]

Believing these national failures a divine referendum on Cromwell's rule, Bishop finally turns to the Protector and exasperatedly demands, "How canst *thou* sleep? How canst *thou* suffer *thine* eye-lids to give *thee* any slumber, whilest it is *thus* with *thee*?"[54] Having thus established the dramatic shift in England's status because of Cromwell's disobedience towards God, Bishop calls on him to "Be *still* therefore, and *cool*," so that he might "let the *witness* of *God* in *thee*, search and try *thee*, and hear *thou* what *it* saith in *this* thing." What follows is a litany of questions, interrogations even, in which Bishop blazes through Cromwell's wartime letters to Parliament for the cause of conscience, his triumphs

on the battlefield as God's instrument, and his speech before the First
Protectorate Parliament in which he identified liberty of conscience
as a natural right and fundamental. Bishop fills page after page with
queries that often cite directly Cromwell's language, confronting the
Protector with his own voice. Having asked that Cromwell be still so
that he might hear the witness of God in his conscience, Bishop uses
these questions perhaps to incite a response from that witness within
or even to play that witness himself: each question is rhetorical, need-
ing no response other than the one implied by the asker. He confronts
Cromwell with his own past, his truth, and what Bishop believes to be
his betrayal.

Turning from the Protector's promising past back to the dismal present, he asks one more question: "Are there *any* that have, and do *groan*
for *Liberty* of *Conscience* that *suffer* because of *it* in these Dominions?"
Bishop bids Cromwell not to seek the answer to this query within, but
rather to allow the *"Prisons* in *most* parts of the *Nation"* to "declare and
speak" the plight of those suffering for the sake of their consciences,
locked away "in *heat* and *cold*, in *hunger* and *nakedness*, shut up from
Friends and *Relations*, and the *wholesome* air, and *conveniences* of *Liveli-
hood*," abhorrent conditions only worsened by "the *inhumane* and *bar-
barous* usages, without regard to *ages* or *sexes*, *young* or *old*, *children*, or
the *hoary-headed men* or *women*, not fit to be related to *modest* ears, without *mercy, reason,* or *compassion*."[55] Bishop thus transfers his hijacking of
the witness's voice within Cromwell's conscience to the prisons themselves, so that they might alarm the Protector with the horrific injustices
committed in his name, the literal witnesses of his iniquities.

Turning once again to *"that* of *God* in *thy* Conscience," Bishop asks
Cromwell to "let *it* search and try *thee*." *"Doth God blesse thee*? Let *his*
Witness in *thee* be heard to speak and answer," he pushes on. "Art *thou*
(*whose* heart *all* the *Sufferings* aforesaid do not *now* melt) in the *same*
spirit as *thou* wast in 1645"? Bishop continues to provide both question and answer in the asking, supposing the responses of Cromwell's
witness evident. Despite the Protector's having fallen away from that
spirit, Bishop believes that God's arms "are yet open to *thee*," if only
he would listen to the light within his conscience and finally fulfil his
former promises of liberty.[56]

Ironically, it was this glimmer of hope that Bishop would ultimately
use against Cromwell when he published this letter four years later in
The Warnings of the Lord to the Men of this Generation (1660). Featuring
a series of letters sent to Richard Cromwell, the restored Rump, the

Council of State, and others, this pamphlet was meant to encourage *"Them* that Remain" to repent their misdeeds towards God before it was too late and they come to share the fate of Cromwell and others who had been overturned.

"Oh! Oliver": Re-locating the "Holy Nation," for Conscience's Sake

In the last years of the Protectorate, Quakers continued to appeal to Cromwell for national change, yet there was a clear shift in their mode of petition: appeals directly to the Protector's conscience ceased almost entirely. During the Rule of the Major-Generals, a fifteen-month period of direct military rule beginning in October 1655, violence against Quakers in various regions of England continued and, in some cases, worsened.[57] Northamptonshire Quakers complained that Major-General William Boteler not only imprisoned them without trial but also ordered their meetings violently broken up by the local militia. *Mercurius Politicus* corroborated such accounts, reporting that the local militia fiercely dispersed a meeting of 800 Quakers on direct orders from Boteler.[58] In her fifth and final letter to Cromwell, Fell cautions him to "consider seriously of these Things [injustices]" for the "good of thy soule, & thy eternall peace." "[God] will not be Mocked," she threatens. Yet her tone in this letter is impersonal and remote, and she neglects to address Cromwell's conscience directly. In fact, while her earlier letters were rife with the language of conscience, it is entirely absent from this final correspondence. Though she still demands that he answer the "cry of the oppression of the Innocent," perhaps she, as Pearson three years prior, feared that there was "nothing left in him of God" (223).

In a series of letters sent to Cromwell in 1657 and 1658, Fox and Burrough similarly alter the nature of their appeals to the Protector. As in past correspondence, they remind Cromwell that God's day of visitation is fleeting, recall his former promises to God regarding liberty of conscience, and confront him with the sufferings of Quakers. Also connecting his failures of conscience to the state of the nation, Burrough asks Cromwell to consider the fact that "thou art but the head of a disjoynted body, which may not easily be bound up to thee." The nation has turned against him, "every one judging themselves to be the greatest sufferers under thee," cutting the body politic off from its head. And, even though they tell the Protector that there is still time to repent, Fox laments what might have been:

> *Oh!* Oliver, Hadst thou been faithful, and thundred down the deceipt, the
> *Hollander* had been thy subject, and tributers; and *Germany* had given up to
> have done thy will; and the *Spaniard* had quivered like a dry leaf, wanting
> the vertue of God; the King of *France* should have bowed under thee his
> neck; the *Pope* should have withered as in winter; the *Turk* in all his fatness
> should have smoaked; thou should not a stood trifling about small things,
> but minded the work of the Lord, as he began with thee at first.

Though God's day of visitation has not yet passed, Cromwell has
squandered precious time that he will never get back. These letters emit
a sense of loss, while at the same time pleading with him finally to "be
awakened."[59]

In addition to expressing loss, Fox and Burrough use the language
of conscience only sparingly, and most often in reference to the unjust
treatment of Friends. Cromwell not only failed to uphold liberty of conscience for God's people, but he has also become the very obstacle to
liberty of conscience himself (15). In a letter sent by Burrough early in
1657, he demands that the Protector "let the light of Christ in thy own
conscience answer" why he "should now suffer that people with whom
the power of the Lord is to be persecuted."[60] While he asks Cromwell
to listen the light in his conscience, Burrough identifies the Protector's
conscience in this case as Cromwell's *own*. He does not assume any
privileged access to that light, as Fell and others had in the past, or that
he can directly address that light. Similarly setting separation between
the Protector's own conscience and himself, Burrough writes again in
March 1658, urging Cromwell to put "all thy objections and doubtings"
regarding the Quakers "into plain positions [...] what thou doubtest of,
or stumblest at, either in respect of our doctrines or practice." "And,"
he continues, "if God permit, a sufficient answer thou maist receive,
to remove all conscienceous scruples."[61] Distancing himself even further from any identification with the light in Cromwell's conscience,
Burrough can only hope that the Protector's "conscienceous scruples"
regarding the Quakers might be dispelled. Perhaps because their many
letters, petitions, and visits had gone unheeded by Cromwell, Friends
no longer believed that he could rule *with* them, standing in the light of
conscience. This long-hoped-for communion abandoned, all that was
left to hope for was sympathy.[62]

Though still moderately optimistic that Cromwell might yet be
God's instrument for transforming the nation into the Kingdom of
God, Friends no longer regarded his conscience as the tool through

which he would accomplish that end. Quakers continued to revise their understanding of the relationship between conscience and the nation as England entered another period of upheaval after Cromwell's death. Writing to the "Rulers" and "such as are in Authority" in 1659, Burrough laments that though many had called for a religious settlement over the last decade, what they really desired was "to have Parliaments to make Lawes, to establish one sect, and throw down and limit all others." Yet, he asks, "can the Laws of Kings or Parliaments settle such Religion, or make people truly religious, or establish a Nation or people, in this Religion?" Burrough responds with a resounding "no," insisting that "only the teaching and leading of the holy spirit of God" can settle religion.[63] Cataloguing England's religious *un*settlement since Henry VIII's reign, Burrough laments that the nature and form of the nation's worship is determined by that of its ruler when, in reality, the "exercise of conscience" is not only "out of their power" but also "over and beyond it." In this traditional model's place, he proposes that those in power "let all sects have their course, and every religion its liberty in a nation or country (so that they doe no violence to one anothers persons and estates) and if thy do, then they fall under the Magistrates power." And, more importantly, while each sect strives "to exalt it selfe, and to overthrow others," the role of the magistrates is to "be all quiet, and looke on in patience, and let their authority be herein exercised, not to limit one, or tollerate one more then an other, onely let them keep mens persons and estates in peace."[64]

Ironically, this plan resembles Cromwell's own hoped-for policy of "liberty of conscience," a policy that Camm and Howgill had reported to Fell with dismay in 1654. Burrough departs from Cromwell, however, in his belief that this competition between sects would eventually lead to the ascendancy of Quakerism as the "true religion."[65] He also departs from Friends' correspondence with the Protector and their belief that his conversion was essential to that of the nation. Burrough asked the magistrates to be passive observers, intervening only when and if physical violence should occur.

Quakers continued to revise this relationship between conscience and the nation into the Restoration. Rosemary Moore argues that the Quaker understanding of conscience shifted after 1660. Prior to this moment, Friends believed that conscience would "inevitably lead people to a Quaker point of view," while after the Restoration, "they were prepared to allow rights of conscience to all kinds of unilluminated people, to accept the existence of a form of 'invincible ignorance' that must be respected."[66] Friends did indeed publish pamphlets advocating for nationwide liberty of conscience, such as Burrough's *The Case of Free Liberty of Conscience in the Exercise of Faith and Religion* (1661) or Howgill, Hubberthorne, John Crook, and Samuel Fisher's *Liberty of Conscience Asserted* (1661). Yet it seems more likely that these and other Friends' calls for religious freedom were still qualified with the hope that such liberty would lead to nationwide and, eventually, worldwide conversion to Quakerism. Writing in 1660, Fox seemed hardly willing to accept the ignorance, however invincible, of non-Quakers: "True religion is ye true rule, and right way of serving God [...] Come Papists, Protestants, Presbiters, and Baptists, with all the severall religions in the world stand forth, and bring your religion to this [Quakerism] & compare them see if they will hold weight and proportion herewith."[67] Similarly, Burrough in 1661 writes that conscience must be free so that it might be guided by the spirit of Christ, leading not to a variety of faiths but rather the "Unity in [...] *Faith* and *Religion*" exemplified by Friends; and even as late as 1666, Fell defends Quakers' practice of "commending our selves to every Man's Conscience," challenging the English ministry to recognize that Friends were "made manifest unto God," and, more importantly, "I trust [that we] are also made manifest in your Consciences."[68]

Rather than ascribe the shift Moore detects to the Quaker understanding of conscience, it seems more likely that it was their changing conception of the nation that affected their use of this language during the Restoration, particularly in their writings to state leaders. Fell sent a dozen letters to the newly seated King Charles II in 1660, many of which she delivered personally. She later refers to these efforts in a letter to King William III: "I was Exercised in this manner [clearing herself and Quakerism to the government], the first Year King Charles the Second came to the Crowne, and laboured Amongst them A whole Year; to Aquainte them and give them to Understand our Principles, in givinge Letters and Papers unto them for that End" (464). In her first letter to the restored King, Fell addresses him as "Deare Friend," and writes that "if thou desire to know the living god, & the eternall truth [...] thou must turne thy minde unto this pure light of xt Jesus." Keeping her message in the conditional tense, she shares her desire that the King might have a portion of the "infinite love, & life of goodnes, & mercy & grace, & virtue that he [God] is Sheddinge abroad in and amonge & upon his people in this Nation." "Many are partakers" of this bounty "in this nation," and she hopes "that you might even partake with us" (277).

While Fell's and others' letters to the Protector called directly upon the light in his conscience with the hopes of converting the nation through Cromwell, she here invites rather than compels the King to turn to Christ within. More importantly, she neither mentions his conscience nor regards him or it as tools through which the Quakers might publicize their message. Indeed in her nearly twenty letters to the King, Fell never once writes directly to the light in his conscience and only mentions Charles's conscience itself in two letters, where she hopes to hold him to his promise of liberty set forth in the Declaration of Breda (1660) (356, 394–5).

Yet Fell's many other writings from the period do not share in this scant mention of conscience or its status as the place where the light of Christ dwelled. What they do share, however, is this perception of the Quakers as a peculiar people within England, rather than England itself as God's peculiar nation. In a letter of June 1660 addressed to the King and to his brothers, the Dukes of York and Gloucester, Fell writes, "Now you are into a Nation, where God hath a suffering people, which he hath owned & will owne, & he hath reproved, & rebuked & overturned the powers of this Nation for their sake." God has set Charles on the throne, she continues, "to try you, what you will doe for his people" (283). Fell looks to King Charles II as she had to Cromwell, with the hope that he might uphold his promise of liberty of conscience; but it is not through the light in his conscience that she tries to reach him or the rest of the nation. In her extensive correspondence with the King, she only once more invites him to partake with Friends in their way of belief (334). Fell instead writes with an eye to protection so this peculiar people of God within the nation might not only survive but also thrive. Writing in September 1660, she implores the King for protection: "Due but Signifie (if it were but one lyne to the Nation) that thou wouldst not have us soe abused, & Imprisoned, & evill Intreated [...] The Judges have done litle or nothinge for us, neither will they, nor can they doe anything for us. It must be thy owne particular act, or else we must Suffer under many hands in the Nation." Fell continues, "if any thinge," including a favourable word towards the Quakers, "preceede from thee (who art the head) it would bynde all others" (304). The English nation, it seems, had become a hostile place against which Friends needed the word of a king to spare their bodies cruel and unjust punishment.

Fell was arrested in 1664 for holding meetings at Swarthmoor Hall and for refusing to take the Oath of Allegiance. During what would be a four-year imprisonment in Lancaster Castle, Fell writes but one letter to the King in which she reminds him again of the terms of the Declaration of Breda and describes the condition of her imprisonment (390–5). She also writes several tracts in defence of Quaker principles, including one that exemplifies her changed view of nationhood, *A Call unto the Seed of Israel* (1668). Beseeching her readers repeatedly to "wait in the Light, which shines in your Consciences," Fell tells them that this light is "now set open for all Nations to flow unto" (3, 2). More importantly, she invites her readers to participate through the light in their consciences in an alternative form of nationhood: "And so the pure Eternal Light, which leads to the Holy Nation, which brings to be a peculiar people, which redeems out of all Nations, Kindreds, People and Tongues, to be Kings, and Priests unto God, unto this pure eternal leader and guider, the Light which shines in your consciences, all be subject" (29). Appropriating the language of 1 Peter 2:9, Fell imagines a transnational "Holy Nation," a spiritual place achieved only through the light in conscience. As Fell writes in the letter she sends King Charles II from prison, England has been rendered a nation "cruell in the eyes of people both within its owne body & in other nations" because of its sustained persecution of the godly (392). She and other Friends no longer look to the English nation as the potential Kingdom of God on earth: rather, the light within conscience has become its own nation, a nation beyond the grasp of carnal laws, angry and unconvinced mobs, and harsh punishments, and a nation set over and against England itself. Fell strives to persuade her readers to take up this nationhood of conscience and to join God's peculiar people as citizens of this most holy of nations.

Chapter Four

Thomas Hobbes's *Leviathan* and the Civilizing Force of Conscience

Samuel Parker begins his notorious – and notoriously Hobbist – *A Discourse of Ecclesiastical Politie* (1670) by presenting readers with a conscience conundrum: "Notwithstanding that Conscience is the best if not the only security of Government, yet has Government never been contrould or disturb'd so much by any thing as Conscience."[1] A spirited opponent of toleration, Parker puzzles over the civil power's dependence upon conscience and its resultant vulnerability. Looking back upon the upheaval of the civil wars, Parker casts conscience as responsible and threatens his readers with a similar state of disorder if those petitioning King Charles II for indulgence prevail. What Parker finds most troubling about conscience, however, is its very necessity: he cannot do away with the concept altogether. Instead, over the course of the next 300 pages, Parker ekes out a way to make conscience most conducive to peace and settlement. In order to tame this potentially volatile concept, he borrows yet another concept from Thomas Hobbes's reviled though oft-cited *Leviathan*: the public conscience.

This process of taming conscience is central to Hobbes's own project in *Leviathan*, as Parker's borrowed terminology indicates. Yet Parker nonetheless hopes to league him with the dissenters, accusing *"Mr. Hobs's Principles in behalf of Liberty of Conscience"* of being "the most powerful Patron of the Fanatick Interest" during the tolerationist campaign because of his endorsement of "free conscience" in *Leviathan* (*A Discourse* 135, 137). Not surprisingly, Parker's opponents similarly accuse him of Hobbism, not wanting to be associated with a man whose reputation ranged from heretic to atheist during the Restoration despite his seeming defence of conscience.[2] As Christopher N. Warren points out, *Leviathan* "came to occupy something of a no man's land in Restoration debates over toleration, as likely to be mined for arguments as castigated."[3] No one was willing to embrace Hobbism openly, but many were willing to borrow furtively from his *Leviathan*.

These accusations of Hobbism on both sides of the toleration debates raise perhaps another conundrum: How can the same text both endorse a program of "liberty of conscience" and circulate the notion of a "public conscience"? Interestingly enough, this conundrum strikes through not only seventeenth-century responses to Hobbes's puzzling text but also twenty-first century criticism. Hobbes's treatment of conscience in *Leviathan* has increasingly become a topic of interest in studies on toleration, forcing critics to reexamine the common contention that "Hobbes does not believe in freedom of conscience" or that he "render[s] conscience null and void."[4] More specifically, some critics credit Hobbes with "founding the liberal approach to politics and religion" because of his separation between the interior space of belief and thought and the exterior world of obedience.[5] Quentin Skinner, for instance, recently argued that Hobbes "explicitly speaks in favour of the arrangement under which everyone is left at liberty to formulate their religious beliefs according to the dictates of conscience, subject only to the civil power."[6]

While many scholars have agreed that Hobbes's separation between the public and private lives of subjects amounts to a "liberal slip" of his "authoritarian pen,"[7] others have argued that Hobbes, as a result, championed both toleration and liberty of conscience. In 1988, Alan Ryan argued for a "'more tolerant' Hobbes,"[8] and others have since followed suit, going so far as to claim that *Leviathan* is "a defense of toleration."[9] More recently, Johan Tralau challenged this prevailing thesis by arguing that Hobbes's championing of this "minimal version" of liberty of conscience is deceptive, with conscience being "first declared free, but then purged of its individual meaning."[10]

It seems that Hobbes's twentieth- and twenty-first-century readers, like his seventeenth-century readers, have only considered his discussion of conscience in fragments. If we focus only on Hobbes's "public conscience," then he seems the destroyer of subjectivity itself; if instead we turn our attention to Hobbes's defence of "free conscience" at the very end of *Leviathan*, then he seems a proponent of toleration in his time and of liberalism in our own. Perhaps most troubling is Tralau's conclusion, when considering Hobbes's public and private constructions of conscience together, that Hobbes sought to deceive his dissenting readers.[11]

In this chapter, I will put Hobbes's public and free consciences back in dialogue with one another in order to gain a more holistic understanding of the relationship he sets out between conscience and the leviathan. This focus will also encourage us to read *Leviathan* as a product of the English Civil Wars, a context that Hobbes himself espoused during the Restoration. In the midst of calls for "liberty of conscience" on behalf of sectarians and *Eikon Basilike* alike, Hobbes engineers his own conception of conscience and its complex relationship to the nation. He imagines public and free forms of conscience that do not compete with one another but rather perform the same function, though in different capacities. Hobbes's conscience – whether public, free, in the condition of war, or in the commonwealth – is a *civilizing force*. It inclines the individual in the condition of war towards peace and concord, and it is the force that sustains the commonwealth from within once the commonwealth is established. In this way, it is the very cornerstone of Hobbes's *Leviathan* and becomes one of its most potent legacies. As the second half of this chapter will explore, Hobbes's revolutionary relationship between conscience and the nation is refashioned by James Harrington during the years of the commonwealth, and becomes a centrepiece of the toleration debates of 1667–72.

What Is the Hobbesian Conscience?

As we have seen, the definition of "conscience" fell along a spectrum in the seventeenth century, especially during and after the Revolution. While for many writers of this period conscience was a private entity with a public life, Hobbes's construct is based purely upon the word's etymology, *con-scire*, or "to know with." He first defines this slippery term in a chapter headed "Of the Ends, or Resolutions of Discourse," emphasizing conscience as socially constructed: "When two, or more men, know of one and the same fact, they are said to be Conscious of it one to another; which is as much as to know it together." This connection between two or more individuals creates a shared *consciousness* – they *know it together* – as well as a sense of accountability based in this joint knowledge. They become "fittest witnesses of the facts of one another, or of a third."[12]

Conscience, like consciousness, arises out of this shared knowledge of fact, with its inviolability based upon the network of witnesses: "it was, and ever will be reputed a very Evill act, for any man to speak against his *Conscience*; or to corrupt, or force another so to do: Insomuch that the plea of Conscience, has been alwayes hearkened unto very diligently in all times" (48). This production of conscience through witness grants it a primarily passive role unless activated at the bar. Even then, conscience neither commands nor judges; rather it exists only to give evidence regarding what two or more persons know together.[13] The unusual nature of this etymological conscience is highlighted by John Eachard in 1673, when he mocks, "*Conscience?* that's good indeed! *Conscience*, you know, is only when one looks over your shoulder, or in at the Key-hole. For, you remember, there must be two at least, to make up a true *Grammatical Conscience*; (because of *cum* and *scio*:)."[14] While ridiculing Hobbes's literalism, Eachard also lodges a deeper criticism against the idea of a conscience whose very existence is based in corroboration.

Yet Hobbes moves on from this precise origin of the concept to when "men made use of the same word metaphorically, for the knowledge of their own secret facts, and secret thoughts; and therefore it is Rhetorically said, that the Conscience is a thousand witnesses" (48). Still relying upon the idea of witness, this proverb transforms conscience itself into the witness, thus making the shared knowledge a fact that one knows with *oneself*. Hobbes's contemporaries believed this classical and Pauline conception of conscience-as-witness more formidable than his socially produced conscience: Richard Sibbes threatens that "conscience is not a private witnesse, it is a thousand witnesses: therefore never sin in hope to have it concealed. It were better that all men should know it, then that thy self shouldest know it."[15] While Sibbes considered conscience-as-witness both infallible and inescapable because "it sees every thing, [and] it heares every thing," Hobbes feared this transition from the literal to the metaphorical.[16]

Once conscience becomes privatized and, more importantly, *unknowable* in the social sphere, its usage slips further and further from fact and towards license. "And last of all," Hobbes laments, "men, vehemently in love with their own new opinions, (though never so absurd,) and obstinately bent to maintain them, gave those their opinions also that reverenced name of Conscience, as if they would have it seem unlawfull, to change or speak against them." Unlike those deeming their own "secret facts" and "secret thoughts" conscience, these individuals only "pretend to know" their opinions are true, "when they know at most, but that they think so" (48). This sense of conscience lacks even a rhetorical social dimension – the "thousand witnesses" – and is hyperindividualized to the point of self-delusion and pretence. Yet those who use the terminology in this dangerous way still capitalize on conscience's "reverenced name," casting their "new *opinions*" as inviolable.[17]

Hobbes's focus on etymology discredits such private claims to conscience. Without a social dimension to account for the *con* in *con*science, the word itself, he contends, loses that "reverenced name."

Conscience in the State of Nature

Considering the inherently social nature of the Hobbesian conscience, it would seem to have no place in his brutally individualistic "Warre *of every one against every one*" (88). Yet, even in the absence of the commonwealth, conscience still emerges as a central and, more importantly, civilizing force. For Hobbes, the condition of war never existed "generally so, over all the world" (89); rather it can occur anywhere and at any time when "men live without a common Power to keep them all in awe" (88). In the absence of absolute sovereign rule, then, individuals live in a state of "continuall feare, and danger of violent death," their lives being "solitary, poore, nasty, brutish, and short" (89).

Though Hobbes threatens that in this condition of war, "there is no Law" and "where no Law, no Injustice" (90), this lack of *civil law* does not preclude the subsistence of *natural law*. Hobbes defines natural law as "a Precept, or general Rule, found out by Reason, by which a man is forbidden to do, that, which is destructive of his life, or taketh away the means of preserving the same" (91). More importantly, even in the condition of war, natural law "*oblige*[s] *in Conscience alwayes*," binding the individual conscientiously to self-preservation (110). In the absence of civil law, the individual cannot commit a *crime*, but he is still capable of committing a sin against natural law, for which his conscience will accuse him. In this state, then, each individual is "his own Judge, and accused onely by his own Conscience" for his sins against natural law, "and cleared by the Uprightnesse of his own Intention" (202).

Hobbes's repetition of the word "own" here emphasizes the onus of self-governance according to conscience in the condition of war. And though this process of governance is internalized, conscience itself does not devolve into the slippery metaphorical usage that Hobbes feared strayed too far from the term's etymological base. Even in the condition of war, conscience is socially constructed, albeit indirectly. The first Law of Nature emblazoned in the individual's conscience is "*to seek Peace, and follow it*" because even though "good" and "evil" are relative and subject to "our Appetites and Aversions" in the condition of war, "all men agree on this, that Peace is Good" (92, 111).[18] Interestingly, this phrase, "seek peace, and follow it," is from David's prayer for safety in Psalm 34:14. David asks, "What man *is he that* desireth life, and loveth *many* days, that he may see good?" and instructs his audience accordingly: "Keep thy tongue from evil, and thy lips from speaking guile. Depart from evil, and do good; seek peace, and pursue it" (34:12–14). Hobbes strips this prayer of its more generalized references to "good" and "evil," maintaining only the activity of seeking peace and pursuing it, which will essentially become *the* prime good that all individuals agree upon.

Similarly, the subsequent laws of nature, including "*Justice, Gratitude, Modesty, Equity, Mercy,* & the rest," are also considered "good" because they are "the way, or means of Peace" (111). By reducing morality to what is most conducive to survival and appointing conscience as the arbiter of that morality, Hobbes creates out of conscience an entity that connects individuals even as they war against each other. Indeed, just as Hobbes earlier described conscience as being produced out of a shared knowledge between "two, or more" individuals, it is not "two, or more" individuals who agree that "Peace is Good," but rather *all individuals*. They are all "CONSCIOUS of it one to another" and so they "know it together," creating a shared consciousness or sense of *conscience* even amid universal discord.

As long as the condition of war exists, however, this mutual knowledge must remain internalized since an outward inclination towards peace in this state is dangerous. For this reason, even though the laws of nature "*oblige in Conscience alwayes,*" they only "oblige *in foro interno*," meaning they "bind to a desire they should take place" even if they are not implemented *in foro externo*. If these laws were to be implemented *in foro externo*, making an individual "modest, and tractable, and performe all he promises" when "no man els should do so," he would "make himselfe a prey to others, and procure his own ruine, contrary to the ground of all Lawes of Nature, which tends to Natures preservation" (110). In this way, by adhering to the first Law of Nature, "*to seek Peace, and follow it,*" an individual could risk transgressing all natural law by provoking his own destruction.

Hobbes elucidates this peculiar relationship with natural law by distinguishing between *the law of nature* and *the right of nature*. While the law of nature forbids an individual from doing anything that would compromise his life, the right of nature gives him license to do anything "for the preservation [...] of his own life." Hobbes distinguishes right and law further by noting that "RIGHT, consisteth in liberty to do, or to forebeare; Whereas LAW, determinith, and bindeth to one of them: so that Law, and Right, differ as much, as Obligation, and Liberty." In the condition of war, then, individuals are in a state of absolute liberty, and thus "every man has a Right to every thing." More importantly, as long as this state of absolute liberty persists, "there can be no security to any man" (91). In this way, it is the rights and liberties of the individual, or the pursuit of such, that force the internalization of conscience's obligation to natural law.[19] Conscience is not a "visible Power" capable of keeping individuals "in awe," tying them "by feare of punishment" to the "observation of those Lawes of Nature" (117). The power necessary to force such obedience must also be "great enough for our security" (118). While David compels his reader to "seek peace, and pursue it," entrusting his security to God, the individual in Hobbes's condition of war has no such recourse for safety.

In this state, then, conscience can only police *intention* and *desire* rather than *action*. Though the individual cannot *"seek Peace, and follow it,"* he still must always *desire* and *intend* to do so for the sake of his conscience. Conscience is thus a *civilizing force* in the condition of war, inclining the individual to give up his absolute liberty for the security and survival a commonwealth offers.

Hobbes's recalibration of conscience first into a social construct and second into an entity that seeks peace dismantles the tradition of conscience as a source of discord and even martyrdom going back as far as the Protestant Reformation. More importantly, it calls into question the claims his contemporaries made and were still making to justify their roles in the Revolution. Rather than cite "liberty of conscience" as a cause for the civil wars, as even Oliver Cromwell himself will do during the Protectorate, Hobbes casts such justifications as divisive, dangerous, and, most poignantly, *unconscientious.* If conscience first and foremost inclines individuals towards peace and concord according to natural law itself, it could never be the very source of discord and dissolution of sovereignty. Also, the calls for "liberty of conscience" so prevalent during these turbulent years would double as a call for the condition of war where absolute liberty and right exists equally for *everyone.* In this way, Hobbes's isolation of conscience itself as a civilizing force is not only revolutionary but also reactionary.

Conscience and Consent: The Leviathan

The formation of the commonwealth revolutionizes the role of the Hobbesian conscience in the public sphere. Whereas in the condition of war, conscience presided only *in foro interno* and over the individual's intentions, in the commonwealth, the shared desire for peace that connected the consciences of everyone can safely be implemented *in foro externo*. Yet this implementation comes with a price.

The commonwealth is formed only through placing restraints upon the absolute liberty possessed by individuals in the condition of war, restraints they willingly embrace for the sake of "their own preservation, and of a more contented life thereby" (117). These restraints require that each individual "conferre all their power and strength upon one Man […] that may reduce all their Wills, by plurality of voices, unto one Will," thereby "submit[ting] their Wills, every one to his Will, and their Judgements, to his Judgement." More importantly, this process creates the leviathan, one man to "beare their Person," with each individual "own[ing], and acknowledge[ing] himselfe to be Author of whatsoever he that so beareth their Person, shall Act, or cause to be Acted, in those things which concerne the Common Peace and Safetie" (120). Members of the commonwealth become passive authors and authorizers of the leviathan's every action by consenting to his aggregate power.

Hobbes is careful to emphasize throughout *Leviathan* that this process of creation is artificial rather than natural. In forging the leviathan, humans play God, with their covenant to one another "resembl[ing] that *Fiat*, or the *Let us make man*, pronounced by God in the Creation" (1–2). And this artificial creation, like God's natural creation, must have an artificial conscience. Hobbes deems this artificial conscience the "publique Conscience," or civil law (223). The artificiality of both the leviathan and his "publique Conscience" is apparent when one turns to the striking visual representation of Hobbes's political theory housed in the text's frontispiece (Figure 4). The engraving features the towering leviathan, torso-deep in a mountainous landscape overlooking a city scene. He wields in his right hand a sword and in his left a bishop's crozier, representing his power in both the civil and ecclesiastical spheres. The panels below him correspond to these powers, comparing left to right the castle to the church, crown to the mitre, and so on. Above the leviathan's head is a phrase from Job 41:24: "*Non est potestas Super Terram quæ Comparetur ei*," "There is no power on earth comparable to him." The engraving visually reinforces this message: though the leviathan's body takes up only one third of the frontispiece, the viewer's eye is constantly drawn back to this striking central image. The leviathan's body comprises a multitude of tiny individual bodies, all gazing up at the face of their sovereign. They look to him as their literal head, and he is dependent upon them for the very existence of his towering body.[20]

Figure 4. Frontispiece of *Leviathan* (1651) by Abraham Bosse in collaboration with Hobbes. By permission of the British Museum.

Figure 5. *Avis au roys*, "The Body Politic" (fourteenth century). By permission of the Pierpont Morgan Library, New York.

What is most important regarding this image is how much it differs from the model that Hobbes intended it to replace: the body politic. Unlike Hobbes's decidedly artificial creation, the body politic is an organic construct derived from the hierarchy that, according to Thomas Elyot, "God hath put generally in all his creatures, begynnynge at the mooste inferiour or base, and assendynge vpwarde."[21] If we compare *Leviathan*'s frontispiece to that from a mid-fourteenth-century representation of the body politic, we notice the King's naked body onto which is mapped his kingdom in descending order of status and occupation from head to foot (Figure 5). The King's head matches that of the leviathan, occupying the prime position within the body, and from there, the seneschals, bailiffs, and provosts comprise the faculties of vision and hearing, the counsellors and wise men the heart, the knights the hands, merchants the legs, and labourers the feet. While the leviathan's body is arbitrarily composed of all his authors – man, woman, labourer, and merchant alike – the body politic mirrors the natural order created by God Himself.

The conscience of this natural body was similarly an outgrowth of God's larger order: the King's conscience was the conscience of the nation. When Charles I puts forth his own conscience as a national entity judging on behalf of the English people in *Eikon Basilike* (1649), he does so as the divinely and naturally appointed head of his nation. His conscience is neither a composite of his subjects' nor a representation of their consent. The persistence of this model was disrupted by the English Revolution, with the notion of a "public conscience" circulating only after significant challenges to Charles's authority.[22] This language begins to emerge in 1646 when John Saltmarsh ponders the nature of the "*State conscience* or *Publike conscience*," and in 1647, when Stephen Marshall weighs the value of an individual's "private fancies" over and against the "publike conscience of the Common-wealth":

> If any one, out of an evill heart, shall break forth into open reviling, scorning, disgracefull words against the present Church-government now established, he shall not be connived at, as a man of tender conscience: for as he giveth himselfe power and liberty to dis-joyn from it, so it is also in his power, not to speak evill of it, but doing it by choice and deliberation; he cannot fall within the compasse of weakenesse. For he that maketh no conscience, of giving offence and scandal to the Christian Magistrate, and all his godly brethren, living in peaceable obedience cannot imagine, that his private fancies though covered with weaknesse, should be more tendered, then the publike conscience of the Common-wealth.[23]

Marshall identifies those dissenters for conscience's sake as falling within the "compasse of weakeness": they dissent because of a tenderness that must be indulged or "connived at" by onlookers. However, an individual's tender conscience – or, in this case, "private fancies" posing as a tender conscience – cannot be valued above the public conscience of the commonwealth. Both Saltmarsh's and Marshall's choices to use this terminology mark the emergence of a new sense of conscience circulating during this period: a single conscience that concerns the nation as a whole, yet one that does not necessarily belong to the sovereign.

Although Hobbes uses the same terminology, his version of this national construct does not allow for the possibility of a genuine "man of tender conscience" who might fall "within the compasse of weakness." Individuals who decide to submit their wills and judgments to a common power that will keep them in awe also agree to be guided by the public conscience (223). More importantly, that public conscience includes their own individual consciences. Just as their crowd of bodies effectively create this artificial man, so their consciences create his artificial conscience. Concretizing this visual representation, Hobbes establishes an inextricable relationship between natural and civil law: they "contain each other," and so "The Law of Nature therefore is a part of the Civill Law in all Common-wealths of the world. Reciprocally also, the Civill Law is a part of the Dictates of Nature" (185). If the *Lawes of Nature oblige in Conscience alwayes*," and the "Civill Law is a part of the Dictates of Nature," then the individual conscience is similarly obliged to the public conscience "*alwayes*." Securing that obligation further, Hobbes tells his reader that "Obedience to the Civill Law is part also of the Law of nature" (185).

This relationship between natural and civil law suggests that the public conscience is in fact an outward manifestation of that enduring obligation between conscience and natural law. In the condition of war, this obligation was confined *in foro interno* as a means of survival; in the commonwealth, however, that obligation and conscience's subsequent role as a civilizing force finally come to fruition. In this way, conscience now not only inclines the individual towards peace from within but also enforces that obligation from without.

Despite this language of enforcement and obligation, Hobbes is careful to note that the public conscience was created through a universal process of consent. The limitations enacted by this construct, then, were self-imposed: just as individuals "have made an Artificiall Man, which we call a Common-wealth; so also have they made Artificiall Chains, called *Civill Lawes*, which they themselves, by mutuall covenants, have fastned at one end, to the lips of that Man, or Assembly, to whom they have given the Soveraigne Power; and at the other end to their own Ears" (147). This shared restraint out of which the public conscience emerges relates back to Hobbes's etymological focus. If conscience is produced when two or more individuals *know together*, then the public conscience is produced out of each individual's shared knowledge and acknowledgment of the civil law (89, 183). And that knowledge is simply an extension of what they always already knew in their own consciences: "*to seek Peace, and follow it*."

Since these bonds are self-imposed, they are also weak. Yet they are "made to hold, by the danger" rather than the "difficulty of breaking them" (147). In the condition of war, individuals lived in a state of "continuall feare, and danger of [...] violent death," the same fear and danger that prompted their covenant (89). As Hobbes suggests, the creation of the commonwealth does not eliminate fear altogether; however, the persistence of that fear allows for the survival of the leviathan. Conscience's role in the commonwealth is central to this necessary production of fear. Whereas fear kept individuals from obeying their consciences *in foro externo* in the condition of war, they are now too fearful *not to obey* the public conscience. While all around him sectarians are using the language of conscience to justify revolution and dissent, Hobbes figures conscience as the very agent of subjection. And, more importantly, this agent operates from within. Indeed, the chains of the public conscience create a self-imposed network of absolute obedience, kept in place by those being restrained rather than by the restrainer.

In addition to manifesting the individual conscience's obligation to natural law, the public conscience also mobilizes that individual conscience's power of judgment between right and wrong. Hobbes labels as a "doctrine repugnant to Civill Society" that *"whatsoever a man does against his Conscience, is Sinne."* In the condition of war, the individual conscience occupied a privileged position "because he ha[d] no other rule to follow but his own reason." Yet the creation of the public conscience curbs both the need for and the safety of each individual "making himselfe judge of Good and Evill." In the presence of the public conscience, the individual conscience becomes synonymous with "judgment" and "private opinions," and so it "may be erroneous." For this reason, if it maintained its role as the judge of good and evil actions, Hobbes fears, "in such diversity, as there is of private Consciences [...] the Common-wealth must needs be distracted, and no man dare to obey the Soveraign Power, farther than it shall seem good in his own eyes" (223). By mobilizing this power of judgment, the public conscience standardizes morality, safeguarding the commonwealth from such "diversity," distraction, and disobedience. And, once again speaking back to Hobbes's etymological focus, this standardized judgment becomes yet another form of knowledge that all participants in the commonwealth share.

"Their Consciences Were Free": Freeing Conscience in the Commonwealth

Having obliged the individual conscience to the public conscience, Hobbes is careful to free it from other sources of potential obligation, particularly doctrinal obligations. As he indicates in his frontispiece, Hobbes envisions the leviathan's jurisdiction extending absolutely over both church and state. In order to maintain that consolidation of power, he limits the independent power that the church might have over the conscience of the individual. If the church were to multiply the obligations placed upon conscience, venturing into the territory of doctrine, it would both threaten the covenantal obedience established with the formation of the commonwealth and allow the church to emerge as a viable legislative authority over conscience. According to Hobbes, Christ sent his apostles out as "Sheep unto Wolves, not as Kings to their Subjects" (361). For this reason, the first converts to Christianity obeyed the apostles "out of Reverence, not by Obligation," their consciences being "free, and their Words and Actions subject to none but the Civill Power" (479).

Like his contemporaries, Hobbes believed that England was entering a special moment in its history as a nation. Also like some of his contemporaries, Hobbes believed that what made this moment so distinct was its potential connection back to a primitive Christianity. The first Christians enjoyed a "free conscience," free from the restraints and obligations of an artificially constructed church government (479). This moment was fleeting as knots upon that liberty were established by the evolving church: first Presbyters, "obliging themselves to teach nothing against the Decrees of their Assemblies," believed the people "thereby obliged to follow their Doctrine"; next, after the number of Presbyters increased, a certain number of them "got themselves an authority over the Parochiall Presbyters, and appropriated to themselves the names of Bishops"; and the final and third knot was the creation of the papacy (479). Those who breached the obligations or knots placed upon conscience by these institutions were excommunicated, according to Hobbes, "not as being Infidels, but as being disobedient" (479). In this way, these knots and obligations were effectively operating in the civil realm rather than the realm of faith.

Hobbes celebrates the untying of these knots in England's most recent history, beginning with Queen Elizabeth by whom "the Power of the Popes was dissolved totally," then moving on to the Presbyterians, who "obtained the putting down of Episcopacy"; and the third knot finally dissolved when "the Power was taken also from the Presbyterians" (479). Believing this process of dissolution complete, Hobbes tells his reader that "we are reduced to the Independency of the Primitive Christians," with consciences freed from the knots of a competing civil power. He replaces the church's power of compulsion with that of persuasion. Hobbes warns against making "new Articles of Faith, by determining every small controversie, which oblige men to a needlesse burthen of Conscience, or provoke them to break the union of the Church" (351). Rather than instigate dissent and nonconformity by binding the conscience unnecessarily, the church should play the primitive role of pedagogue:

> Our Saviour Christs Commission to his Apostles, and Disciples, was to Proclaim his Kingdome (not present, but) to come; and to Teach all Nations; and to Baptize them that should beleeve; and to enter into the houses of them that should receive them; and where they were not received, to shake off the dust of their feet against them; but not to call for fire from heaven to destroy them, nor to compell them to obedience by the Sword. In all which there is nothing of Power, but of Perswasion. (360–1)

"Faith," after all, "hath no relation to, no dependence at all upon Compulsion, or Commandment; but onely upon certainty, or probability of Arguments drawn from Reason" (342). Individuals were driven towards faith by reason, not by force.

Such a defence of conscience and faith would seem to cast Hobbes alongside the most fervent defenders of liberty of conscience in 1651. Hobbes maintains, after all, that "internall Faith is in its own nature invisible, and consequently exempted from all humane jurisdiction," and that "the inward *thought*, and *beleef* of men, which humane Governours can take no notice of," "fall not under obligation" of the civil law (360, 323). Moreover, it is a grave "Errour" in "Civill Philosophy" to "extend the power of the Law, which is the Rule of Actions onely, to the very Thoughts, and Consciences of men" (471). While many scholars have recently read these final pages of *Leviathan* as a testament to Hobbes's being more tolerant than previously thought, or even the "father of liberalism," it is important for us to recall his definition of the word "conscience" before we group him with the likes of those he feared most.

After all, the phrase "liberty of conscience" was more than familiar by *Leviathan*'s publication in 1651. Cromwell himself would declare "liberty of conscience" a fundamental only a few years later, a belief that he and many of his sectarian contemporaries and allies held long before his ascendancy as Lord Protector. As early as 1644, Milton implores the Long Parliament for "the liberty to know, to utter, and to argue freely according to conscience, above all liberties." Yet *Leviathan*, however it may have been used after its publication, was not an argument for the sort of liberty Cromwell encouraged or for the liberty that Milton felt entitled to as an Englishman. In fact, Hobbes talks not of *liberty of conscience*, a phrase that would have aligned him with sectarians; rather he references only a *free conscience*. While that conscience is free from the knots of a burdensome ecclesiastical doctrine, Hobbes does not liberate it to act freely in the world, allowing individuals to "know, to utter," or to "argue freely" according to their consciences. As soon as "internall Faith" is translated into words and actions, it becomes subject to the civil power (360).

Just as conscience in the condition of war, the individual conscience's connection to faith also has an inherently social dimension. *Conscience* for Hobbes means "to know with," an etymological focus that precludes the possibility of many forms of "liberty of conscience." Hobbes declares that "there ought to be no Power over the Consciences of men, but of the Word it selfe, working Faith in *every one*" (480). This production of faith is universal: even in the condition of war, every individual's conscience created a desire within him for peace and concord that was similarly mutual but kept invisible. Now, within the confines of the commonwealth, the Word of God – a public institution – works upon every one's conscience, ensuring not only faith but also obedience. This production of a quasi-public sphere within the very agent of civil obedience and subjection seems in part an iteration of the production of the leviathan itself. The creation of the public conscience through an obligation already upon the individual conscience eliminated the possibility of dissent from that public conscience or civil law. Similarly, the dissolution of doctrinal knots upon the individual conscience eliminates both the possibility of and need for religious dissent from the church and sovereign. The cooperative space that is created within the conscience, moreover, is one swayed only by persuasion rather than compulsion. For this reason, any faith working within the conscience as a result of the Word and evangelism – both agents of the public sphere – is self-imposed, just as the chains that bind one's ears to the mouth of the leviathan.

Most important for Hobbes's purposes, the level of freedom enjoyed by conscience seconds as a measure of the sovereign's absolute power in both the civil and ecclesiastical realms. If we reconsider Parker's conscience conundrum, Hobbes's *Leviathan* works to harness the potentially destructive power of conscience in order to ensure that it be "the best if not the only security of Government." Through his creation of the public conscience, then, Hobbes makes conscience itself the very cornerstone of the commonwealth. And, while this construct is revolutionary, it also disables – or aims to – conscience as a potential agent of revolution.

James Harrington's *The Commonwealth of Oceana* (1656) and the National Conscience

Hobbes's grappling with the conscience conundrum put into circulation a revolutionary relationship between conscience and the nation, one that his contemporaries borrow, appropriate, and even try to perfect over the next several decades. After the establishment of the Protectorate in 1653, very few were "prepared to state that they were straightforward disciples of Hobbes," yet "almost everyone could admit that some of the things he said were very well said indeed."[24] Jonathan Scott deems James Harrington, a former intimate of the imprisoned Charles I and later republican theorist, "the greatest English disciple [...] of Hobbes," a supposition even recognized in his own time.[25] Matthew Wren, politician and polemicist, wrote of Harrington, "though Mr. Harrington professes a great Enmity to Mr. Hobs in his politiques, underhand notwithstanding he holds a correspondence with him, and does silently swallow down such Notions as Mr. Hobs hath chewed for him."[26] In *The Prerogative of Popular Government* (1657), Harrington responds to Wren's attack, admitting that "It is true, I have opposed the Politicks of Mr. *Hobbs* to shew him what he taught me [...] my Conscience bears me witnesse, that I have done my duty: Nevertheless in most other things I firmly believe that Mr. *Hobbs* is, and will in future Ages be accounted the best Writer, at this day, in the World."[27]

Harrington demonstrates this complex relationship with Hobbes in his construction of the "national conscience" in *The Commonwealth of Oceana* (1656), a hybrid of Hobbes's "public conscience" and, at least on the surface, Oliver Cromwell's church settlement. Like both Hobbes and Cromwell, Harrington recognized a careful treatment of conscience as central to England's peace and settlement. In order to apply and adapt Hobbes's theory to Cromwell's policy of liberty of conscience, he fashions a commonwealth through which he might show the Protector the way towards what Harrington hoped would be his eventual abdication. Crucial to Harrington's vision of this perpetual and Protectorless stability, however, was the disarming of conscience in the civil sphere, revealing that he, like Hobbes, similarly feared and distrusted this concept.

Harrington's *Oceana* describes in great detail the founding of the commonwealth of Oceana, a fictionalized model of and for the English nation. The ultimate end of his enterprise was to fashion an immortal commonwealth, one that would never again have to fear the tumults of civil war.[28] In "The Corollary" to the text, Oceana's lawgiver Lycurgus, "when he saw that his government had taken root and was in the very plantation strong enough to stand by itself,"

> conceived such a delight within him, as God is described by Plato to have done, when he had finished the creation of the world, and saw his own orbs move below him. For in the art of man, being the imitation of nature which is the art of God, there is nothing so like the first call of beautiful order out of chaos and confusion as the architecture of a well-ordered commonwealth.

His next step was to consider how he might render this government "unalterable and immortal."[29] As in Hobbes's *Leviathan*, Harrington imagines the commonwealth an artificial creation imitating God's own art. He oscillates between this image of the commonwealth as the world itself and as a human body, much like Hobbes's "Artificial Man."[30] And also like Hobbes's creation, Harrington's too possesses its own conscience.

In opposition to Henry Vane's and others' calls for a separation of civil and spiritual authority, Harrington imagines a commonwealth where the former encompasses the latter, creating a system of civil religion.[31] He erects a Council of Religion that presides over not only the national church but also matters of conscience, guaranteeing that "'true religion' remained a business of state."[32] This consolidation of power, Harrington insists, is the only condition under which liberty of conscience can subsist. If the magistrate, for example, is beholden to the pope, and the pope denies "liberty of conscience unto princes and commonwealths, they cannot give that unto their subjects which they have not" (40). With civil and spiritual powers consolidated in Oceana, Harrington envisions two levels of liberty of conscience – the individual and the national – that are contingent upon one another: "But as a governor pretending unto liberty, and suppressing the liberty of conscience which [...] is the main, must be a contradiction; so a man that, pleading for the liberty of private conscience, refuseth liberty unto the national conscience, must be absurd." "A commonwealth," he continues, "is nothing else but the national conscience. And if the conviction of a man's private conscience produce his private religion, the conviction of the national conscience must produce a national religion" (39). Harrington affords the same liberty of conscience – a liberty that he describes as the "main" or chief freedom a government can offer – to the nation that he affords to the individual as a matter of logic: if one should exist without the other, such conditions would be without reason.

More importantly, much like the Cromwellian church settlement, Harrington extends public expressions of liberty of conscience to "gathered congregations" outside of the national religion, as long as they are "not Popish, Jewish nor idolatrous" (81). This break from Hobbes's conception of this freedom also accounts for Harrington's choice of the word "national" rather than "public" to categorize his aggregate conscience in *Oceana*.[33] Hobbes's "public conscience" is the law to which all individuals in a commonwealth must consent for their own safety: this construct and its name precludes any alternate public expressions of conscience. Harrington's "national conscience," being the commonwealth, whose "materials [...] are the people," similarly represents the unified expression of the nation (75). However, its existence does not preclude other public shows of liberty of conscience since it is simply the national rather than *the* public conscience. To establish precedent for this model, Harrington looks to the commonwealth of Israel, where "the law ecclesiastical and civil was the same," but "as the national religion appertained unto the jurisdiction of the Sanhedrim, so the liberty of conscience appertained from the same date and by the same right unto the prophets and their disciples." Looking forward even to John the Baptist and Christ himself, Harrington maintains that it was "by this right" that they "had their disciples, and taught the people, whence is derived our present right of *Gathered Congregations*" (39–40).

Yet despite the importance that he attaches to liberty of conscience, Harrington too must contend with the conscience conundrum. Liberty of conscience, though foundational to the commonwealth, must be safely contained so as to prevent its most tragic disturbances. After all, Harrington's first priority in *Oceana* was not establishing liberty, whether civil or religious, but rather establishing peace and settlement.[34] Harrington claims that he "contracted a disease," presumably a mental breakdown, after Charles I's execution.[35] His acute distress following the regicide, it seems, fuels his desire to establish both a commonwealth immune to political turbulences and a citizenry free from the desire for such insurrections. In this quest, Harrington appropriates and safeguards Cromwell's church settlement from both enthusiasm and the usurping clergy.[36] He thinks most dangerous those "who, holding that the saints must govern, go about to reduce the commonwealth unto a party," perhaps a reference to the looming threat of the Fifth Monarchists (63). Harrington goes on to caution that "pretence of religion hath always been turbulent in broken government, so where the government hath been sound and steady, religion hath never shown herself with any other face than that of her natural sweetness and tranquillity" (64).

Despite his support of Cromwell's church settlement, Harrington's image of religion as naturally sweet and tranquil also dismantles the Protector's own narrative regarding the civil wars. In his second speech before the First Protectorate Parliament, Cromwell cites religion – and liberty of conscience more particularly – as the cause of the revolution. While the Protector too sought peace and settlement for England, his characterization of the wars and the continued strain placed upon his government for the cause of conscience cast his most beloved liberty as potentially volatile and contentious. The tenuous peace that Cromwell established during the years of the Protectorate was a far cry from Harrington's vision of an immortal commonwealth. Through his theorization of Cromwell's church settlement, Harrington offers him counsel, showing how liberty of conscience might safely be contained within the confines of the civil power, protected without the need of a Protector.[37] Through his system of contingent liberties of conscience – the national and the individual – Harrington incited an irresistible deference to the national conscience on behalf of those who chose to exercise their liberty of conscience outside of the state religion. This deference to the liberty that secured the gathered congregations' freedom also guaranteed that the system based on Cromwell's own church settlement was defended and immortalized from within.

Harrington perfects Hobbes's vision of the "public conscience" as well: whereas he feared that Hobbes had yet left the leviathan vulnerable to conscience and its most nefarious manifestations, Harrington secures Oceana from conscience by granting it public liberty. He eliminates, in other words, any desire for revolution for the sake of conscience, uprisings much like the civil wars themselves. Indeed, as Jonathan Scott remarks, "Alone among republicans Harrington claimed to have extinguished the possibility of rebellion."[38] He had learned well from Hobbes, and feared with him the possibility of England's back-sliding into tumults once again.

Unfortunately for Harrington, Cromwell rejected his efforts. John Toland, Harrington's biographer, describes the Protector's reaction to his *Oceana*:

> He did accordingly inscribe it to OLIVER CROMWELL, who, after the perusal of it, said, the Gentleman had like to trapan him out of his Power, that what he got by the Sword he would not quit for a little paper Shot: adding in his usual cant, that he approv'd the Government of a single Person as little as any of 'em, but that he was forc'd to take upon him the Office of a High Constable, to preserve the Peace among the several Partys in the Nation, since he saw that being left to themselves, they would never agree to any certain form of Government, and would only spend their whole Power in defeating the Designs, or destroying the Persons of one another.[39]

Despite Harrington's carefully constructed commonwealth, Cromwell, at least according to this account, still considered his own firm grip on power the key to peace and settlement.

Conscience and Conformity: Revisiting Hobbes's Public Conscience during the Toleration Debates (1667–72)

Nearly a decade into the Restoration, Hobbes's public conscience resurfaces once again with the publication of Samuel Parker's controversial *A Discourse of Ecclesiastical Polity*.[40] Parker became a chaplain to Gilbert Sheldon, the archbishop of Canterbury, in 1667 and would earn a reputation as "one of the most aggressive opponents of religious toleration" during the toleration debates of 1667–72.[41] Like Hobbes and Harrington, Parker too is concerned with the *"Publick Peace and Settlement"* of the nation, a phrase that becomes his mantra throughout the lengthy tract (*A Discourse* iv). He also hopes to solve the conscience conundrum by appropriating in part the Hobbesian public conscience, a move that inspires an uproar at the press as tolerationists disparage Parker's use and abuse of *Leviathan*.

Gary De Krey deems the toleration debates of this period the first Restoration crisis, and more specifically, a crisis about conscience.[42] Dissenters in London openly challenged the authority of the restored Church of England and the second Conventicle Act (passed in 1670) in the pulpits, in print, and even in the streets.[43] Anglican apologists like Bishop Benjamin Laney, preaching before Charles II in 1665, maligned already mounting defences of conscience by casting conscience as the victimizer rather than the victim: "There is a great complaint in the world of domineering over the Conscience; but have we not rather cause to complain of the domineering of the Conscience?" Laney cautions the King further, asking him to recall the dangers of this domineering concept during the civil wars: "when the Conscience was loose for a while; one would think Hell had broke loose, so fill'd was on a sudden the Church with sects, and the Common-wealth with confusion."[44] Through Laney's and other Anglican polemicists' efforts, conscience emerged as the most potent of "traumatic legacies" of the English Revolution.[45]

Parker's *A Discourse* similarly connects contemporary calls for toleration to the "late Confusions" of the civil wars, a time when "Liberty of Conscience was laid as the Foundation of Settlement": "How was Sect built upon Sect, and Church upon Church, till they were advanced to such a height of Folly, that the Usurpers themselves could find no other way to work their subversion, and put an end to their extravagancies, but by overturning their own Foundations, and checking their growth by Laws and Penalties" (*A Discourse* 22). Parker paints a fearful picture of toleration, threatening that if tender consciences were indulged, their folly would increase without an end or limit in sight. This connection between chaos and conscience undoes the work of Hobbes's *Leviathan* where he redefines conscience as a civilizing force and foundational to peace and settlement. For Parker, rather than the condition of war, "to be a Subject is as natural upon being born, as to be a Man," a natural state disrupted rather than encouraged by free conscience (*A Discourse* 124).

For this reason, he casts tender conscience as a veritable public enemy. Parker focuses on the concept of the "public" throughout *A Discourse*, and more specifically public worship whose "proper End and Usefulness is to express Mens Agreement in giving Honour to the Divine Majesty." "And therefore," he concludes, "unless the Signs by which this Honour is signified be Publick and Uniform, 'tis not Publick Worship, because there is not Publick signification of Honour" (*A Discourse* 108–9). More importantly, the sense of agreement central to the production of public worship is not based on consent but rather the magistrate sets its terms. Any worship that falls outside of that established by the magistrate is thus deemed "Private Worship; in that they are not Publick, but Private Signs of Honour" to God (*A Discourse* 109). This separation between public and private worship delegitimizes calls for indulgence in the public sphere. Such tender consciences only threaten the uniformity of the public worship and risk becoming "unruly," "boisterous," "vicious and diseased," "untoward," and "Wild and Fanatick" (*A Discourse* 9, 18, 11, 16, 21).

Instead, Parker insists, tender consciences, as the "Product of a weak Understanding," ought to be "apt to comply with the Commands of its Superiours," and particularly the "Determinations of the Publick Wisdom" (*A Discourse* 269, 283, 280). In addition to the public wisdom, the "Voice of the Publick Laws cannot but drown the uncertain Whispers of a Tender Conscience; all its Scruples are hush'd and silenced by the Commands of Authority: it dares not whimper, when that forbids; and the Nod of a Prince awes it into Silence and Submission" (*A Discourse* 304). Parker imagines a conscience whose voice is literally silenced by these forms of public authority. Not content with the public wisdom and public laws alone, Parker also submits the private conscience to the judgments of the "Publick Conscience." "In Cases and Disputes of a Publick Concern," he maintains, "private men are not properly *sui Juris*, they have no Power over their own Actions, they are not to be directed by their own Judgments, or determined by their own Wills; but by the Commands and determinations of the Publick Conscience." Parker replaces the Hobbesian public conscience – an aggregate of the civilizing force within all consciences – with a nullifying entity, one that overrides the private consciences of subjects. After all, he continues, those in authority are "more competent Judges of Publick Concerns, than mens own Private Perswasions; and so must have a Superiour Authority over them, and bind them to yield and submit to their Determinations" (*A Discourse* 308, 309).

More importantly, individuals are bound to the commands of the public conscience whether or not they are correct. "'Tis better to Erre with Authority," Parker counsels his reader, "than be in the Right against it" since the "Duty of Obedience" outweighs all others in religion. He fears that, if this hierarchy between conscience and authority were to be disrupted, "we immediately dissolve all Government" (*A Discourse* 308, 309). Having identified the private conscience as a prime public enemy, Parker finally strips it of its most fatal power – dissent – by displacing its authority with that of the public conscience. He thus tries to solve the conscience conundrum by leaning in part on Hobbes's revolutionary construct.

Despite his borrowings from *Leviathan*, Parker attempts to dissociate his work from Hobbes's. Nevertheless, his opponents notice and expose the damning connections:[46] John Humfrey, calling Parker "a young *Leviathan*," remarks that his setting up a "power in any Mortal state above [conscience]" "does but do the same thing in a lower degree, as Mr. *Hobbs* does."[47] While Humfrey considers Parker but "a young *Leviathan*," Andrew Marvell in his *The Rehearsal Transpros'd: The Second Part* (1673) believes that Parker's "*Behemoth* exceeds his *Leviathan* some foot long, in whatsoever he saith of the Power of the Magistrate."[48] More pointedly, others resoundingly attacked his appropriation of Hobbes's public conscience, a hailstorm that helped to define the nature and terms of the defence of conscience during the toleration debates. The anonymous author of *Insolence and Impudence Triumphant* (1669) fears what beliefs might be forced on subjects through Parker's public conscience: "*I am apt to think from his discourse of a public Conscience, should Church or State command the* Mass *or* Alchoran *to be used in room of the Liturgy, he* [Parker] *would conform to it. Nay, should* Jupiter, *or any other Heathen Deity be set up, he would not be a* Nonconformist."[49] Scoffing at his opponent's vision of the public conscience, this author pushes Parker's fear of nonconformity into the realm of the absurd.

Similarly taking aim at Parker, Marvell calls *A Discourse* a "Haloo to Princes and all mankind to fall upon Tender Consciences with the severest rigour." Even worse than this war declared on tender consciences, he condemns, Parker's public conscience makes "mens private Consciences" "very inconsiderable."[50] Mocking Parker's preoccupation with the word "public," Marvell refashions his public conscience into a prostitute:

> She [*publick Conscience*] is a Lady doubtless of great Quality and Virtue, I should be glad to know her lodging and be better acquainted with her: though often it happens that there is little difference betwixt Publick and Prostitute. But she being very generous, *if there be any sin in her Commands will her self answer for it*, and discharge you of all danger *she will warrant your Obedience, and hallow, or at least excuse your Action*. Do what you will with her, *She will secure you from Sin, if not from Errour*. She *will render your Actions virtuous, whatever they are in themselves*. 'Tis the best Woman that ever was born.

Marvell imagines Parker's construct as prostituting out the services of conscience for the profit of public uniformity. And while Parker reassured his readers that they could not err even if the public conscience erred so long as they remained obedient, Marvell casts this reassurance as a moral leniency just as debased as this "best Woman." More importantly, his conflation of public and prostitute emphasizes the commonness of Parker's concept, an attribute that contradicts the very essence of what he believes conscience to be. Marvell laments that, while Parker renders the individual conscience a "thing so inconsiderable," "the mischief is this, that this is that by which every man must be excused or accused." Despite the role private conscience must play in salvation, Parker transforms it into "a meer Trollop," "an old Beldam superannuate, and a Bulbegger fit to fright Children."[51] His public conscience would have the private seem an obsolete spectre, Marvell cautions, inciting but a baseless terror in the believer.

Going beyond accusations of prostitution, John Owen calls Parker's public conscience "*Circes Rod*, one stroke whereof turned men into Hoggs." He continues in this fantastical strain, supposing that Parker "would find hard work" "to perswade men to put out their own eyes, or blind themselves, that they might see all by one publick Eye." Compounding his Circean and cyclopean imagery, Owen hopes his readers would find this construct just as absurd, "considering especially that that publick Conscience it self is a meer *Tragelaphus*, which never had existence in *Rerum natura*." In response to Parker's attempt to make obedience to the public conscience seem most natural, Owen accuses his opponent of having created a mythological beast, the stuff of makebelieve. After all, he argues, individual conscience is the very "Yoke of God," a burden "placed in them by him who made them, to rule in them and over their actions in his name, and with respect to their dependence on him." In opposition to Parker's dangerous imitation of God's yoke, this private conscience is both divine and natural, being part of the "order of things."[52]

Parker responds to this criticism in *A Defence and Continuation of the Ecclesiastical Politie* (1671), hoping to distance himself from Hobbes's *Leviathan* and, more importantly, from Hobbes's "public conscience." Citing the same passage that caught the attention of Humfrey, Marvell, Owen, and others, Parker concedes, "This is somewhat rank Doctrine, and favours not a little of the Leviathan. But yet how can I avoid it? are not these my own words?" Yet Parker follows this confession by insisting that his use of the "public conscience" has been abused by his detractors. Parker fires back that, while this concept only "concern[ed] such nice and petty things as are liable to doubt, scruple, and Disputation" in *A Discourse*, Owen in particular would have it seem as though he "speaks *of the most important parts* of Religion" by splicing together different passages.[53] He makes a similar argument in *A Reproof to the Rehearsal Transposed* (1673), this time challenging Marvell's attack upon his public conscience:

> And here all your Plot to is borrowed from *J.O.* and the great subtilty of it lies no deeper than only in representing what I have determined in the Case of a doubting, scrupulous and unsatisfied Conscience, as if I had intended it of Conscience in general in all matters and as to all events [...] and the People have swalled it with a glib and round Assurance that I have exhorted them to disgorge their Consciences instead of their Scruples, and to renounce all Obligations of Vertue and Religion but what are tied upon them by the Laws of the Common-wealth, and to know no other Rule or Measure of their Duty, but the will and Pleasure of their Prince, and when once the outcry is taken, 'tis to no purpose for me to plead that this is the very Divinity of the *Leviathan*, that I have labour'd to oppose.[54]

While admitting that he has borrowed Hobbes's vocabulary, Parker condemns the "very Divinity of the *Leviathan*," which he believes his own contradicts.

Despite Parker's self-defence, his opponents' responses to *A Discourse* transform his public conscience into a reflection of the monstrous nature of conformity itself. More importantly, dissenting writers offer up alternative models of "peace and settlement" that do not require a public or national conscience at all. Rather than solve the conscience conundrum, they discredit it, prompting a rethinking of conscience's role in Restoration politics and worship. Despite this disagreement with Hobbes, Harrington, and Parker, however, dissenting writers too were invested in presenting conscience as a "civilizing force," or perhaps more appropriately, a *civilized* force. Owen, for example, argues that "primitive Christians" refused "to observe the Religion required by Law," all the while "exercising themselves in the Worship of God, which was strictly forbidden," yet "neither Anarchy, nor Confusion, or any disturbance of publick Tranquility did ensue thereon." "So did the Protestants," Owen adds, "here in *England* in the dayes of Queen *Mary*, and sometime before."[55] He identifies the punishing of dissent rather than dissent itself as the cause for disruptions to the "publick Tranquility." Owen asks, "What quietness, what peace is there like to be in the world, whilst the sword of vengeance must be continually drawn about these things?" His repetition of Parker's refrain, "publick Peace, Tranquility and Welfare," undoes the work of *A Discourse*, showing nonconformists to be obedient subjects who "willingly employ themselves for the publick good and welfare" of the nation.[56]

The author of *Insolence and Impudence* pushes further than Owen's call for clemency and peace through toleration, reimagining altogether the idea of unity: he wishes for "a happy end of all our Differences and Divisions, the blotting out all Names of Distinction, and the promoting of *Catholick Charity* amongst Brethren: That all true Christians may endeavour to preserve *the Unity of the Spirit in the Bond of Peace*."[57] Citing Ephesians 4:3, this writer draws on Paul's goals of unification and peace among a divided congregation. The apostle addresses former Gentiles and Jews, reminding them that "he is our peace, who hath made both one, and hath broken down the middle wall of partition *between us*" (2:14). This sense of peace and unity need not be created or enforced artificially by the civil power: it already exists in Christ and needs only to be recognized.

The legacy of Hobbes's "public conscience," mediated through the hysteria Parker hoped to incite against nonconformity, thus helped to shape such arguments in favour of toleration. Dissenting writers find in that legacy the very embodiment of tyranny over conscience. Hobbes's construct is transformed from the representation of conscience's civilizing force to a monstrosity in and of itself, and one capable of inciting rebellion, the very thing Hobbes had hoped to eliminate. In order to civilize conscience anew, then, dissenting writers discredit this public iteration.

Chapter Five

Lucy Hutchinson's Revisions of Conscience

Perhaps the most dramatic episode in the whole of Lucy Hutchinson's *Memoirs of the Life of Colonel Hutchinson* is her singular moment of wifely disobedience. In May 1660, she sensed that her husband was "ambitious of being a publick sacrifice" for the republican cause. As a result, "herein only in her whole life" Lucy Hutchinson "resolv'd to disobey him" by forging a written retraction in her husband's name to the Speaker of the House of Commons.[1] James Sutherland argues that "nothing else that she says or does in her long narrative is likely to please [her audience] more" (xviii). Most scholars, including recent editors of the *Memoirs*, have accepted her account of the forged letter as truth; yet its veracity has rightly been called into question on several occasions.[2] Soon after the discovery of John Hutchinson's petition, C.H. Firth points out that "Mrs. Hutchinson conceals much of the truth, and misrepresents many of the facts" in the *Memoirs*, especially in regard to this particular episode. Citing a second petition sent to the House of Lords six weeks after the original letter, as well as John Hutchinson's endorsement of the first letter – "A copy of my letter to ye house of Commons" – Firth argues convincingly that "[John] Hutchinson's share in this matter was not confined to the passive and silent acceptance of his wife's expedient."[3] It seems more likely, as Firth and more recently Derek Hirst conclude, that Lucy Hutchinson may have been the colonel's amanuensis in this case rather than the sole author of the recantation; or, as David Norbrook argues, the document might even have been "some kind of collaboration" between husband and wife.[4]

Such speculation provokes the question, why would Lucy Hutchinson claim sole authorship of the petition? Also, considering her claim, why does she fail to disclose the terms of this recantation in the *Memoirs*, a text that is otherwise meticulous in its attention to detail? This petition, it seems, is an absent presence in the text: Lucy Hutchinson, after all, calls attention to it by trying to make it disappear. And scholars who want to focus on the Hutchinsons as stalwart republicans similarly elide this explicit submission to monarchy. Despite scholarly fascination with Lucy Hutchinson's alleged moment of wifely disobedience, only recently has attention been given to the petition itself.[5] This chapter will use this little-explored document to shed light on the *Memoirs*. More specifically, I will examine the use of the word "conscience" in the recantation and in the *Memoirs* to show how Lucy Hutchinson strives to recover her husband's reputation as a staunch republican.

While scholars have noted that the *Memoirs* is a redemptive text, they have failed to recognize that it is also a very anxious text.[6] The language of conscience throughout is insistent and reiterated precisely because Lucy Hutchinson has something to hide. The *Memoirs* confronts readers with a seemingly flawless – if constructed – picture of John Hutchinson. He is at once an Englishman, a republican, *and* a man of conscience, with each of these attributes being inseparable from the next. "He never did anything," she insists, "without measuring it by the rule of conscience" (6). Yet, as N.H. Keeble points out, the "collapse of the Good Old Cause posed for [Lucy Hutchinson], as for all the defeated Puritans and their nonconformist successors, a daunting case of conscience. The 'revolution' of 1660 […] tempted her, and them, to betray their Puritan allegiance, to doubt God's providential dealings with his elect nation, and to despair."[7] Whether the sentiment of John Hutchinson's petition is genuine or not, it suggests that he may have momentarily failed this test of conscience. In the recantation, he twice maintains that it was for his conscience's sake that he had returned his loyalties to Charles II and repented his role in the regicide. This language of conscience at once makes the colonel's petition more credible (he was pardoned soon after its delivery) and sullies his reputation as a republican, regicide, and advocate of the cause. Considering these two incriminating appeals to conscience, it seems no accident that the *Memoirs* is rife with references to John Hutchinson's decidedly republican conscience.

Yet Lucy Hutchinson's project in the *Memoirs* is not simply a recovery effort: she also seeks to inspire hope that the English nation might yet be a republic through this portrait of her husband's revised conscience. Because the colonel's character uses the "rule of conscience" to determine his actions – especially his decision to sign Charles I's death warrant – Lucy Hutchinson roots his (and her own) cause to establish an English republic in divine providence. She creates out of her husband's character, then, a martyr for the republican cause whose peaceful conscience heartens her readers to remain confident in "God's providential dealings with his elect nation." In this way, the *Memoirs* is both retrospective and forward looking in its desire to spark a new republican future for the English nation out of a failed republican past – a failure, ironically, shared by John Hutchinson, the anxious text's hero and unremitting "man of conscience."

John Hutchinson's Petition to the Commons and the Politics of Seduction

Though Lucy Hutchinson's failure to disclose the terms of her husband's recantation in the *Memoirs* is surprising, this fact becomes much less baffling upon a single reading of the document. A copy of the petition itself was not discovered until the nineteenth century by Mrs M.A. Everett Green in the Public Record Office and was published in the *Athenaeum* on 3 March 1860. Green's finding was a draft of the original in Lucy Hutchinson's hand and without a signature, the original having been destroyed in a fire in 1834.[8] Despite its obvious importance to the narrative of the *Memoirs*, some editors have not included the text of the petition in their editions; others have included it but with little commentary.[9] On the whole, more attention has been paid to the fact that Lucy Hutchinson claimed the letter as her own than to the actual letter itself. Ironically, it seems that her deliberate inattention has successfully prompted many scholars' own neglect of its terms. Yet the petition and its damaging language, I would argue, had a profound effect on the way in which Lucy Hutchinson fashioned her husband's defence in the *Memoirs*.

The letter begins with an expression of "that deepe and sorrowfull sence which so heavily presses my soule, for the unfortunate guilt that lies upon it." Such profound "penitent sorrow," as John Hutchinson terms it, transforms this letter into an act of contrition, meant to acquit the colonel and to alleviate his guilty conscience. In his own defence, John Hutchinson assures the Commons that he leagued with Parliament during the wars not for "my owne mallice, avarice, or ambition" but rather because "an ill-guided judgement led me." Though the colonel begins with a confession of wrongdoing, he also constructs his disobedience as largely passive: it was Parliament with their "seeming sanctity" and "subtile arts" who "seduc'd not only me, but thousands more" to fight against the King. Once he realized his error, John Hutchinson insists, he immediately "stopt and left acting with them"; and, once he defected, "no person with a more perfect abhorrency detested both the heinous fact and authors of it [the execution of Charles I]." Distancing himself further from Parliament, he claims to have abandoned the cause even before Oliver Cromwell's dissolution of the Rump Parliament in 1653 – the point after which most republicans ceased to support Cromwell – desiring more than anything "to returne to that loyall subjection to the right Prince, from which I had bene so horridly misled." Moreover, the colonel argues, after Cromwell's death in 1658, a time when many republicans hoped for the revival of the cause, "the same desires [to be loyal to the king] continued in me" (290–1).

Yet John Hutchinson's seduction, this letter suggests, reached beyond his "ill-guided judgement" and into the inner sanctum of his conscience. He assures the Commons that it was "God's greate mercy, a thorough conviction of my former misled judgment and conscience and not a regard of my particular safety that drove me to [repent]." This construction is most troubling since, for devout Puritans like the Hutchinsons, conscience should be led by God through the scriptures rather than by the "arts of those men." Now that he realized his error, it was the colonel's conscience and not his instinctual drive for self-preservation that returned his allegiance to the Crown. Earlier in the petition, he had similarly appealed to his conscientious obedience, asserting that he was not "driven to this [repentance] through feare, but the conviction of my conscience that I ought so to act." "Conviction" in this sense has two meanings: first, convincement, or convincing someone of the truth, and second, finding one guilty of a past misdeed, or finding one in error.[10] By employing this language, then, John Hutchinson hoped to convince the Commons that he had already been accused in his conscience for his rebellion and that his present obedience to the King was thus sealed by his conscience – a seal that the colonel's colleagues would have known he did not take lightly (290–1).

To substantiate this grand claim to conscience, the colonel appeals to his past actions as evidence of his convincement. Such proof, he is confident, would confirm that his "repentance [...] [had] bene long since, and not of late expresst; that it was reall, rather declard by deeds then words." More specifically, he notes that he "hindred the oath of renuntiation," an oath introduced on 2 January 1660 by the restored Rump meant to renounce the *title of his* Majesty *and the whole line of King* James";[11] "endeavoured the release of Sir G. Booth," the head of a royalist uprising in 1659; and sought the "restoring of the secluded members" of Parliament, members who had been forcibly removed by the New Model Army during Pride's Purge in December 1648 for their attempt to negotiate a settlement with Charles I (291).

Only by neglecting to disclose the details of this petition and by claiming authorship of it could Lucy Hutchinson hope to recover her husband's conscience for the republican cause. What is more, this was not the only episode in the *Memoirs* where she omits incriminating information. On 11 May 1660, before John Hutchinson's petition was sent to the Commons, the Convention Parliament demanded that he account for his actions during the civil wars and regicide in person. Lucy Hutchinson describes this speech in the *Memoirs*: "[Colonel Hutchinson] told them that for his actings in those dayes, if he had err'd, it was the inexperience of his age and the defect of his judgement, and not the mallice of his heart, which had ever prompted him to pursue the generall advantage of his country more than his owne." She continues, "The vaine expence of his age and the greate debts his publick employments had runne him into" during the course of the wars "yielded him just cause to repent that ever he forsooke his owne blessed quiett to embarque in such a troubled sea, where he had made shipwrack of all thing but a good conscience" (228). This report of his speech renders the colonel's "repentance" inconclusive. He only admits to the possibility of erring – *if* he had erred – and he only repents compromising his quiet life for public engagements. More importantly, drawing on 1 Timothy 1:19, John Hutchinson maintains that he made a shipwreck of all things *except a good conscience*. In other words, all of his actions were performed in good faith, including his signature on Charles I's death warrant. Aware of this ambiguity, Lucy Hutchinson reports that one gentleman in the House exclaimed, "When a man's words might admitt of two interpretations, it befitted gentlemen allwayes to receive that which might be most favourable" (228).

This uncertainty, however, like her story about the petition, is a result of Lucy Hutchinson's partial omission of her husband's confession. In William Bankes's diary, held at the Lancashire Record Office, there is a second account of John Hutchinson's speech before Parliament that day. The diarist records,

> John Hutchinson saith w^t was donne by him was out of noe ill intent that hee hath seene ye ill effects of it, & hath since endea[voured] to bring ye k[ing] back he hath not advanta[ged] himselfe by these turnes & throwes himselfe upon ye mercy of ye Par[liament].[12]

The colonel's claim that he "endea[voured] to bring y[e] k[ing] back" is telling: it not only dispels the ambiguity in Lucy Hutchinson's representation of the speech but also suggests that *if* he preserved his good conscience up to the present moment, then his conscience *must* have approved of his endeavours to bring the King back. By eliminating this line, then, Lucy Hutchinson once again shielded her husband from this damning association with the Restoration.[13]

The colonel's former republican allies, Edmund Ludlow and Algernon Sidney, corroborated these outward manifestations of John Hutchinson's "recovered" conscience, though they doubted how conscientious his repentance truly was. In a letter dated 30 August 1660, Sidney writes, "If I could write and talk like Col. Hutchinson […] I believe I might be quiet. Contempt might procure my safety, but I had rather be a vagabond all my life than buy my being in my own country at so dear a rate."[14] Similarly, John Hutchinson's fellow regicide, Edmund Ludlow, records in his memoirs that "Colonell Hutchinson […] had gotten the King's pardon before his coming over, and had joyned with Monke in his treachery, pressing the Howse to execute their sentence against the emynent patriot Sir Henry Vane, and improving all opportunityes against the honest party, of which he formerly professed to be a zealous wel-wisher."[15] Though Ludlow incorrectly claims that John Hutchinson had been pardoned before Charles II's return, his accusation regarding the colonel's actions against Vane and the "honest party" as a whole has more truth to it.[16] Moreover, both Ludlow's and Sidney's comments confirm at least the appearance of a "change of conscience" in John Hutchinson at the dawn of the Restoration, a change that the colonel himself sought to prove.

John Hutchinson's speech of 11 May alone was not sufficient for Parliament to grant him pardon. As a result, the colonel's petition was read aloud before the House of Commons on 9 June 1660 and was recorded in the Commons Journals as the "humble Petition of *John Hutchinson*." The Commons resolved that day that he would lose his position as an MP and be barred from holding public office in the future, but "*John Hutchinson* Esquire, in respect of his signal Repentance, shall not be within that Clause of Exception in the Act of general Pardon and Oblivion, as to any Fine, or Forfeiture of any Part of his Estate not purchased of, or belonging to, the Publick."[17] The colonel's petition, or "signal Repentance," spared him his life and property. More importantly, on 23 June 1660, John Hutchinson's name was struck from the record of those present at the King's trial, effacing the history that his wife would later seek to restore in the *Memoirs*.

Revising History from the "Defense of John Hutchinson" to the *Memoirs*

In order to undo the damage done by this "abject and dishonoring petition," Lucy Hutchinson created an insurmountable tension between the *Memoirs* and the historical record regarding her husband's loyalties.[18] This fact becomes only more apparent when considering the first defence that she wrote on the colonel's behalf. Twenty years prior to writing the *Memoirs*, Lucy Hutchinson had written a document justifying her husband's actions as governor of Nottingham Castle during the civil wars.[19] Norbrook appropriately titled this unpublished manuscript the "Defense of John Hutchinson" because of the text's clear rhetorical purpose.[20] The extensive use of the pronoun "our" in reference to the colonel's forces in the "Defense" as well as its meticulous detail suggest that Lucy Hutchinson drew heavily on her husband's own notes while compiling this narrative.[21] She would later transport much of this material from the "Defense," which takes up about one third of the *Memoirs*, to her new project. Her recycling of text, however, was not without revision, reframing, and in some cases, rewriting. For this reason, the differences between the "Defense" and the *Memoirs* are noteworthy and reveal her shift in focus regarding her husband's conscience. In the *Memoirs*, Lucy Hutchinson often enhanced the barebones narrative approach of the "Defense" so that she might have room to comment on her husband's conscience – a word used sparingly in the "Defense" – during various trying episodes of his time as governor.

She made one such revision in an incident regarding the Cannoneers, the gunners of the castle and religious separatists. According to Lucy Hutchinson's account in both the *Memoirs* and the "Defense," pressure from military officials in Nottingham and local ministers had forced John Hutchinson, then governor of Nottingham Castle, to imprison the Cannoneers in order to avoid a mutiny. Aside from being nonconformists, as Lucy Hutchinson writes in the *Memoirs*, the Cannoneers were "honest, obedient and peacefull" (131). The Cannoneers were to be held until Huntingdon Plumtre, a member of the committee, received orders from then general Thomas Fairfax as to how he might proceed. As a result, John Hutchinson wrote to the general to inform him of the situation. In the "Defense," Lucy Hutchinson briefly relayed the result of this correspondence:

> The Lieft. Coll[onel] went immediately to my Lord General who upon y[e] Go[vernor] [Hutchinson's] letters sent Plumtre a letter to discharge him y[e] Garrison & likewise sent to y[e] Go[vernor] to release the Canoneers.[22]

She augmented this moment in the *Memoirs* in order to reveal the nature of her husband's conscience and his regard for the consciences of others:

> The Generall, upon the Governor's letters, sent down a letter to Plumtre to discharge him the Garrison, and another to the Governor to release the Cannoneers; which he accordingly did to the satisfaction of his owne conscience, which was not satisfied in keeping men prisoners for their consciences so long as they liv'd honestly and inoffensively. (131)

In order for this revision to be possible, Lucy Hutchinson had to exclude an earlier episode from the "Defense" regarding the colonel's troubled relationship with the Cannoneers. According to this account, John Hutchinson granted permission to a Mr Collins and Anthony Smith to worship privately in their chambers on Sundays on the condition that "none else should be with them" save their chamber fellows. When he discovered several weeks later that there were "some more y^n he gave allowance for" worshipping with Smith and Collins, John Hutchinson "surprised them at unawares" and imprisoned both men.[23] He later released them not for any scruple of conscience but rather because he needed their aid against the royalists.[24] Lucy Hutchinson omitted this incident and revised the colonel's later relations with the Cannoneers so that he might appear a champion of conscience, when, in reality, he had taken action against the Cannoneers in the past.

Subsequent revisions continued to develop this portrayal of her husband as a man of conscience. Sir John Meldrum and the local committee appointed John Hutchinson governor of Nottingham Castle on 29 June 1643, and soon thereafter Parliament and Lord Fairfax appointed him governor of both the castle and town. Since his power remained largely undefined, especially his power over the local forces, he often came in conflict with the local committee, who accused him of conspiring with royalists.[25] In the "Defense," Lucy Hutchinson records the moment her husband became governor of both town and castle, casting the local committee in a negative light:

> While it [the garrison at Nottingham] was in soe low & dangerous a condition they all [the committee] courted the Governor both to accept & keep it [the appointment as governor of the town] themselues not daring to undergoe the hassard but when there was likelihood of any profitt by it they then were as ready to catch at it & envie the fruites of other mans labours as unable to deserue anithing themselues.[26]

In writing against this committee in the *Memoirs*, or as she preferred to called them in this later text, the "conspirators," Lucy Hutchinson puts the consciences of her husband's detractors to work on his behalf:

> When the Governor undertook this employment, the Parliament's interest in those parts was so low, and the hazard so desperate, that these pittifull wretches, as well as all the other faithfull-hearted to the publique cause, courted him to accept and keepe the place [as governor], and though their fowle spiritts hated the day light of his more vertuous conversation, yet were they willing enough to let him beare the brunt of all the hazard and toyle of their defence, willinger to be secur'd by his indefatigable industry and courage than to render him the just acknowledgment of his good deserts; which ingratitude did not at all abate his zeale for the publick service, for as he sought not prayse, so he was well enough satisfied in doing well. Yet even through their envious eies they tooke in a generall good esteeme of him, and sin'd against their owne consciences in persecuting him, whereof he had after acknowledgments and testimonies from many of them. (136–7)

Lucy Hutchinson altered this passage to expose that those committee members who persecuted her husband sinned against themselves. Their consciences, after all, supported John Hutchinson against their own wrongful actions, a conclusion she claims to have drawn from their own later testimonies.

One final example illustrates again how Lucy Hutchinson inserted her husband's attention to conscience into the *Memoirs* where it had not been in the "Defense." This episode, regarding a seemingly unjust excise tax issued in Nottingham, appears in the "Defense" as such:

> Mr Salusbury & one Siluester for their owne profitt had gotten a commission to sett on foote ye excise in this garrison ^and countie^ & ioyned with them our Sherwin these two were such pragmaticall knaves that they grew odious to all men & ye towne generally refused to pay & that wch made them & the thing more odious was that when ye Yorkeshire horse came into ye country & lay upon free quarter they made the poore country pay excise for that very meate & drinke wch ye souldiers plundred from them & they neuer tasted of wch oppression was soe great y^t when they came to desire souldiers of ye Governor to helpe gather it the soulders were rather readie to mutinie for it & when it was ordered y^t ye mony should be payd to ye souldiers they refused to take any of it yet these

men came still urging ye Governor to compell it whereupon ye Governor told them he would first call a hall & see if he could perswade them [the soldiers to collect the tax].[27]

In the *Memoirs*, conscience appears twice, effectively changing the original purpose of this passage:

> Salsbury and one Silvester had, for their owne profitt, gotten a Commission to sett on foote the excise in the County, and joyn'd with them one Sherwin. These two were such pragmaticall Knaves that they justly became odious to all men, and allthough necessity might excuse the tax in other places, yett here is was such a burthen that no men of any honesty or conscience could have acted in it; for when plund'ring troopes kill'd all the poore countriemen's sheepe and swine and other provisions, whereby many honest famelies were ruin'd and beggar'd, these unmercifull people would force excise out of them for those very goods which the other had rob'd them of, insomuch that the religious souldiers sayd they would sterve before they would be employ'd in forcing it, or take any of it for their pay. The Governor, being enclin'd in conscience to assist the poore county, was very active in endeavours to relieve them from this oppression, which they highly urg'd in their Articles against him, and these Excise men came very pressingly to urge the Governor to enforce the payment of it in the Towne. The Governor told them before he would use compulsion he would trie faire meanes, and call a Hall to see whether they [the soldiers] would be perswaded [to collect the tax]; which accordingly he did. (153)

Here, not only have the soldiers who objected to the tax become "religious souldiers," but also the colonel's conscience was in harmony with all "men of any honesty and conscience" in his unwillingness to enforce the tax on the "poor county."

Sydney Race argues that when revising the "Defense" for her *Memoirs*, Lucy Hutchinson omitted passages that "might have been considered by the Colonel's enemies to reflect on his character and conduct," citing an episode where John Hutchinson was complicit in the torture of a boy spy and one of the soldiers of the garrison.[28] In addition to excising such unfavourable material, Race claims, she also "heightened by little touches here and there" "the actual part which he plays in the history" so that "he becomes the central figure of the story" (37). Norbrook similarly points out that "this version [the "Defense"] includes some vivid touches which seem to have been omitted from her later version in the name of literary decorum."[29] It seems that Lucy Hutchinson also recast the material in the "Defense" in order to shape her husband's character into a bona fide man of conscience.

There are traces in the "Defense" of the John Hutchinson that readers would later meet in the *Memoirs*: after delineating her husband's reasons for hesitating when offered the position of governor of Nottingham, Lucy Hutchinson notes, "But for all this & many things elce since yᵉ State & my Lord Fairfax had bene pleased to conferre yᵗ burthensome honor on him he resolved ^not^ to refuse it, but in this as in all this other actions to maintaine an upright and cleare conscience before god and to despise all yᵗ yᵉ malice of fortune or wicked men could endeavour against him."[30] Yet the scarcity of such declarations in the "Defense" confirms that revisions like those cited here were deliberate and are significant. Since both the "Defense" and the *Memoirs* justify John Hutchinson, Lucy Hutchinson clearly shifted her presentation in the twenty-year lapse between the two texts in order to accommodate an event that occurred after she had already completed the "Defense." And that event, I would argue, was John Hutchinson's retraction of June 1660 – a retraction grounded upon the supposed misguidance of his own conscience.

John Hutchinson, Man of Conscience

In addition to her efforts to obfuscate the offending petition, Lucy Hutchinson uses the language of conscience extensively in the *Memoirs* to forge an inextricable bond between her husband's dedication to a "free Republick" and his sense of himself as a good Christian (214). She opens the *Memoirs* with a vivid description of her husband entitled "To My Children": she deems her work a "naked undrest narrative, speaking the simple truth of him," though at the same time she hopes to be "pardon'd for drawing an imperfect image of him" since the extent of his glory could not possibly be captured by her words (1–2). When describing his Christian virtues, Lucy Hutchinson asserts that his "life and joy was most in resignation and submission to God." More specifically,

> He never did aniething without measuring it by the rule of conscience, and for the gaine of the whole world would not have committed one sinne or omitted one duty against his conscience, that being perswaded neither his estate, honor, wife, children, nor his owne life weigh'd aniething with him in the ballance against Christe and his interest, and having often

cheerefully sett them att the hazard, he att last joyfully parted with them
all att God's call and for God's cause. (6)

This portrait of the colonel differs dramatically from the man represented in the petition of 1660. Here he is mathematically precise in his
attention to conscience, a man whose conscience could not be easily
misled since it was linked to Christ's own interests. Not only did the
colonel measure all of his potential actions by the "rule of conscience,"
but also he was ruled by conscience, setting it before all earthly posses-
sions, relationships, and honours.

Ironically, the colonel's petition to the House of Commons had made
a similar argument for him as a "man of conscience": it was his misled conscience, after all, that he had followed into sin, and his rightly
led conscience that made him repent and return his allegiance to the
King. In order to offset such irony, Lucy Hutchinson was at pains to
prove the opposite: that it was his rightly led conscience, rather, that led
him to Parliament's cause. She recalls that during the Irish Rebellion of
1641, the colonel first "applied himself to understand the things then
in dispute":

> [He] read all the publick papers that came forth between the King and
> Parliament, besides many other private treatises, both concerning the
> present and foregoing times; whereby he became abundantly inform'd in
> his understanding, and convinc'd in conscience of the righteousness of
> Parliament's cause. (53)

Rather than being seduced to Parliament's side, his decision was careful and the result of much private study and devout reflection. This
John Hutchinson was not a passive victim seduced by Parliament;
instead, he was an active and informed advocate. And as Nottingham
became a key factor in Parliament's war against the royalist forces, John
Hutchinson was even more "perswaded in his conscience of the cause,
and of God's calling him to undertake the defence of it," even though
"in all humane probabillity he was more like to loose than save" the
town (76). Lucy Hutchinson presents her husband's conscience, then,
as a mediating agent between his understanding of God's providence
and his actions in the world. It was "Conscience to God," after all, that
"engag'd him in that party he tooke" (91).

This portrait of the colonel as the quintessential man of conscience,
careful in his decision-making and calculated in his actions, spills over

into what was considered his most reprehensible crime by the King's party: John Hutchinson's decision to sign Charles I's death warrant. Lucy Hutchinson's primary concern was to present her husband not merely as a good Christian but also as a good republican, for his conscience's sake. Indeed, she deems the civil wars "that greate cause of God's and England's rights," suggesting that "encroaching princes" violated God and Englishmen and women alike (24). On 16 March 1646, John Hutchinson became an MP for Nottingham, a position formerly held by his father. On 18 September 1648, negotiations with the King, also known as the Treaty of Newport, opened. Throughout this process of negotiation, Parliament received petitions from Oxfordshire, Leicestershire, Newcastle, and elsewhere demanding that the King be held to account for the loss of English lives during the civil unrest. Despite such demands and despite Charles's unsatisfactory answers to the terms of the treaty, the Commons voted 129–83 to continue negotiations with the King after sitting all night on 4–5 December 1648. As a result of this vote, the colonel was "convinc'd in his conscience that both the cause, and all those who had with an upright honest heart asserted and maintain'd it, were betrey'd and sold for nothing." The King's power being "inconsistent with the liberty of the people," John Hutchinson felt that the vote was "contrary to their former engagements to God" regarding the future of the English nation. Thus unable to be "satisfied in conscience" with Parliament's decision, the colonel and several other MPs "enter'd into the House Book a protestation against that night's votes and proceedings" (187).[31]

Regardless of John Hutchinson's public protest to this vote, his wife claims that he also detested Colonel Thomas Pride's decision on 6 December to purge Parliament of the King's supporters. He remained an MP, nevertheless, and was soon appointed by the court to help try the King later that month. The colonel acted as part of this commission, she records, against his own will, but held himself "oblige'd by the Covenant of God and the publick trust of his country reposed in him" to partake in this unprecedented trial. Speaking directly to this simultaneous obligation to the nation and to God, Lucy Hutchinson claims that when the court saw in Charles a "disposition so bent to the ruine of all that had oppos'd him, and of all the righteous and just things they had contended for" the judges and "divers others" present thought it "upon the[ir] consciences [...] that if they did not execute justice upon him, God would require at their hands all the blood and desolation which should ensue by their suffering him to escape" (189–90). In other words, if they did not prosecute the King for his past crimes, his future crimes would lie on *their* consciences. The members of the commission, for this reason, believed that they "ought to cast themselves upon God while they acted with a good conscience for him and their country" even with their fear of the political consequences (190).

Though her husband was certainly included among those who felt it upon their consciences to indict Charles, Lucy Hutchinson stresses, once again, that his decision was an individual and painstaking one. Objecting to her husband being considered part of a faction earlier in the text, she had insisted that "they very little knew him that could say he was of any faction, for he had a strength of judgement able to consider things himselfe, and propound them to his conscience, which was so upright that the veneration of no man's person allive […] could make him doe the least thing without a full perswasion of conscience that it was his duty so to act" (166–7). And so it was with his decision to support the regicide. He was "very much confirm'd in his judgement concerning the cause," but since he was being called to such "an extraordinary action," the colonel

> addresst himselfe to God by prayer, desiring the Lord that, if through humane frailty he were led into any error or false opinion in these great transactions, that he would open his eies, and not suffer him to proceed, but that he would confirme his spiritt in the truth, and lead him by a right enlight'ned conscience.

The colonel desired to be freed from exactly what he would later claim in his petition to have been subject to: seduction, or being "led" into error. In response to his prayer, however, he felt "no check, but a confirmation in his conscience that it was his duty to act as he did" in signing the King's death warrant. Moreover, this decision, as his earlier decision to league with Parliament, came after "serious debate, both privately in his addresses to God, and in conferences with conscientious, upright, unbiassed persons." Having thus distinguished his decision-making from that of the "Gentlemen that were appoynted his [Charles's] judges, and divers others" in the courtroom, Lucy Hutchinson brought him back into the fold by asserting, as she had with the those trying the King, that her husband, too, "cast himselfe upon God's protection, acting according to the dictates of a conscience which he had sought the Lord to guide" (189, 190).

What is perhaps most remarkable about this passage is Lucy Hutchinson's direct affront to her husband's petition: no longer seduced by Parliament with "thousands more," the colonel's decision to sign Charles I's death warrant was the result of much prayer, debate, and a *rightly guided* conscience. She also establishes that the dictates of her husband's conscience were in agreement with the conscientious decisions of the larger godly community. Though Lucy Hutchinson throughout fashions her husband as exceptional in his virtue and attention to his conscience, she was hesitant to present his conscience itself as exceptional. Rather, it was more important for the larger function of this text and its connection to the future of the English nation that John Hutchinson and the dictates of his conscience appeared representative rather than extraordinary.

John Hutchinson's Republican Conscience and the Future of the English Nation

In the *Memoirs*, Lucy Hutchinson represents her husband's death as the death of a republican martyr – a martyr, that is, who died as all martyrs do: with a peaceful conscience. As a result of his efforts to seek pardon, the colonel escaped the fate of many of his fellow regicides, execution and imprisonment. Most of the signatories of Charles I's death warrant were either hanged or drawn and quartered or died in prison, and the bodies of Oliver Cromwell, Henry Ireton, and John Bradshaw (who presided over the King's trial) were exhumed and executed posthumously in a gory display of Restoration justice. With John Hutchinson being one of two signatories pardoned (Richard Ingoldsby being the other), his wife blasts his detractors who "because he was not hang'd at first [in 1660], imagin'd and spoke among themselves all the scandalls that could be devis'd of him, as one that had deserted the cause, and lay private here in the country to trapan all the party and to gather and transmitt all intelligence to the Court" (244). The colonel himself, as he saw his former colleagues go to the scaffold, "suffer'd with them in his mind" and believed himself "judg'd in their judgement, and executed in their execution" (234). Thus, whatever part John Hutchinson played in attaining his pardon, it seems, he soon came to regret. There is no account recording when he had this change of heart, but perhaps it was a result of his own guilty conscience. Imprisoned first in the Tower and then in Sandown Castle on suspicion of involvement in a plot against the restored government in 1663, the colonel told his wife that "this captivity was the happiest release in the world" (255).

Rather than focus on his "signal Repentance" that delayed the colonel's punishment, Lucy Hutchinson as both character and narrator emphasizes that it was "God's eminent appearance" which had "singled him out for preservation" (234). The colonel's supposed "eminent deliverance" was pivotal to Lucy Hutchinson's picture of his imprisonment and death as part of God's plan for the future of the cause. Scholars have recently acknowledged that the *Memoirs* were "confined to manuscript because she *could* not, rather than *would* not, reach a wider public."[32] She opens the *Memoirs*, after all, by setting out the hoped-for end of her husband's death and, by extension, of her text: first, "to discover the deformities of this wicked age," and second, "to instruct the erring children of this generation" (1). Thus, though the text would only circulate in manuscript during her lifetime, Lucy Hutchinson does not sell it short of these grand aspirations. She told her audience that she "celebrate[d] the glories of a saint" in writing the *Memoirs*, confident that her husband "and all his excellencies came from God, and flow'd back into theire owne spring." "There [in the fountaine of God] lett us seeke them," she encourages her readers, "thither lett us hasten after him" (2).

This call for her readers to "hasten after him" was not altogether metaphorical. Speaking to her husband's "delight in the study of devinity" soon after their marriage in 1638, Lucy Hutchinson digresses to compare "how God tooke this time to instruct him" to the "preparation of Moses in the wilderness with his father in law." Moses's training at that time, she argues, was similar to her husband's in that "he was thus prepar'd to be a leader of God's people out of bondage" (35). During his own period of contemplation, the colonel too had "beheld the burning bush still unconsum'd" and "had the call to goe back [to public life] to deliver his country, groaning under spirituall and civill bondage." She admits that this parallel breaks down since Moses was God's "sole Viceroy" while her husband "was joyn'd with many partners equally sharing the worke" of deliverance during the civil wars. Yet, she continues, "whosoe considers the following history," the subsequent pages of the *Memoirs*, "shall find that Mr. Hutchinson againe might often take up the paralell of the greate Hebrew Prince" (36). Writing in the future conditional tense, Lucy Hutchison guarantees her audience that if they considered this comparison while reading, the colonel would again and again become a Moses-like leader of the Israelites out of slavery.

Beyond the future of the text, she also looks to the future of the nation. Lucy Hutchinson encourages her readers to view his time of imprisonment in Sandown Castle, where the colonel would die on 11 September 1664, as the "bleake mountaines of afliction" where "the Lord instructed him in his law, and shew'd him a patterne of his glorious tabernacle," just as God had with Moses on Mount Sinai. Pushing this parallel to its logical end, she claims that before he died, her husband saw the "promis'd land," and "tooke possession of future glory, and resign'd himself in the assured hope of returning with the Lord and his greate Armie of Saints" (36). Like Moses, the colonel was only allowed a glimpse of the promised land just before his death; but he found solace in "future glory," the glory of Lucy Hutchinson's readers to establish this promised land in England with the memory of John Hutchinson, man of conscience, as their leader out of bondage.

This digression comes early in the *Memoirs*, yet Lucy Hutchinson returns to the idea of her husband as a Moses-like leader once again when recounting the colonel's imprisonment in Sandown Castle. While there, he diligently studies the scriptures and experiences "dayly greater enlightenings" (234). As a result of his studies, the colonel assures his wife's character that the cause would be revived because "the interest of God was so much involv'd in it that he [God] was entitled to it." And, he believed, the best thing he could do to further the cause in England was to die a martyr's death: "my blood will be so innocent I shall advance the cause more by my death, hasting the vengeance of God upon my unjust enemies, than I could doe by all the actions of my life" (264). Lucy Hutchinson substantiates his hope for martyrdom in her description of his death. Though his "pulse grew very low, and his head allready was earth in the upper part," the colonel asks the doctor "'why [do] you thinke me dying; I feele nothing in my selfe; my head is well, my heart is well, and I have no payne nor sicknesse anywhere.'" Not only did he seem free from the agonies of his condition, but his facial expression after death, according to his wife's description, resembled his expression in life when most happy. Moreover, his doctors were so moved when he passed that they wept, and one claimed that he "never in his whole life saw any one receive death with more Christian courage, and constancy of mind, and stedfastnesse of faith, than the Collonell had exprest from the first to the last." Lucy Hutchinson readily attributes his demeanour both before and after death to the "peace and joy which crownes the Lord's constant martirs," confident in their own salvation (272, 273).

Yet she redefines this martyr trope by adding that his self-assuredness also lay in his confidence that the cause would revive. Fashioning the colonel as not only a martyr but also a prophet, Lucy Hutchinson reports how her husband "foresaw that the courses that the King and his party tooke to establish themselves would be their ruine" and "he was very confident God would bring them downe" (265, 269). Continuing in this prophetic vein, he also feared that the pride of his own party would lead to certain ruin once again. A subtext running throughout the *Memoirs* was one of profound human failure: responding to the fear that the Restoration might indicate God's abandonment of his elect nation, Lucy Hutchinson repeatedly identifies humanity's shortcomings as the culprit for the collapse of the cause.[33] It was not God, after all, who had betrayed the "most glorious cause that was ever contended for," but rather his people (167). Despite their failures, John Hutchinson insisted that "if God had a people in the land, as he was confident he had, it was among them [the republican party] and not among the Cavaliers," and so he would adhere to them for "the cause they own'd" rather than their merits. Foreseeing that his party's pride would once again bring the cause to ruin, the colonel advised his son not to league with the "hot spirited people" who would first drag the nation into confusion after the King's demise, but to wait for the more "sober party" that would afterward strive for settlement (265).

As this prophecy suggests, the colonel still believed his party – or at least part of it – capable of victory. And, more than anything else, Lucy Hutchinson tried to capture in the final moments of her husband's life and in his death just that: victory. Through this story of her husband's life, and relaying of the dictates of his conscience, she was at pains to prove that the cause remained God's. In the text, it was God who continually convinced the colonel's conscience of the integrity of his actions against the King. During his darkest moment of despair, he watched those who had most supported the cause defect from it, calling it "rebellion and murther" in the face of the Restoration. The colonel once again sought reassurance from God for his actions and found that the "more he examin'd the cause from the first, the more he became confirm'd in it" (234). His subsequent study of the scriptures continued to confirm the cause in his conscience, preparing him for his martyrdom.

As with his guidance during Charles I's trial, however, these revelations through the scriptures were not for the colonel's conscience alone: rather than construct her husband's conscience as extraordinary, Lucy

Hutchinson presents it as a model for those readers of the *Memoirs*. Keeble notes that the Restoration caused many republicans to despair of God's support for the cause, and Lucy Hutchinson combats such despair with the assurance of her husband's conscience through which she hopes her readers would attain a similar faith in the cause. Indeed, she outlines his Bible-reading rituals within in the *Memoirs*, noting that his most prized text was Paul's Epistle to the Romans, a letter more rife with the language of conscience than any other gospel (270). Moreover, though never before published by one of the text's editors, she also included an appendix to the original manuscript of the *Memoirs* cataloguing extensively the scriptural passages that he had marked in his Bible while imprisoned in Sandown Castle.[34] This appendix functions as a florilegium of sorts, an anthology of the Bible's greatest hits organized according to descriptive subtitles for ease of reading: "Concerning his enemies"; "Concerning a mighty Adversary," which, not surprisingly, lists many snippets from scriptures written against princes; "For the 30th of January," the anniversary of the regicide; "Grounds of encouragement wch he had selected with some choyce promises"; "Spirituall Triumphs and exercises of faith very suitable to his professions to those that were with him to the last," with a particular emphasis on Corinthians 15:23, "All shall be made alive in Christ," which was underlined; "Some more threats to wicked princes and people"; "Rules Gathered for sundry things out of the scripture Concerning Magistracy and Magistrates for the choyce of them"; "Magistrates Duties"; "Concerning Subiects," and so forth.

Norbrook points out that these passages "not only provide an intellectual portrait of her husband, leaving the manuscript a memorial to him in a further sense, but also bring out messages for the future: in defiantly linking her husband's political positions with the prophets of the Old Testament, Lucy Hutchinson provides inspiration and guidelines for her children and other sympathetic readers of the manuscript."[35] In addition to providing an intellectual portrait, these bits of scripture piece together the inner workings of John Hutchinson's conscience just before he died – a conscience certain of the integrity of the cause. In this way, the "messages for the future" relayed through this portrait are meant to work upon the conscience of the reader so that he or she might also be confirmed in the cause and find similar solace in God's plan for His chosen nation. Since he could not claim a military victory over his opponents, after all, it was this victory – the victory of an assured conscience, confident in the future of the nation – that the colonel wielded "in life and death," making him finally "victorious over the Lord's and his enemies," the penultimate line of the *Memoirs*.[36] It was also this sort of victory that she hoped to pass onto readers. Prior to his imprisonment in Sandown Castle, John Hutchinson had a dream which, though he was not "superstitious of dreames," "stuck a little in his mind":

> He dreamt one night that he saw certeine men in a boate upon the Thames, labouring against the wind and tide to bring their boate, which stuck in the sands, to shore; att which he being in the boate was angrie with them, and told them they toyl'd in vaine and would never effect their purpose. 'But,' sayd he, 'lett it alone and lett me try.' Whereupon he lay'd him downe in the boate, and applying his breast to the head of it, gently shoov'd it allong till he came to land on Southworke side, and there, going out of the boate, walk'd in the most pleasant lovely fields, so greene and flourishing and so embellisht with the cheerefull sunne that shone upon them as he never saw aniething so delightfull; and that there he mett his father, who gave him certeine leaves of lawrell which had many words written in them which he could not read.

Lucy Hutchinson offers one reading of this dream, with the boat representing the commonwealth, "which severall unquiet people sought to enfranchise by vaine endeavours against wind and tide," and the colonel's "lying downe and shooving it with his breast might signifie the advancement of the Cause by the patient suffering of the Martyrs, among which his own was to be eminent." Moreover, the laurel leaves given to him by his father (then dead) with "unintelligible characters fortold him those triumphs which he could not read in his mortall state" (242).

According to Lucy Hutchinson's interpretation of the dream, it was patient suffering that would bring the fulfilment of the cause within reach. The colonel was only able to earn his laurel leaves, a symbol of his victory, by painfully pushing his chest against the bow of the boat rather than labouring against the elements. This was the legacy that Lucy Hutchinson hoped the colonel's story would finally produce: the legacy that his wife fashioned in order to erase his own moments of weakness and to exorcise the conscience he appealed to in his damning petition. Through the *Memoirs*, she sought the survival of the cause in the minds, and the assurance of the cause in the consciences, of her readers. In this way, the *Memoirs* were meant as a working text: John

Hutchinson emerges as a flawless man of conscience so that the readers' memory of him might similarly work upon their own consciences and eventually lead the commonwealth to victory. Until England would once again find the strength to rid itself of kingship, it was in the minds, memories, hearts, and, most importantly, the consciences of believers that the cause would thrive and the future of the nation persevere.

In the opening lines of the *Memoirs*, Lucy Hutchinson tells her readers that, in accordance with her husband's last wishes, she must discover some way to "moderate my woe." And she finds nothing more consolatory than the "preservation of his memory" that would follow in the ensuing pages (1). Preserving his memory was a way for Lucy Hutchinson to keep the colonel alive far past his death; but preservation in this sense also meant to protect or save from an undesirable eventuality.[37] When considering both John Hutchinson's petition and his speech before Parliament, it seems that his wife was at pains to protect him from himself. It also seems that the conscience she fashions for her husband in the *Memoirs* may have been closer to her own conscience than his. In shaping her husband into the ultimate republican hero, Lucy Hutchinson had, perhaps unknowingly, actually become that hero herself. It was *her* firm belief in the integrity of the republican cause for conscience's sake, after all, that drove Lucy Hutchinson to excise her husband's conscientious concessions of 1660. It was also her certainty that the republican cause was God's cause that gave her the confidence to rewrite her husband's conscience in the *Memoirs*.

Lucy Hutchinson exudes this same confidence regarding others' consciences in the *Memoirs* as well. Referring to those men during Charles I's trial who refused to partake in the proceedings, she claims to have "certaine knowledge that many – yea, most of them – retreated not for conscience," as they stated, "but for feare and worldly prudence." She also attacks those who, after the Restoration, sought pardon on the grounds that they were seduced by Parliament into supporting the regicide rather than convinced in their consciences, claiming once again that it is "certaine that all men herein were left to their free liberty of acting, neither perswaded nor compelled" "by Cromwell, and like" (190). More importantly, Lucy Hutchinson does not confine this jarring relationship between a good conscience and monarchy to the *Memoirs*. In her biblical epic *Order and Disorder*,[38] she comments on Isaac's unjust exile at the hands of King Abimelech in canto 17:

> Could mortals but with true discerning eyes
> Behold the state of kings, they would despise

What now, regarding with unsteady view,
The general wishes of mankind pursue:
Not seeing that all who to the high throne climb
Must wade through blood and strife, check at no crime,
Tread on contemnèd piety and faith,
Quit every virtue in that horrid path,
Encounter sorrow, danger and affright,
With a guilt-stainèd conscience hourly fight.[39]

If mortals could see, she argues, "the state of kings" with "true discerning eyes," they would know for certain that monarchy was antithetical to God's laws. Indeed, according to her formulation, not only must would-be kings forgo any sense of virtue or faith before ascending the throne, but also, once there, they "with a guilt-stainèd conscience hourly fight" in order to maintain their position of power. As in the *Memoirs*, at several key junctures in *Order and Disorder*, a poem that Norbrook classifies as "Eve's version of Genesis," Lucy Hutchinson continues to mine the scriptures for this vexed connection between an upright conscience and kingship.[40]

Also in the opening pages to the *Memoirs*, Lucy Hutchinson, referring to herself in the third person as she does throughout the text, claims that "if he [the colonel] esteem'd her at a higher rate than she in her selfe could have deserv'd, he was the author of that vertue he doted on, while she only reflected his owne glories upon him" (10). When considering the man of conscience that Lucy Hutchinson fashioned for the *Memoirs*, however, it seems more likely that *she* was the author of her husband's virtue, a virtue she hoped others would dote on. And, more than just authoring his virtue, she also authored that most private and sacred part of his being: his conscience. In this way, reflecting her own glories upon her husband, Lucy Hutchinson rewrites his past so that she might write the future of the English nation.

Chapter Six

Milton's Nation of Conscience

In the second edition of *The Readie and Easie Way to Establish a Free Commonwealth*, published just a month before King Charles II's return in May 1660, John Milton hopes that "our governors beware in time, least thir hard measure to liberty of conscience be found the rock whereon they shipwrack themselves as others have now don before them in the cours wherin God was directing their stearage to a free Commonwealth." At several key junctures in this urgent treatise and elsewhere, Milton draws on the ship of state metaphor, maintaining that the "ship of the Commonwealth is alwaies under sail." He thus imagines the nation afloat, directed by God Himself towards a free commonwealth, a course that "is plane, easie, and open before us."[1]

While the way towards freedom may be ready and easy, Milton nevertheless warns the soon-to-be-elected Parliament of its own potential shipwreck, a tragedy of self-destruction played out time and again by their predecessors. Milton had just reminded the English nation that liberty of conscience "above all other things ought to be to all men dearest and most precious." Yet because of attempts to hinder this "best part of our libertie," the ship of state has repeatedly wrecked itself while on its God-given course (*CPW* 7:456, 420). The nation's greatest – and only – peril at sea is, it seems, itself.

In this passage, Milton exemplifies the centrality of conscience to his idea of a free nation. He also captures how his unyielding dedication to conscience and its liberty complicates and, in the post-revolutionary years, would even thwart his sense of national identity. On the cusp of the Restoration, Milton can only imagine a nation fractured, composed at once of an "abundance of sensible and ingenuous men" and a "misguided and abus'd multitude" who risk pitching England over a "precipice of destruction" (*CPW* 7:463). For Milton, these fault lines were set most deeply for the cause of conscience.

Scholars have recently shown considerable interest in Milton's nationalism, yet the role of conscience in Milton's writing of the nation remains untreated.[2] Conversely, the scholarly conversation on conscience in Milton has not, for the most part, considered politics in general or nationalism more specifically.[3] As this chapter will demonstrate, this yoking not only complicates our understanding of both conscience and the nation in Milton's corpus; it also sets Milton firmly in conversation with contemporary writers who similarly turned to conscience to bind the revolutionary nation.

Why, of all potential hazards, must the beleaguered English nation mind its own measure towards liberty of conscience? From the start of the civil wars, the relationship that Milton imagines between conscience and the nation is precarious. Sharon Achinstein deems Milton's conception of conscience "awkward and malleable," being born out of the "heat of the civil war fires."[4] Yet, I would argue, far more awkward and malleable is his conception of the nation. As Milton imagines and reimagines the nation during the turbulent years of the Revolution and disheartening years of the Restoration, free conscience remains the foundation upon which that nation is constructed, an essential forerunner of both civil liberty and godly nationhood. The very representative of individual faith and spiritual discernment, conscience seems an odd and even capricious choice for Milton's national vision. Yet it is in what Milton calls the "brotherly dissimilitudes" produced by free consciences at work that he hopes England will find a sense of coherence and shared identity. As this chapter will demonstrate, as early as 1641, Milton aspires to write into being an English nation coterminous with his imagined nation of conscience. This revolutionary project begins with the nation that Milton believes to be God's elect and evolves into a nation whose boundaries are determined not by borders but rather by conscientious dissent: a nationhood experienced in and through free conscience itself.

Returning to the ship of state metaphor, Milton considers godly nationhood the terminus of England's journey, and liberty of conscience her compass. After all, Milton passionately defends liberty of conscience not simply for liberty's sake, but rather because it is fundamental to the process of realizing true Reformation. In fact, it *is* the process, without which the ship of state would remain adrift.

Conscience Embattled: Revolution

In June 1641, when Milton published his first of five antiprelatical tracts, *Of Reformation*, he could not have imagined that, in just over a year's time, King Charles I would unfurl his royal standard in Nottingham, launching the First Civil War. Milton then held that there was no government "more divinely and harmoniously tun'd, more equally ballanc'd as it were by the hand and scale of Justice, then is the Common-wealth of *England*" (*CPW* 1:599). Yet the poet-polemicist's picture of England in *Of Reformation* is, like all of his national renderings, complex. At the same time that he praises England as God's elect nation, he also laments her backsliding. Rather than think on Charles's standard, he instead puzzles over how England, having been "the first that should set up a Standard for the recovery of *lost Truth*, and blow the first *Evangelick Trumpet* to the *Nations*, holding up, as from a Hill, the new Lampe of *saving light* to all Christendome," "should now be last, and most unsettl'd in the enjoyment of that *Peace*, whereof she taught the way to others" (*CPW* 1:525). Milton proposes to solve this riddle, discovering those causes that hinder England's reformation.

Exercising a grotesque flourish, he chiefly advises that the nation "cut away from the publick body the noysom, and diseased tumor of Prelacie," a popish system of church government barring England's union with "our neighbour Reformed sister Churches" (*CPW* 1:598). Milton saw in 1641 the inklings of revolution: William Laud, archbishop of Canterbury and a staunch advocate for conformity, was imprisoned in the Tower on 1 March; Thomas Wentworth, Earl of Strafford, the King's chief advisor after 1639, was executed on 12 May; and on 27 May, Oliver St John's bill for the abolition of episcopacy was presented to the Commons by Sir Edward Dering. The time was ripe for change, or even, as Milton hoped, reformation.

In *Of Reformation*, the poet-polemicist proposes the beginnings of his national program, a program that must start with an assessment of England's status as a nation. Prelacy, after all, not only halts England's reformation but also threatens its national integrity. Milton vividly imagines "our dear Mother England" appearing in "a mourning weed, with ashes upon her head, and tears abundantly flowing from her eyes" for those of her children who have "forsake[n] their dearest home" for "the savage deserts of *America*" because "their conscience could not assent to things which the Bishops thought *indifferent*."[5] Published in 1640, *Constitutions and Canons Ecclesiastical* declared those rites and ceremonies "indifferent" that were "neither commanded nor condemned by the Word of God," including the placement of a "holy Table" or altar and where and how worshippers would receive "the divine Mysteries." Robert Greville, Lord Brooke, shares Milton's invective against this doctrine of indifference, accusing bishops of having "pressed Consciences, even unto Gasping: yea, and would not be satisfied, though they daily heard the sighes and groanes of those bleeding hearts, which themselves had stabd with the poysoned sword of *Church-Indifference*."[6] Whereas Brooke's imagery is violently visceral, Milton's is a picture of national degeneration. "Mother England" mourns the loss of "numbers of faithfull, and freeborn Englishmen, and good Christians," the very types she needs to incite reformation. Yet, Milton asks, "What more binding then Conscience?" (*CPW* 1:585). This rhetorical question sets the force of conscience above all others, including that of nation: in order to protect their consciences, the godly are fleeing to the "savage deserts of *America*." Prelacy, then, creates out of conscience a thing of national division when its free exercise ought to be the very driving force of England's reformation. Only by ridding itself of this "diseased tumor" and allowing conscience its due liberty might England realize its national destiny.

With the outbreak of the civil war in August 1642, that promise of revolution was finally in sight. Milton writes *Areopagitica* (1644), an optimistic tour de force celebrating England as a nation "not beneath the reach of any point the highest that human capacity can soar," at the height of the first phase of the English Revolution, once again forwarding his national program. He casts aside the image of England in her mourning clothes, instead seeing "a noble and puissant Nation rousing herself like a strong man after sleep, and shaking her invincible locks," and "an Eagle muing her mighty youth, and kindling her undazl'd eyes at the midday beam; purging and unscaling her long abused sight at the fountain it self of heav'nly radiance." England no longer mourns her loss but rather wakes with a newfound strength and purpose as a rousing Samson, Israel's champion who "is holy unto the Lord,"[7] and as the eagle who, in molting and staring into the sun, renews its youth.[8] The source of this rebirth is the "true liberty" that Parliament's "own valorous and happy counsels have purchast us" (*CPW* 2:551, 558, 559).

Amid this celebration of England's awakening, however, Milton finds himself in what will become a familiar position: a petitioner for the cause of conscience against a nation always teetering on the edge of self-destruction.[9] In June 1643, Parliament issued a Licensing Order calling for pre-publication censorship, a threat, as Milton saw it, to the very lifeblood of the "true liberty" Parliament purchased, liberty of conscience. Recalling the "noysom, and diseased tumor" in *Of Reformation*, he begins *Areopagitica* by cataloguing the papist origins of censorship, a history grounded in the suppression of conscience. Looking back to "primitive Councels and Bishops," Milton argues that they "were wont only to declare what Books were not commendable, passing no furder, but leaving it to each ones conscience to read or to lay by" (*CPW* 2:501). Once the papacy was "provkt and troubl'd at the first entrance of Reformation" and pre-publication censorship founded, books were subject to a "wors condition then a peccant soul," made "to stand before a Jury ere it be borne into the World, and undergo yet in darknesse the judgement of *Radamanth* and his Collegues, ere it can passe the ferry backward into light" (*CPW* 2:505–6). This cruel treatment of unpublished books, Milton advises, runs counter to the "true liberty" that Parliament has only recently restored to England. It would not only stymie Reformation, but also cause the nation to backslide towards prelatical tyranny.

The England Milton envisions comprises an active citizenry, exercising its liberty of conscience through "much arguing, much writing, [and] many opinions" as it unites "into one generall and brotherly search after Truth" (*CPW* 2:554). Whereas in *The Readie and Easie Way* Milton believes that England is destined to be a free commonwealth, he here envisions its endpoint as Christ's Second Coming, which will coincide with the revelation of truth. Indeed, this "brotherly search after Truth," whose "perfect shape" came into the world with Christ only to be hewn to pieces by "a wicked race of deceivers" after his death, will continue until Christ returns to "bring together every joynt and member" of her torn body "and shall mould them into an immortall feature of loveliness and perfection" (*CPW* 2:549). So that England's "obsequies to the torn body of our martyr'd saint" might continue in this search, Milton implores Parliament to "forgoe this Prelaticall tradition of crowding free consciences" (*CPW* 2:550, 554).

More importantly, embodying the voice of England's citizens, Milton demands, "Give me the liberty to know, to utter, and to argue freely according to conscience, above all liberties" (*CPW* 2:560). He assigns to conscience a tripartite liberty that ought to be cultivated by Parliament: liberty of thought, liberty of speech, and the liberty to disagree within the larger Protestant framework.[10] These public and private liberties, exercised "according to conscience," will help to forge a nation of scholar-citizens, all contributing to England's journey towards truth. They also allow for what Milton calls "neighboring differences" between believers, differences that Parliament need not fear as the source of schism or sectarianism (*CPW* 2:565). Rather, he imagines the nation itself as a process, as its scholar-citizens continually exercise their consciences, prompting not only spiritual and intellectual conflict but also, and more importantly, progress. Those who may be erroneous in their beliefs need only "gentle meetings and gentle dismissions," and for their matter of disagreement to be examined "thoroughly with liberall and frequent audience" (*CPW* 2:567). In this way, and only in this way, might England's citizens be united in their exercise of free conscience to become "a knowing people, a Nation of Prophets, of Sages, and of Worthies" (*CPW* 2:554). Liberty of conscience, Milton argues, is what will constitute England as a nation, fashioning bonds of spiritual unity rather than ecclesiastical uniformity.

The spectre of prelacy continues to drive Milton's advocacy for liberty of conscience even after Parliament passes an ordinance for the establishment of a limited Presbyterian church order in March 1646. As he demonstrates in *Of Reformation* and *Areopagitica*, nothing short of a full system of liberty of conscience for Protestant believers could sustain England's journey towards reformation. Fearing that the Presbyterians have taken up the prelate's mantle of intolerance, Milton once again takes on the voice of his imagined nation of conscience to appeal to Parliament, albeit indirectly. In "On the New Forcers of Conscience under the Long Parliament" (ca. 1646–7), Milton establishes for both the Presbyterians and Parliament the proper relationship between civil power and the individual conscience. The sonnet opens with a scathing attack on the Presbyterians, the "New Forcers of Conscience" and Milton's former allies against prelacy:

> Because you have thrown off your Prelate Lord,
> > And with stiff Vowes renounc'd his Liturgie
> > To seise the widdow'd whore Pluralitie
> > From them whose sin ye envi'd, not abhor'd, .
>
> Dare ye for this adjure the Civill Sword
> > To force our Consciences that Christ set free
> > And ride us with a classic Hierarchy.
> > > > >   (1–7)[11]

Milton establishes the Presbyterians' hypocrisy in this lengthy catalogue. Though they had "thrown off [their] Prelate Lord" by abolishing episcopacy in October 1646, and with "stiff Vowes renounc'd his Liturgy," banning the Book of Common Prayer in 1645, the Presbyterians went on to "seise the widdow'd whore Pluralitie," the practice of one minister holding two or more ministerial livings which they had formerly condemned and now adopted. Couching his opponents' duplicity in a lengthy subordinate clause, Milton finally delivers his central challenge: "Dare ye for this adjure the civil sword / To force our consciences that Christ set free?" The year 1646 marked the height of the campaign in London for a full Presbyterian system that would "repress errors, both religious and civil."[12] Members of the Westminster Assembly of Divines, as well as Presbyterian clergyman and controversialist Thomas Edwards ("shallow *Edwards*" (12)) and Scottish Presbyterian minister and author Robert Baillie ("Scotch what d'ye call" (12)), labelled Independents and other Protestant sectarians heretics in an effort to establish compulsory religious conformity.

It was not the Presbyterians' intolerance alone that Milton critiqued, but specifically their attempt to "adjure the Civill Sword" in support of this campaign. Edwards addressed the Long Parliament in his best-selling *Gangraena* (1646), warning MPs that "the great opinion of an universal Toleration, tends to the laying all waste and dissolution of all Religion and good manners."[13] Edwards, like his Presbyterian brethren, believed it the magistrates' God-given duty to enforce religious conformity.[14] According to Edwards, whether MPs actively cultivated a "universal Toleration" or passively turned a blind eye to sectarianism, they compromised their own salvation. Milton considers such use of the civil power against the sects an aggressive act, warranting a similarly aggressive interrogation: "Dare ye," he demands, "for this adjure the Civill Sword." Would they dare, because they have thrown off their "Prelate Lord" only to occupy his former place, "to force our Consciences that Christ set free"? While Edwards threatens the MPs with God's wrath for failing to use the civil sword in the realm of conscience, Milton accuses Edwards and his ilk of sacrilege for attempting to do so.

In this way, Milton sets explicit limits on civil power in the realm of conscience. Here, as elsewhere, he uses the potent verb "force" to characterize the civil power's violation – or potential violation – of conscience. Such forcing of conscience, Milton argues, is an abuse not only of the individual, but also of Christ's own sacrifice. It was Christ, not Parliament or its army, who set conscience free, and it is now the Presbyterians, like their "Prelate Lord" before them, who threaten this fundamental Christian liberty. Rather than exert force in the realm of conscience, the role of the civil power is to buttress Christ's own rule by protecting the liberty that his sacrifice granted. "But we do hope," Milton continues in the sonnet, "to find out all [the Presbyterians'] tricks" so that Parliament might perform its civil duty where conscience is concerned (13). Parliament, Milton expects, will league with the violated rather than the violators, and

> with their wholsom and preventative Shears
> Clip your Phylacteries, though bauk your Ears
>   And succour our just Fears
> When they shall read this clearly in your charge
> *New Presbyter* is but *Old Priest* writ Large.
>
> (16–20)

He imagines Parliament armed with both curative and precautionary "Shears," whose violent act of clipping was reserved for the Presbyterians' phylacteries (small leather boxes containing the Hebrew scriptures worn by Orthodox Jewish men), rather than their ears, as the ears of John Bastwick, Henry Burton, and William Prynne had been notoriously clipped under Charles I. In Matthew 23, Jesus admonishes the Pharisees for making "broad their phylacteries" so that they might "outwardly appear righteous unto men" while being "full of hypocrisy and iniquity." By clipping the Presbyterians' phylacteries, Parliament, like Christ, would expose their hypocrisy, checking their desire to use force against conscience.

Though this sonnet is not directly addressed to Parliament, Milton places pressure upon Parliament to fulfil the role he has set out for the civil power: protector of free conscience. Milton includes his own conscience among those potentially threatened by the Presbyterians' campaign – "To force our Consciences that Christ set free" – and he includes himself amid the petitioners – "we do hope" – who will inspire Parliament to take their "wholesome and preventative" action against the Presbyterians. Out of his plural poetic voice emerges the accusatory voice of a nation liberated in conscience and in need of "succour" to maintain that liberty. The enjambment of line 16 puts emphasis on "May," which in turn emphasizes Parliament's power and ability to take action against the Presbyterians. And it is not merely Parliament's power that will "succour our just Fears," but also the fact that Parliament "shall read this clearly in [the Presbyterians'] charge / *New Presbyter* is but *Old Priest* writ Large" (19–20). "Shall" suggests that Parliament's charge is a necessary condition following upon the collective voice's discovery of the Presbyterians' "tricks," "plots and packings" (13–14). More importantly, the poem itself, beginning with a catalogue of the Presbyterians' machinations, essentially fulfils the collective voice's hope to discover their hypocrisy. Even the title, labelling the Presbyterians the "New Forcers of Conscience," performs this petitioning function. With Milton having exposed the Presbyterian's hypocrisy, it is now Parliament's obligation – what they may and shall do – to charge the Presbyterians with the same charge the poem itself establishes. Parliament's role, in other words, is to protect free conscience from the force that the Presbyterians hoped to exercise against it – Parliament's own civil power.

Conscience Freed: Regicide

Milton's fear of these "New Forcers of Conscience" continues through the Second Civil War and even the days leading up to Charles's trial and execution. During these turbulent and unprecedented moments in English history, Milton came to believe that the regicide was England's door to liberty, both spiritual and civil. For this reason, he considered the onslaught of publications protesting Pride's Purge on 6 December 1648 and the King's impending trial to be dangerous roadblocks. In response, Milton published *Tenure of Kings and Magistrates* on 13 February 1649, just two weeks after Charles's execution. In this timely text, he not only crafts a republican political theory and defends tyrannicide but also once again attacks the Presbyterians for backsliding from the revolutionary cause.

Scoffing in *Tenure* at the Presbyterian ministers' opposition to the trial of Charles I, Milton refers to their "Printed letters which they send subscrib'd with the ostentation of great Characters and little moment" (*CPW* 3:242). However, Milton's language of conscience in this tract indicates that he was also concerned about the clergymen's potential sway. After all, Presbyterian ministers were very influential in London, and many of them now appealed to their congregants' consciences against the actions of the Rump and army.[15] The fifty-eight London Presbyterian ministers who signed their names to *A Vindication of the Ministers of the Gospel* (1649) deem their protest a "discharge of our consciences," a phrase invoked often in tracts and letters protesting on behalf of the King.[16] Similarly, the nineteen signatories of *The Humble Advice and Earnest Desires of Certain Well-Affected Ministers* (1649) declare, "We cannot without wounding our own consciences [...] sit down in silence." Fearing for the army's consciences and the national repercussions of regicide, they also implore Sir Thomas Fairfax, commander-in-chief of the army, and his soldiers to "forbear doing ought in the premises, which may wound the conscience, or pierce the hearts of any of Gods people" and "which may rend and tear the bowels of this your and our native Country."[17]

Such publications coupled with the Presbyterians' similar pronouncements in the pulpit attracted the attention of the Rump Parliament. On 3 February 1649, the Commons appointed a committee to consider *A Vindication of the Ministers of the Gospel* and "to restrain publick Preaching and Printing any thing against the Proceedings of this House, and the High Court of Justice, in relations to bring [...] the King to Justice."[18] Despite these measures, many Presbyterian ministers continued to defy the Rump.[19] Milton was similarly aware of the nascent republic's need for clerical support and feared that the Presbyterians' insolence could prove fatal in the realm of conscience. Hence he depicts them as hypocrites, who, at the start of the First Civil War, "devested [thir King], disannointed him, nay curs'd him all over in thir Pulpits and thir Pamphlets," and who now ally themselves with the king for nefarious motives (*CPW* 3:191). Barbara Lewalski senses in Milton's tone a "seething rage against these backsliders from the revolution."[20] To that, I would add a touch of anxiety. Fearing the influence that these ministers might have upon the consciences of believers, Milton implores them to take up the office of "good Pastors" to the people and embrace the "true end and reason" of the gospel, learning "what a world it differs from the censorious and supercilious lording over conscience." And, Milton cautions, if they refuse to take up the mantle of reformation, instead "aspiring [...] to sit the closest & heaviest of all Tyrants, upon the conscience," they will meet the same fate as the prelates before them (*CPW* 3:241, 242).

Milton imagines conscience as a potential victim: for the present, it seems, the Presbyterians can only aspire to tyrannize over it. Conscience is thus placed in a most precarious position as the Presbyterians threaten its freedom and, through it, that of the nation itself. To counter their efforts at the pulpits and in print, Milton crafts a casuistry of sorts, treating the case of conscience now pressing upon the populace: What lawful actions might be taken against the tyrant of a nation? Moving through classical, biblical, and finally historical cases of tyrannicide, Milton finally lights upon John Knox, "a most famous Divine and the reformer of *Scotland* to the Presbyterian discipline." When Knox argued that monarchs were subject to the law at a general assembly, Milton recounts, he was "commanded by the Nobilitie to write to *Calvin* and other lerned men for thir judgement in that question," to which he responded that "both himself was fully resolv'd in conscience, and had heard thir judgements, and had the same opinion under handwriting of many the most godly and most lerned that he knew in Europe" (*CPW* 3:223, 224). In this way, Milton hopes to disable the Presbyterian support for Charles through one of their most prominent fathers. In the second edition of *Tenure*, he adds the words of Martin Luther, John Calvin, Huldrych Zwingli, and other Protestant authorities to those of Knox in order to strengthen his case.

Milton heightens this comparison in the final pages of *Tenure* by setting the backsliding Presbyterian ministers, referred to as "they" for much of this closing diatribe, in opposition to an imagined "we." Pulling the audience onto his side of the debate, Milton interrogates his adversaries through the collective voice of the nation: "They tell us that the Law of nature justifies any man to defend himself, eev'n against the King in Person: let them shew us then why the same Law, may not justifie much more a State or whole people, to doe justice upon him, against whom each privat man may lawfully defend himself" (*CPW* 3:254). This assumption of a plural voice forces the reader to Milton's side as he aggressively questions the authority of the Presbyterian ministers. It also creates an irresistible response to the case of conscience treated within the text as a whole. Pointing to the catalogue of revered Protestant authorities, "the best and chief of Protestant Divines," Milton maintains that "we may follow them for faithful Guides, and without doubting may receive them, as Witnesses abundant of what wee heer affirme concerning Tyrants" (*CPW* 3:257). By speaking with and for his readers, Milton hopes to convince them to "love freedom heartilie" at a moment when their most precious freedom – that of conscience – is treacherously hunted by "a pack of hungrie Church-wolves" (*CPW* 3:190, 257).

Milton's anxiety about the effect of the Presbyterian ministers' hostility towards the newly established republic persisted beyond *Tenure*. In *Eikonoklastes* (1650), Milton argues that he cannot ascribe "dejection and debasement of mind" to the "natural disposition of an Englishman, but rather to two other causes": "the Prelats and thir fellow-teachers, though of another Name and Sect, whose Pulpit stuff, both first and last, hath bin the Doctrin and perpetual infusion of servility and wretchedness to all thir hearers" (*CPW* 3:344). This deferral of blame to the Anglicans and Presbyterians demonstrates the poet-polemicist's lingering hope that the English people might still come to embrace their "native liberty" (*CPW* 3:407).[21] Though both *Tenure* and *Eikonoklastes* lack the optimism of *Areopagitica*, Milton nonetheless imagines England as entering a new period in its identity as a nation. In *Tenure*, when looking forward to the King's impending trial and execution, Milton held that "truth and conscience" were about to be "freed," one factor, he believed, instigating the Presbyterians' backsliding (*CPW* 3:196). This contingency between regicide and liberty of conscience paves the way for one of Milton's most formidable undertakings, his attack on the King's book.

In between his penning of *Tenure* and *Eikonoklastes*, Milton was appointed Secretary of Foreign Tongues of the Commonwealth. Thus, whereas he wrote *Tenure* as a private person in support of the regicide, Milton was "bidden to reply" to *Eikon Basilike* on behalf of the budding republic (*CPW* 4.1:627). *Eikon Basilike* undermined the authority of the commonwealth in its attempt to hold the nation in a state of conscientious obedience to the Stuart line. While I discussed *Eikonoklastes* and Milton's assault on Charles's conscience in chapter 1, I will here consider how Milton more broadly connects Charles's execution and the liberty of English consciences. In his response to the King's book, Milton replaces the Presbyterians with Charles himself as the "closest & heaviest of all Tyrants" for his abuse of his subjects' free consciences. Most remarkable, however, is Milton's use of this dynamic to overturn the explicit associations between Charles and Christ prevalent throughout *Eikon Basilike*: not only is Charles holding a crown of thorns in the book's iconic frontispiece, but he also uses Christ's words – asking God to forgive his people, *"for they know not what they do"* – and compares his negotiations with Parliament to Christ's temptation on the pinnacle of the temple.[22]

Milton rebuts *Eikon Basilike*'s portrait of Charles as a martyr for conscience's sake with the image of a remorseless King ready to "bereave a Christian conscience of libertie" for the "narrowness of his own" (*CPW* 3:469). What is worse, his persecution of conscience was both self-serving and something he actually relishes, "never d[oing a] thing more eagerly then to molest and persecute the consciences of most Religious men." In fact, Charles's violation of his subjects' consciences was so widespread that, Milton argues, the word "persecution" should be replaced with "plain Warr" (*CPW* 3:488, 457). Reclaiming *Eikon Basilike*'s ubiquitous language of conscience, Milton transforms the civil wars into Charles's war on his subjects' consciences. It was the "church of God" who "was compell'd to implore the aid of Parlament, to remove [the King's] force and heavy hands from off our consciences" (*CPW* 3:492). Parliament loosened the royal grasp through the regicide, an act that at once freed conscience and England from the bonds of tyranny.

Milton ends *Eikonoklastes* with the image of a nation both hopeful and hopeless. First, there is the "inconstant, irrational, and Image-doting rabble" who idolize the King. Also imperiled are those who have been misled by error and who, Milton hopes, "may find the grace and good guidance to bethink themselves, and recover." Both types subsist alongside the "knowing Christian," immune to the King's posthumous machinations (*CPW* 3:341, 601). Through its freeing of conscience, the regicide catalysed a national transformation, albeit one that can only ever be incomplete, with the rabble and the misled impeding Milton's vision of a nation unified in its exercise of free conscience. Nevertheless, now rid of "that little pest at sea," "the *Remora*," who had tried to "arrest and stopp the Common-wealth stearing under full saile to a Reformation," England keeps its course, with free conscience at the helm (*CPW* 3:501).

Conscience Protected: The Commonwealth and Protectorate

Milton's anxieties regarding England's path towards reformation continue to mount during the years of the commonwealth. With new threats to liberty of conscience arising in Parliament in 1652, Milton is once again forced to revise his national vision in service of this freedom closest to his heart. More specifically, he loses faith in Parliament as a vehicle of his national program. Turning away from this representative body, Milton turns towards one of its most prominent members, Oliver Cromwell, a man representative of his vision for England as a nation of conscience. In his sonnet "To the Lord General Cromwell," Milton appeals to England's national hero, imploring him to fight for the nation in a new capacity.

Milton begins by lauding Cromwell's victories on the battlefield:

> Cromwell, our cheif of men, who through a cloud
>> Not of warr onely, but detractions rude,
>> Guided by faith & matchless Fortitude
>> To peace & truth thy glorious way hast plough'd,

And on the neck of crowned Fortune proud
    Hast reard Gods Trophies & his work pursu'd,
    While Darwe*n* stream wth blood of Scotts imbru'd,
    And [Dunbarr field] resounds thy praises loud,
    And Worsters laureat wreath.
                  (1–9; brackets in original)

Praising Cromwell's martial victories, Milton also recognizes that Cromwell's reputation has suffered "detractions rude" from both satiric royalist accounts and Presbyterian attacks for his toleration.[23] He completes this retrospective glance at Cromwell's conquests with a nod to his greatest triumphs over the Scots at Preston on the banks of Darwen in 1648, at Dunbar in 1650, and Worcester in 1651. Breaking convention, he inserts the *volta* in the middle of line 9, a deferral that emphasizes his transition from past to present:

      yet much remains
    To conquer still; peace hath her victories
    No less renownd then warr, new foes arise

Threatning to bind our soules wth secular chains:
    Helpe us to save free Conscience from the paw
    Of hireling wolves whose Gospell is their maw.
                  (9–14)

Though not printed until 1694 in *Letters of State*, the sonnet was composed in May 1652, as indicated by the deleted title from the Trinity Manuscript: "*To the Lord Generall Cromwell May 1652. On the proposalls of certaine ministers at y[e] Commttee for Propagation of the Gospell.*" The most immediate occasion for this poem, as the title suggests, began with a petition to Parliament in February 1652 on behalf of several Independent divines, including John Owen, Cromwell's army chaplain during his campaigns in Ireland and Scotland, regarding a "heretical" book. When Owen and his supporters submitted their petition, fears in Parliament and London of sectarianism and heterodoxy were at an all-time high.[24] In the midst of this anxiety, the question of religious toleration was once again brought to the fore with the publication of *The Racovian Catechism* (1652), a Socinian book denying both Christ's divinity and the trinity, a version of which Milton allegedly licensed.[25] Owen and his associates protested the book's publication, leaving behind a copy so that Parliament might consider their petition. Parliament resolved to create a committee to consider more closely with the Independent ministers "such Proposals as shall be offered for the better Propagation of the Gospel; and to report the same, with their Opinion therein, to the House," a committee to which Cromwell was appointed.[26]

On 18 February 1652, the ministers presented this Committee for the Propagation of the Gospel with fifteen proposals that called for the continuance of a state church and a licensing system for preachers while also allowing for a degree of toleration towards those "persons dissenting from the Doctrine and Way of Worship owned by the State."[27] Although their proposals were not published until 31 March, the committee's consideration of them raised much intrigue before then.[28] While some saw the ministers' proposals as too radical, others questioned both the committee's and Parliament's power to rule over spiritual matters. In early March, William Boteler, an army officer and a commissioner on the Committee for the Propagation of the Gospel in Wales, presented the committee with four proposals questioning the persecution of even "damnable Heresies" and the right of "Civil powers to assume a Judgement in Spirituals."[29] The day before the publication of the ministers' *Humble Proposals*, Roger Williams, the religious controversialist and founder of Providence, Rhode Island, published an annotated version of Boteler's proposals, complete with a dedicatory letter titled "To the Truly Christian Reader" and the ministers' own proposals. Hoping that there might yet be a chance to influence Owen and his supporters, Williams asks God "graciously to stir up the Hearts of these Worthy Men to put in some *Christian Retraction*."[30]

Significantly, Williams, like Milton, addresses Cromwell himself in defence of the cause of conscience. In his dedicatory epistle, Williams includes "*two excellent late Speeches of his* Excellency *the* Lord General, *upon occasion of these Papers*," and calls Cromwell's conviction a spirit "*from* God, *and the* Lamb *of* God," and the only one "*like to guard this* Nation *from the* Terrours *of* Ecclipses, *of* Pestilencies, *of* Navies, *of* Armies, *of* Men *and* Devils." Rather than fight offensively for the nation on the battlefield, Cromwell will now "*guard this* Nation" defensively from the scourges of both man and God, guiding it safely towards "Peace *and* Tranquility." While entrenched in the committee debates of 1652, Williams was also in contact with Milton as the two men traded language lessons and perhaps even expressed their shared abhorrence of the ministers' fifteen proposals.[31] In 1652, as we have seen, they considered Cromwell an ally, even leader, in their fight for liberty of conscience.

While Cromwell was being pressured to carry through radical reforms on behalf of the godly, fear-mongering letters published in the Rump's official newspaper, *Several Proceedings in Parliament*, urged Parliament to limit the spread of "blasphemies, and such things as tend to the beating down of the fundamentals of Religion."[32] In the midst of these expectations, Milton composes his sonnet to the man Williams and others claimed for the cause of conscience. He begins by addressing Cromwell with a telling epithet, "our cheif of men," a phrase that not only confirms but also endorses and celebrates Cromwell's pre-eminence over his contemporaries. The subsequent enjambed lines relay with speed Cromwell's military and personal triumphs, ploughing through a cloud "Not of warr onely, but detractions rude." His pursuit was fuelled not by glory but rather "faith & matchless Fortitude," emphasizing Cromwell's conviction and, once again, his exceptionality. Moreover, his path was one not of destruction but rather of production: Milton's choice of the verb "plough'd" suggests the both laborious and "glorious" path he carved towards "peace & truth," the oft-stated goals of the war.[33] The next quatrain charges forward at a similar pace, stacking victory upon victory all while pursuing God's "work" at the scaffold and against the Scots.

Cromwell, it seems, is unstoppable – or, as Milton's past tense verbs suggest, was unstoppable. He has "plough'd" his "glorious way," "reard Gods Trophies," and "his work pursu'd," with Milton's continual end and internal rhyme on the consonant "d" throughout the octave emphasizing both this sense of accomplishment and its pastness. Cromwell's victories are such, in fact, that they cannot be contained by the strictures of the sonnet form: as mentioned, Milton defers his *volta* until the middle of line 9, allowing for the dramatic contrast between highest distinction for work accomplished – "Worsters laureat wreath" – and the yet-to-be-accomplished – "yet much remaines." Whereas Milton's earlier use of enjambment propelled the poem forward, the enjambment of line 9 instead forces the reader to pause on its incompleteness. The intrusion of "yet" in this catalogue of victories heightens the comparison of done and undone, and the verb tense of "remaines" has a similar effect while also breaking the pattern of unrelenting "d" rhymes.

"To conquer still" completes the line, a reminder of the sonnet's now halting motion or stillness where Cromwell has not yet paved his "glorious way." Milton appropriates a martial lexicon amid this stillness in order to redefine the parameters of the revolution for Cromwell, a military man accustomed to measuring his success on the battlefield. He may have ploughed his way "To peace & truth," but "peace hath her victories" as well. While the octave is rife with past tense verbs hurtling the reader forward through Cromwell's victories, the stillness of these final moments resonates. They take their power not from swift movement but rather from the threat of potential movement: souls about to be bound with "secular chaines" and free conscience about to be consumed by "hireling wolves." Milton fears the threat posed by Owen and his supporters, and dramatizes that fear in his closing couplet. The striking end rhyme of "paw" and "maw" makes imminent the terrifying possibility of free conscience falling victim to these ravenous beasts, while the plea reminds readers that there is still time. The deferral of the sonnet's main verb, "Helpe" has the effect of isolating the poem's first line of address, "Cromwell, our cheif of men," and the final couplet as a stand-alone plea to the Lord General, a distillation of the sonnet's power into three direct and irresistible lines.

Most significant is the role that Milton asks Cromwell to fulfil. In his 1646 sonnet regarding the "New Forcers of Conscience," Milton imagined the Long Parliament as a check on the Presbyterians' desire to exercise the civil sword in the realm of conscience. He expected Parliament, in other words, to curb its own power where conscience was concerned. Yet, by 1652, rather than rely on Parliament and its "wholsom and preventative Shears," Milton appeals to its most prominent member, Cromwell. The Rump was failing in its essential civil role of buttressing Christ's kingdom in the conscience, and so Milton must seek help elsewhere. As a result, this singular reliance upon Cromwell as "our cheif of men" forges a new identity for both Cromwell and the speaker of the poem. Milton chooses a plural pronoun as the voice of his sonnet, once again transforming his poem into a representative call to arms. Perhaps this petition's most striking feature is its rhyming couplet; in addition to its rhetorical power, it is the only Miltonic sonnet to end with this distinctively English rhyme scheme. Milton, appealing to "our cheif of men" to "Helpe us to save free Conscience," does so in a plural voice that speaks for the English nation in its own signature poetic style. He imagines a nation that recognizes Cromwell as its head as well as its reliance upon him alone for the safety of its Christian liberty. Cromwell, on the other hand, emerges as the agent of a Protestant nationalism based in liberty of conscience.[34] It was Cromwell that this voice could rely upon to protect "our Consciences that Christ set free," and thus Cromwell who would help to create out of England the new Israel.

Milton's hope that Cromwell would "Helpe us to save free Conscience" resonates into the Protectorate. Indeed, his prose writings between the time of Cromwell's installation as Lord Protector and King Charles II's return continue to appeal to Cromwell to champion free conscience even as they express Milton's own frustration with parliaments past and present for their inaction regarding the same cause. Having once celebrated Parliament's removal of Charles's "force and heavy hands from off our consciences," Milton seemingly now seeks a pair of heavy hands to force England to become his imagined nation of conscience.

While Milton's sonnet to Cromwell as Lord General pointed out that "peace hath her victories / No less renownd then warr," Milton's *Defensio Secunda* (1654) depicts a Cromwell who is "as mighty in deliberation as in the arts of war" as he "Daily [...] toiled in Parliament." Turning to the dissolution of the Rump, Milton describes Cromwell's actions in terms remarkably similar to Cromwell's own speech before the Nominated Assembly on 4 July 1653.[35] Milton goes on to dismiss the Nominated Assembly as one who "did nothing" until "they of their own accord dissolved the Parliament" (*CPW* 4.1:671). He follows these two brief accounts with a telling appeal that verbally installs the Protector anew and intensifies the sentiment of his earlier poetic appeal: "Cromwell, we are deserted! You alone remain. On you has fallen the whole burden of our affairs. On you alone they depend." This passive construction – "Deserimur Cromuelle" – emphasizes both the nation's vulnerability and Cromwell's lack of force in the transference of power from Parliament to Protector. Rather than violate the nation's liberty, this "cheif of men" remains – as Milton had already regarded him in 1652 – its only hope.[36]

Nonetheless, Milton once again adjures Cromwell to maintain the cause closest to his heart: liberty of conscience. At this point, Milton had cause to be disappointed with some of Cromwell's recent legislation regarding the church. In March 1654, several months before Milton publishes *Defensio Secunda*, Cromwell established a national body of "Triers" to assess new clergy in an effort to improve the quality of the ministry.[37] Milton registers his disappointment in Cromwell's intervention through his request that the Protector "leave the church to the church." Yet he also tries to overcome it by separating his critique of Cromwell's ecclesiastical policies from his appeal for liberty of conscience.[38] By allowing each request to stand on its own, Milton eliminates any contingency between liberty of conscience and the separation of church and state:

> Lastly, may you yourself never be afraid to listen to truth or falsehood, whichever it is, but may you least of all listen to those who do not believe themselves free unless they deny freedom to others, and who do nothing with greater enthusiasm or vigor than cast into chains, not just the bodies, but also the consciences of their brothers, and impose on the state and the church the worst of all tyrannies, that of their own base customs or opinions. (*CPW* 4.1:679)

Milton fears what those who will "cast into chains" the bodies and consciences of their brethren might impose on the state and church. If they have the power to corrupt both of these institutions through Cromwell – "may you least of all listen to those" – then Milton assumes that despite the fact that the state and church are under one power – Cromwell's – the Protector nonetheless is capable of defending liberty of conscience.

Echoing his hope that Cromwell "Helpe us to save free conscience," Milton reserves his advice regarding conscience until the end of his catalogue, heightening its rhetorical impact and perhaps prioritizing it before his hope regarding the separation of church and state. Cromwell's adherence to this counsel was so unyielding that it would impede his ability to establish productive working relationships with either the First or Second Protectoral Parliaments. Patrick Little and David L. Smith argue that the "heart of the problem lay in Cromwell's desire to use a body designed as 'the representative of the whole realm' to advance what remained a minority agenda, 'liberty of conscience.'"[39] And while this "minority agenda" brought tension between Cromwell and Parliament, in this case, Milton and Cromwell belonged to the same minority.

Cromwell's relationship with Parliament over the course of the Protectorate was defined by his insistence that it fulfil the role Milton assigned to this body as early as 1646: protector of free conscience. Moreover, his dedication to this cause cost him both political stability and popular support. Despite differences over the separation of church and state, in this conscience-centred agenda, Cromwell was aligned with Milton, who would keep his post as Secretary of Foreign Tongues into the Protectorate. And, with the exception of the revised edition of the first *Defensio* in 1658, after *Defensio Secunda*, Milton would not publish another polemical text until Richard Cromwell's term as Protector in 1659. Because Milton breaks this silence only after Cromwell's death, and for the cause of conscience, he had, it seems, no need to write on behalf of conscience while Cromwell was in power.

Milton takes up the mantle of defender of conscience once again only after Cromwell's death, and then even draws upon some of Cromwell's own appeals to Parliament. Addressing the Parliament called during Richard Cromwell's brief term as Lord Protector in *A Treatise of Civil Power in Ecclesiastical Causes* (1659), Milton asks that they "regard other mens consciences, as you would your own should be regarded in the power of others" (*CPW* 7:240). Also similar to Cromwell, he maintains that "for beleef or practise in religion according to this conscientious perswasion no man ought to be punishd or molested by any outward force on earth whatsoever" (*CPW* 7:242). If Cromwell desired to employ Parliament to advance a minority agenda, Milton as polemicist followed in his path.

In the days leading up to Charles II's restoration, Milton reiterates a tragic reading of England's failure to live up to the ideals of the Revolution. As we have seen, in *The Readie and Easie Way*, he casts his nation's most recent history as a series of shipwrecks, each precipitated by a "hard measure to libertie of conscience." Though Milton pleads with Parliament, hoping that some of his readers might "become children of reviving libertie," he admits that "they seem now chusing them a captain back for *Egypt*" (*CPW* 7:463). Worse than shipwreck, this ship of state, he fears, is sailing in the wrong direction.

Dissenting Conscience: A Nation of Believers

Writing on 6 June 1666, Peter Heimbach, an admirer from Cleves, expresses his relief that Milton had not, in fact, "been restored to your heavenly *patria*," as had been rumoured. He closes his letter on flattering terms, naming the poet-polemicist "a most noble and celebrated man, John Milton, Englishman." In his response, Milton laments that his patriotism, "after having allured me by her lovely name, has almost *expatriated* me, as it were." Six years after King Charles II's return to the throne, Milton declares that it was his very love of nation that prompts his feelings of national exclusion. Only *almost* expatriated, Milton has a relationship to his nation that is dubious at best: his passionate service has been repaid with inhospitality, leading him to conclude that "one's *Patria* is wherever it is well with him" (*CPW* 8:2–3, 4). The Restoration thwarted Milton's vision of England as a nation of conscience, and this tragedy forces him to redefine once again his concept of nation, a project that he undertakes in *Paradise Lost*.

The language of conscience that proliferated in revolutionary England continued to flourish amid urban dissenting communities after the King's return. This discourse, once a point of contention between Presbyterians and other nonconformists, now bound "dissenters of all persuasions" into a "community for conscience," however diverse politically and theologically they may have been.[40] In response to the rigidly conformist policies of the 1660s, dissenters flooded the presses with arguments for the toleration of tender or overly scrupulous consciences. Scholars of the past two decades have seen *Paradise Lost* as deeply responsive to Restoration politics.[41] Yet, as mentioned earlier, critics who have examined Milton's treatment of conscience in the epic have focused on it primarily in theological terms, assuming it to be private in nature and thus far from contemporary calls for conscientious dissent.[42] I would argue, however, that it is precisely in its depiction of the private experience of conscience – its internal horrors and peace – that *Paradise Lost* coheres most dramatically with Restoration politics and Milton's own attempts to reimagine the nation. Indeed, while Milton's use of the word "conscience" in *Paradise Lost* identifies him as a member of this "community for conscience," it is not toleration that he seeks.[43]

Rather, in his great epic, Milton shapes a dissenting identity based on unconditional obedience to God-given conscience. This alternative allegiance at once heightens and resolves the tension between conscience and the nation present throughout Milton's corpus: finally unable to imagine an England willing to be guided by free conscience, the poet-polemicist abandons his efforts to force onto the nation an identity that it repeatedly rejects. Instead, he crafts a nation of believers, fit readers who, guided by conscience, will "safe arrive," an arrival the ship of state never would have achieved. Free conscience thus enables a revolutionary type of nationhood, one that looks forward to a "New Heav'n and Earth, wherein the just shall dwell," God's promise of future paradise for his followers (3:335).[44]

More importantly for Milton's contemporary readers, free conscience also acts as a conduit for this apocalyptic nationhood in the present. In order to convince his audience to obey their consciences even in the face of persecution, Milton dramatizes both the negative and the positive: the horrors of a guilty conscience – horrors worse than persecution and worse than the physical torments of hell itself – and the "paradise within" of a free conscience. This "paradise within" unites believers in spirit, while also heartening them with a taste of what it will be finally to "safe arrive." In this way, liberty of conscience in *Paradise Lost* is both a means towards an end – paradise – and that end itself.

The Restoration was ushered in with a promise of liberty of conscience: in the conciliatory Declaration of Breda (1660), Charles II pledged "a liberty to tender consciences, and that no man shall be disquieted or called in question for differences of opinion in matter of religion, which do not disturb the peace of the kingdom."[45] Many religious radicals initially embraced this assurance of liberty to tender consciences, yet it would remain unfulfilled.[46] During the first year of the Restoration, Charles attempted to compromise with Presbyterians on church affairs as promised, yet his efforts were persistently thwarted by the Anglican clergy. Parliament proved similarly intolerant, passing the Act of Uniformity of 1662, which not only ensured that Presbyterians would be expelled from the national church but also resulted in the removal of nearly one thousand parish ministers.[47] After the expulsion of such ministers, the Restoration Church, and its clergy in particular, sought the active persecution of nonconformity in order to force dissenters back into the church.[48] Clerics such as Reverend Nathaniel Aske, after all, believed that if dissenters were required to attend church and hear its sermons, "constant hearers doe many tymes become conscientious hearers."[49] However, threats of excommunication and persecution and even the Act of Uniformity itself could not quell nonconformity or the popularity of many ejected preachers. Instead, conscience became a rallying cry against persecution.

While all dissenters knew that a heavenly reward awaited them for this suffering, many also believed that the consolation of a good conscience rewarded them even in this world. It is this consolation that nonconformist pamphlets offered to those afraid of persecution. This idea was expressed explicitly in the first bestseller of the Restoration, a book aptly named *Farewel Sermons* (1663), and condemned by Roger L'Estrange as "one of the most *Audacious*, and *Dangerous Libels*, that hath been made publique under any Government" in "Defiance of the *Law*."[50] Memorialized in this dangerous book, Edmund Calamy preaches that the straits to which martyrs were driven "for God and a good Conscience" were "so sweetned to them by the consolations and supportations of God's spirit" that "a Prison was a Paradise to them."[51] Focusing on 2 Samuel 24:14, Calamy distinguishes between hardships suffered for "guilt of sin," like David's, and those suffered for "God and a good Conscience." The former "awaken[ed] Conscience" and "fill[ed] it full of perplexities," while the latter were "no troubles at all."[52]

Published alongside Calamy, Mr Watson reminds his readers that "we see a godly man in misery; but we see not his comforts; we see his prison grates, but we hear not that sweet musick that he enjoys in his conscience"; Thomas Jacombe shares that "when the burden is heavy upon the back, then the peace of Conscience is great within"; and Mr Jenkins closes his sermon by reminding his congregation that "either thy conscience doth comfort thee, or it shall."[53] Beyond *Farewel Sermons*, George Whitehead, a Quaker leader, similarly tells his readers in *An Epistle of Consolation* (1664) that those persecuted for conscience's sake "do know a sweet repose in their deepest sufferings and tryals […] and herein joy, and peace, and everlasting glory and triumph is seen and felt by all the faithful and sincere in heart over all their oppressors."[54] Even Zachary Cawdrey, a conformist clergyman who late in his career was, according to Philip Henry, "much maligned and reproached by some people for his moderation toward dissenters,"[55] advises his readers that "peace of Conscience is certainly the best feast that any can invite himself to next to the supper of the Lamb the glory of Heaven."[56] This transformation of prisons into paradises allowed the persecuted to transcend England's failings, finding that their "heavenly *patria*" dwelled within their consciences.

As we turn from the religious tracts on the consolation of a good conscience in the face of persecution to Milton, we can recognize a deeper resonance and topical significance in the language of conscience that pervades *Paradise Lost*. Milton's God identifies the role of conscience in *Paradise Lost* when He speaks of placing His "Umpire *Conscience*" in fallen humanity. Leading up to this moment, God had stressed the importance of free will in his creation: humankind not only "ordain'd thir [own] fall" but also after their restoration by way of divine grace, they must once again stand of their own accord (3:128). In order to help humankind freely choose the right path after the fall, God promises to

> place within them as a guide
> My Umpire *Conscience*, whom if they will hear,
> Light after light well us'd they shall attain,
> And to the end persisting, safe arrive.
>
> (3.194–7)

Restored to freedom by God's grace, humanity can be guided by conscience towards the good.[57] What is more, God calls conscience

"My Umpire," asserting his ownership over conscience as well as the degree to which conscience should be obeyed. Derived from the Middle and Old French words meaning "peerless," as an "umpire," conscience would thus be an arbiter who "surpasses all others."[58] This language of conscience as supreme arbiter and guide implicitly dismantles the arguments of those conformist Restoration divines who dismiss conscience as "every private mans perswasion" or "weak, silly, and ignorant things."[59]

Yet the most salient word in this passage from *Paradise Lost* is not "umpire" or even "conscience" but rather "if." *If* they will hear conscience, they will "safe arrive," but *if* they will not, they will "stumble on, and deeper fall" (3.198–201). Hence, it is not the predetermined reprobate who shall suffer damnation but rather the wilful neglectors of conscience. And "none but such," God asserts, "from mercy I exclude" (3.202). Interestingly, it is here, when setting out the rule of conscience, that God stops to ask for the "charity so dear" that the Son will offer (3.216). It is also here that the world of the text comes into contact with the world of the reader: by speaking directly to the importance of fealty to conscience, Milton's God also speaks to the reader's present struggle between competing loyalties to his conscience and to the restored state and church. The language of "conscience" here would have both signalled to and exhorted Milton's readers. Stressing that hearing conscience is a free choice, Milton's God puts the responsibility of obedience upon each individual regardless of state compulsion or persecution: just as Adam and Eve, those who "deeper fall," "enthrall themselves" (3.125). Although the power to save remains God's alone, each individual has the power through conscience to choose the good and to express "true allegiance."

Significantly, most of *Paradise Lost* focuses not on this conscience-guided "true allegiance" to God but rather on wilful disobedience – namely that of Satan as the archetypal disobeyer and, later, Eve and Adam's transgression. The price of disobedience proves to be agonizing. Recalling Calamy's idea of a good conscience creating the internalized space of paradise even within a physical prison, here, the horrors created by a guilty conscience create within the culprit nothing short of hell. The poem opens with Satan's inner horror at the thought of "lost happiness and lasting pain" (1.55). Satan hides his mental anguish from his fallen crew through his heroic rhetoric and seemingly "unconquerable Will," yet the narrator assures the reader that although "vaunting aloud" Satan is "rackt with deep despair" (1.106, 126). Satan's mental torment, however, only comes to the fore once he has left the physical place of hell behind and is in sight of paradise in the opening lines of book 4. Satan finally understands the profundity of his punishment when, having escaped the Stygian pool, he realizes he nevertheless carries hell within him – the hell of a guilty conscience (4.75).

Satan's daughter-lover, Sin, earlier emblematizes this mental anguish when she describes her hellish offspring as:

> yelling Monsters that with ceaseless cry
> Surround me, as thou saw'st, hourly conceiv'd
> And hourly born, with sorrow infinite
> To me, for when they list, into the womb
> That bred them they return, and howl and gnaw
> My Bowels, thir repast; then bursting forth
> Afresh with conscious terrors vex me round,
> That rest or intermission none I find.
>
> (2.795–802)

In one 1667 copy of *Paradise Lost*, a contemporary hand has aptly written beside this grotesque description, "Horrors of Conscience."[60] These "horrors," or as Sin calls them, "conscious terrors," "vex" her "round" in the form of her cannibalistic progeny. Encircling her with their "ceaseless cry," they continuously gnaw at her bowels, causing her "sorrow infinite."[61] In Satan, this visceral process of infinite torment is internalized to become the horrors of conscience identified by that early reader. The narrator's description of the fiend in book 4 performs the same function as Sin's monstrous offspring: Satan's "dire attempt"

> Now rolling, boils in his tumultuous breast,
> And like a devilish Engine back recoils
> Upon himself; horror and doubt distract
> His troubl'd thoughts, and from the bottom stir
> The Hell within him, for within him Hell
> He brings, and round about him.
>
> (4.16–21)

In the first part of the passage, the words mimic the cyclical and self-damaging movement of Satan's "horror and doubt," recalling the description of Sin's litter (4.18). The enjambment of lines 17–18 enacts this recoiling effect. In the next few lines, Milton creates a different but related effect through chiasmus, as horror and doubt stir up the hell that Satan thinks he has left behind, revealing that hell is a permanent inner state rather than a place that can be escaped.[62]

Folding back on itself, this language paves the way for the catalyst of Satan's horror:

now conscience wakes despair
That slumber'd, wakes the bitter memory
Of what he was, what is, and what must be
Worse.

(4.23–6)

As this passage makes clear, it is Satan's conscience that recreates the space of hell within him by awakening a stunning sense of self-awareness. Satan's first line in the poem expressed his horror at Beelzebub's change from "what he was": he asked "If thou beest hee" in disbelief, "But O how fall'n! how chang'd" (1.84). As his soliloquy in book 4 demonstrates, now Satan's conscience forces him to look to himself and vexes him with the conscious terrors of his own change, culpability, and self-inflicted fall from grace:

Pride and worse Ambition threw me down
Warring in Heav'n against Heav'n's matchless King:
Ah wherefore! he deserv'd no such return
From me.

(4.40–3)

And, just as Sin's progeny goes forth from her womb only to return to their maker to fill her with terror and agony, Satan's attempts to curse God's love "dealt equally to all" only redound upon his own head. After he curses God, his conscience interjects, literally turning his words back upon himself: "Nay curs'd be thou; since against his thy will / Chose freely what it now so justly rues" (4.71–2).[63] In response to this timely revelation, Satan cries out, "Me miserable!" (4.73). He finally realizes that, because of his conscience, "Which way I fly is Hell; myself am Hell," a statement once again employing the verbal repetition characteristic of the poem's conscience-laden scenes, while also restating the narrator's earlier description of Satan (4.75). This knowledge of his own evil *is* Satan's hell, the "hot Hell" of a guilty conscience "that always in him burns," making paradise itself his prison (9.467).

Adam is similarly tormented by the horrors of a guilty conscience for his wilful disobedience. The serpent's words seem to Eve to be "impregn'd / With Reason" and "Truth," yet, when Adam is tempted by Eve, "to himself he inward silence broke" (9.737–8, 895). This moment dramatizes Adam's striking failure to listen to the knowledge within him and to obey his conscience. He acknowledges that Eve has "yielded to transgress / The strict forbiddance," but he resolves that he too must violate God's law and so share in her fate (9.902–3). The narrator amplifies Adam's self-consciousness throughout this temptation scene, noting that Adam

> scrupl'd not to eat
> Against his better knowledge not deceiv'd,
> But fondly overcome with Female charm.
>   (9.997–9)

Just as the rebel angels refuse "Right reason" or conscience "for thir Law," so Adam consciously transgresses against what he knows to be right and good (6.42).[64] And, like Satan, Adam suffers for his transgression.

After the Son's mild judgment of Adam and Eve, Adam witnesses around him the "growing miseries" of his fallen paradise (10.649–714). While these miseries "were from without," Adam "worse felt within" (10.714, 717). Once again recalling Sin's progeny, he calls his horrors of conscience a "deathless pain," a "deathless Death," and an "endless misery" worse than the quick death he had imagined (10.775, 798, 810). Moreover, Adam's fear of this pain's perpetuity "Both in me, and without me [...] / Comes thund'ring back with dreadful revolution / On my defenseless head" like Sin's tormenters who are "hourly born" (10.812–14). Adam longs to become "earth / Insensible" only so that God's "voice no more / Would thunder in my ears" and "no fear of worse / To me and to my offspring would torment me / With cruel expectation" (10.776, 778–82).

His persistent queries throughout this soliloquy, like the narrator's description of Satan's psychologically tormented state, create for the reader the experience of a conscience heavy with sin. His reason now fallen, Adam's plagued conscience forces him to question God's sense of justice, mercy, and his own just punishment. Like those fallen angels in Pandemonium who "reason'd high / Of Providence, Foreknowledge, Will, and Fate, / Fixt Fate, Free will, Foreknowledge absolute" yet "found no end, in wand'ring mazes lost," so Adam's queries only lead him deeper into anguish (2.558–61). Unrepentant and consumed with despair, Adam finally identifies the culprit, crying out

> O conscience, into what Abyss of fears
> And horrors hast thou driv'n me; out of which
> I find no way, from deep to deeper plung'd!
>   (10.842–4)

Just as with Satan, then, Adam's guilty conscience creates within him the unbearable experience of hell – the "peerless" and unsurpassed punishment of disobedience. His "evil conscience," or consciousness of his own evil as Milton defines it in *De Doctrina Christiana*, torments him further, "represent[ing] / All things with double terror" like the "conscious terrors" produced by Sin's hellish offspring (10.849–50).[65]

The intensity of Adam's psychological anguish and the time that Milton takes in representing it (this soliloquy is one of the longest in the poem) suggest that Adam experiences the fall – or his paradise lost – most dramatically in his conscience. It is his conscience's representation of "All things with double terror," after all, which amplifies the "dreadful gloom" of the fallen world around him and exacerbates his "fierce passion" towards himself and his "stern regard" of Eve (10.847, 865–6). Having abandoned his consciousness of good and right reason when he "Against his better knowledge" ate the forbidden fruit, Adam now suffers the "degradation of the mind" attendant on the fall, including "mind and conscience" (*CPW* 6:394). As Milton also points out in *De Doctrina*, the spiritual death that followed the fall consisted first in the "loss or at least the extensive darkening of that right reason, whose function it was to discern the chief good, and which was, as it were, the life of the understanding." Humanity thus loses righteousness and "liberty to do good," which is replaced by "slavish subjection to sin and the devil," a conscience weighted down with the guilt of sin, and the necessity for the law of the Old Testament (*CPW* 6:394–5).

Up to this point, *Paradise Lost* demonstrates the horrors of a guilty, fallen conscience through both Satan and Adam. While the heavenly dialogue sets out the importance of obedience, much of the epic shows the consequences of disobedience, consequences that include the creation of a physical hell and the birth of a more agonizing hell within. Though both Adam and Satan despair, Adam, unlike Satan, "shall find grace" – a grace that Milton identifies in part as freedom from the horrors of sin, or the freedom of conscience (3.131). In this way, Adam functions as a model of primal disobedience *and* as the subject of redemption, both experienced through conscience. The horrors of Adam's guilty conscience are finally overcome by the Son's sacrifice, proleptically presented at two points in the poem so that it might prefigure the psychological effects that redemption will finally have on fallen humankind. In book 3, the Son offers himself as the vehicle for God's grace: "Behold mee then, mee for him, life for life / I offer, on mee let thine anger fall; / Account mee man" (236–8). His sacrifice, moreover, would guarantee "peace assur'd, / And reconcilement" between humanity and God

(3.263–4). The Son's speech in book 11 similarly prefigures this peer-less sacrifice when he intercedes on Adam and Eve's behalf, present-ing their penitent prayers before God. Similar in his repetition of the pronoun "mee" to his speech in book 3, the Son implores the Father to bend his ear to penitent humankind:

>   hear his sighs though mute;
>   Unskilful with what words to pray, let mee
>   Interpret for him, mee his Advocate
>   And propitiation, all his works on mee
>   Good or not good ingraft, my Merit those
>   Shall perfet, and for these my Death shall pay.
>   Accept me, and in mee from these receive
>   The smell of peace toward Mankind, let him live
>   Before thee reconcil'd.
>
>   (11.30–9)

These two moments prefigure the Son's ultimate sacrifice for human-kind after which humanity could live before God "reconcil'd." In initi-ating this new relationship between God and humankind, his offering will also alleviate the hellish experience of the guilty consciences of God's fallen creation. The Son's sacrifice itself, then, was made in order to inaugurate a new relationship between God and humanity – a rela-tionship experienced through the regenerated conscience rather than through the law. In this way, the pattern of echoes between his mono-logues in books 3 and 11 suggests a positive version of the recoiling and folding language so common in the episodes where conscience is not at peace.

Although this intercession looks forward to the time when the Son, as Christ, shall fully expiate Adam and Eve's sin, it does have certain immediate effects even at this point. God, at the Son's request, accepts human prayer and grants Adam and Eve "Strength added from above" and "new hope" "Out of despair" (11.138–9). More than that, Adam, believing he was "heard with favor," tells Eve that "peace return'd / Home to [his] Breast" – a reference back not only to the Son's request for peace from the Father but also to the "Abyss of fears / And horrors" produced earlier by his sin-burdened conscience (11.153–4; 10.842). The statement also looks forward to the "paradise within" that Michael will promise. Adam twice more refers to this change within him as Michael tells him the future in book 12: Adam claims that his "heart" is "much eas'd, / Erewhile perplext with thoughts," and he tells Michael that he leaves paradise in "peace of thought" (12.274–5, 558). In Adam's case, his peace is derived from the Son's promise of redemption rather than its fulfilment. Nevertheless, his transition from the horrors produced by his guilty conscience to this state of inner tranquillity dramatizes for the reader the "peace of conscience" made available to him through the Son's sacrifice – available, that is, if the reader, like Adam, chooses to hear.

While the horrors of a guilty conscience and the peace of a restored conscience might seem private in nature, their very intimacy places *Paradise Lost* into the political mêlée of the 1660s. Nonconformists such as Calamy used the private experience of conscience, especially their fear of compromising the peace of their consciences, to justify dissent. Similarly, through Michael's prophecy, *Paradise Lost* offers a radical account of the role conscience plays in the politicized world of religious dissent. Having established the need for absolute obedience to God's "umpire," Milton polarizes worldly and divine power, with each vying for humanity's allegiance in a war that will rage on until those who hear "safe arrive."

In the epic, the dangers of conscience in a fallen world and the courage of the righteous under persecution are not directly shown but narrated as part of Michael's prophetic vision in books 11 and 12. Michael's narrative is initially a story of the few righteous – Enoch, Noah, Abraham, and Moses against the multitude of the unrighteous (11.664–73, 808–21; 12.111–26, 169–72). And, once the Son's sacrifice restores the "peace / Of Conscience" to those suffering under the law, conscience emerges as the locus of an epic battle between the "enemies of truth" and the "few / His faithful" (12.480–2). The wolves that "shall succeed" the apostles "for teachers" (12.508) – the loathed hirelings of Milton's *Considerations Touching the Likeliest Means to Remove Hirelings out of the Church* (1659) – will threaten this peace granted by Christ himself by joining with "Secular power, though feigning still to act / By spiritual" (12.517–18). Indeed,

> from that pretense,
> Spiritual Laws by carnal power shall force
> On every conscience; Laws which none shall find
> Left them inroll'd, or what the Spirit within
> Shall on the heart engrave.
>
> (12.520–4)

Through such laws, the "wolves" will effectively undo Christ's sacrifice by stripping conscience of its freedom; and "Without this freedom," as Milton argues in *De Doctrina*, "we are still enslaved: not, as once, by the law of God but, what is vilest of all, by human law" or, better yet, "inhuman tyranny" (*CPW* 6:123).

At this tragic juncture, Michael interrupts his narrative so the world of the text might once again come into contact with the world of the reader:

> What will they then
> But force the Spirit of Grace itself, and bind
> His consort Liberty; what, but unbuild
> His living Temples, built by Faith to stand,
> Thir own Faith not another's: for on Earth
> Who against Faith and Conscience can be heard
> Infallible?
>
> (12.524–30)

Michael's rhetorical questions force the reader to consider what the (now obvious) answer must be. In book 3, God had promised paradise to those who choose to hear His umpire conscience, and here Michael confirms once again the superiority of conscience's voice over all others. More importantly, once the reader responds to Michael's questions, she too must corroborate conscience's authority.

Michael continues, "many will presume" to be heard infallible against conscience; and the "far greater part" will willingly consent to this violation of their own freedom (12.530, 533). Forfeiting their Christian liberty because they "deem in outward Rites and specious forms / Religion satisfi'd," this "far greater part" (12.534–5) will conform to unjust and unholy laws. As such, they will suffer the hell of a conscience heavy with sin and ultimately dissolve with Satan and his "perverted World" (12.547). On the other hand, those who disobey unjust authorities in order to obey their consciences and God, as Michael tells Adam, face "heavy persecution" (12.531). These obedient few, however, do not suffer under this worldly abuse. As do the sermons of Calamy, Watson, Jacombe, and other nonconformists, Milton's poem similarly suggests that the righteous will find solace in their peaceful consciences:

> What man can do against them, not afraid,
> Though to the death, against such cruelties
> With inward consolations recompens't.
>
> (12.493–5)

Even in the face of the heaviest of persecutions – death – Milton's martyrs are rewarded with the "inward consolations" of a free and peaceful conscience.

The martyrs' experience of this consolation in *Paradise Lost*, however, goes beyond the passive dissent encouraged by the nonconformist preachers: Milton's martyrs are so "oft supported" by their consolations "so as shall amaze / Thir proudest persecutors" (12.496–7). The consolations enjoyed by those obedient to God's will in this way become the dissenters' greatest weapon through which they might "amaze" the enemies of truth. As opposed to the gnawing, guilty conscience that consumes the sinner from within, this free conscience, preserving the inner person, allows him to engage in spiritual warfare against even his "proudest persecutors," including Satan. Armed with "spiritual armor," God's obedient can "resist" or oppose "*Satan's* assaults" and "quench his fiery darts" (12.491–2). According to this model, dissent against both humanity and Satan is defensive in that it protects the liberty of conscience; yet it is also offensive because, through that liberty, it actively opposes the enemies of truth.

In *A Treatise of Civil Power* (1659), Milton wrote in similarly violent terms regarding the standoff between the conscientious believer and his persecutor. Commenting on 1 Corinthians 1:27, "*God hath chosen the weak things of the world to confound the things which are mighty*," Milton argues, "Surely [God] hath not chosen the force of this world to subdue conscience and conscientious men, who in this world are counted weakest; but rather conscience, as being weakest, to subdue and regulate force, his adversarie, not his aide or instrument in governing the church" (*CPW* 7:257). For Milton, conscience is the regulator and oppressor of force. Anticipating book 12 of *Paradise Lost*, this passage similarly imbues individuals with the power to "amaze / Their proudest persecutors" (496–7) through their use of conscience. Milton then comments on another biblical verse (this one from 2 Corinthians), arguing that Paul, when claiming that "*the weapons of our warfare are not carnal*," was speaking of "that spiritual power by which Christ governs his church, how all-sufficient it is, how powerful to reach the conscience and the inner man with whom it chiefly deals and whom no power els can deal with," and in comparison how "uneffectual and weak is outward force with all her boistrous tooles" (*CPW* 7:257). Such force, Milton concludes, is "oft times fatal to them who use it" (*CPW* 7:261–2). In this spiritual battle, the conscientious prevail, not only amazing their enemies with their consolations but also subduing and regulating the agents of persecution and witnessing their ultimate self-destruction.

Adam learns this same dual lesson from Michael's narrative. He now knows that to "obey [God] is best," but also that "by things deem'd weak" he might "Subver[t] the worldly strong." Similarly, "suffering for Truth's sake" – undoubtedly through persecution – is, at the same time, "fortitude to the highest victory" (12.561, 567–70). Similar to *A Treatise of Civil Power*, in *Paradise Lost*, the lesson learned is that victory is achieved through conscientious obedience, obedience sustained even through suffering, persecution, and, if necessary, death. Such victory is not a retreat inward but instead the highest form of outward dissent. Thomas N. Corns argues that by the end of *Paradise Lost*, Adam and Eve are "impotent against the forces which, as Michael reveals, will all but overwhelm them." "The strategies available to them," he continues, "are strategies for surviving, not for winning."[66] Yet the poem's closing pattern of references to conscience suggests a present and future victory for the "fit though few" who choose to hear conscience over their "proudest persecutors." And this victory, more than for Adam and Eve, is for the fit reader who can, if he or she chooses, experience the paradise within of a peaceful conscience.

Participating in the larger nonconformist conversation arguing for liberty of conscience, Milton's great epic contributed to the Restoration's vibrant culture of dissent. Indeed, he invites his audience to join the nation of believers, to defend their liberty of conscience and find comfort in both God's promise of a future paradise and the preview of that comfort through the "paradise within." Whether its dictates are tolerated or not, Milton shows his audience that conscience is free and that to forfeit its freedom to conformity is to repeat the archetypal fall itself – a failure to stand that inevitably leads to the unbearable horrors of conscience emblematized by Sin and experienced by Satan and Adam. In *A Treatise of Civil Power*, Milton argues that God "hath not only given us this gift [of liberty] as a special privilege and excellence of the free gospel above the servile law, but strictly hath commanded us to keep it and enjoy it" (*CPW* 7:263). In this way, enjoying that paradise of a peaceful conscience and cultivating it are both requisite parts of the obedience owed to God. In a world fraught with persecution and compulsion, Milton, like Calamy, hoped that his fit audience, his nation of conscience, would make *"conscience what we hear and how we hear."*[67] And, as God ensures in book 3, "if [they] will hear," and only if they will hear, will they "safe arrive."

It is not surprising that Milton's last major foray into poetry is about a man who, after being blinded and imprisoned by his enemies, finally hears his conscience (372). Milton publishes *Samson Agonistes* with *Paradise Regain'd* in 1671, two poems that explore the drama of "one mans firm obedience," or, in the case of Samson, *reaffirmed* obedience.[68] In "The Argument," he recounts that Samson, visited *"by a publick Officer to require his coming to the Feast before the Lords and People," "at first refuses, dismissing the publick Officer with absolute denyal to come"* (69). In the poem itself, Samson's *"absolute denyal"* doubles as an effort to preserve his "conscience and internal peace," even at the cost of his life (1334). Throughout *Samson Agonistes*, readers witness Samson's despair, a hopelessness dispelled through the series of agons that finally reaffirm the fallen hero's faith in himself. This transformation is confirmed when the officer asks Samson to "Regard thy self" after he refuses to obey the Philistine Lords' commands, and Samson responds, "My self?," more concerned with his restored paradise within than his bodily safety (1333–4).

Yet, only moments later, Samson tells the Chorus that "I begin to feel / Some rouzing motions in me which dispose / To something extraordinary my thoughts. / I with this Messenger will go along" (1381–4). Critics have called into question the source of Samson's "rouzing motions," but Loewenstein asks that we "not adopt a position of extreme skepticism that prompts us to doubt" Samson's spiritual inspiration.[69] Samson assures the Chorus that he will do nothing "that may dishonour / Our Law, or stain my vow of *Nazarite*" – in other words, nothing that might disturb that which he had earlier hoped to protect, his "conscience and internal peace" (1385–6). Samson's violent act of dissent, inspired by these "rouzing motions," is both conscientious and the highest form of obedience towards God.

Samson's adherence to his own conscience and "internal peace" in these final moments mobilizes the nation of conscience that Milton so carefully crafts in *Paradise Lost*. Just as Michael predicts that the "inward consolations" of the faithful "shall amaze / Thir proudest persecutors," so Samson promises the Philistines that what he means to "shew you of my strength" "As with amaze shall strike all who behold" (1634–5). Fulfilling in part Michael's prophecy, Samson amazes the Philistines with the consolations of his conscience.

More important is the intended effect of Samson's conscientious dissent on Milton's readers. In his introduction, Milton cites Aristotle, reminding his audience that tragedy, "by raising pity and fear, or terror," has the power "to purge the mind of those and such like passions, that is to temper and reduce them to just measure with a kind of delight, stirr'd up by reading or seeing those passions well imitated" (66). Tragedy thus profits the reader by prompting catharsis, a process of emotional temperance. What is the nature of the catharsis produced by the poem's dramatic and violent finale? In the midst of his own self-deprecation, Samson disparages "*Israel*'s Governours, and Heads of Tribes" who "Acknowledg'd not" the "Deliverance offerd" through his own "great acts" (243–6). This tension between the nation and its intended deliverer heightens Samson's status as an outsider of sorts. The word "Nazarite" comes from the Hebrew *nazār*, meaning "to separate or consecrate oneself," suggesting that Samson occupies an extra-national space, at once a part of Israel and not.[70]

In this way, his status is akin to Milton's, an expatriate within the borders of his own nation. Through his obedience to the "rouzing motions" of his conscience, Samson reconciles himself not to Israel but rather to Milton's nation of conscience. Moreover, Samson's end is meant to produce for readers a feeling of "peace and consolation," language reminiscent of the "paradise within" of a free conscience. God's champion thus provides fit readers with a vicarious initiation into the nation of conscience. And to Milton's lost nation, Israel, he has left freedom, if only it would "Find courage to lay hold on this occasion" (1706). Perhaps this last exhortation to Israel – Samson's final and most dramatic act on its behalf – is the last vestige of Milton's bygone hope that England would or could "safe arrive" with the "best part of our libertie" intact.

Afterword

In the mid-nineteenth century – and in the most unlikely of places – we find a witness to the enduring impact of the connection this study recovers between conscience, the nation, and the English Revolution. Matthew Arnold, Victorian writer, social conservative, and enemy of narrow-minded Philistinism, revisits the English Revolution as a foil of the French Revolution in his "The Function of Criticism at the Present Time" (1865): "1789 asked of a thing, Is it rational? 1642 asked of a thing, Is it legal? or, when it went furthest, Is it according to conscience?" For Arnold, the French Revolution's preoccupation with reason is what made it a "more spiritual event than our Revolution, an event of much more powerful and world-wide interest, though practically less successful." While its ideals were "universal, certain, permanent," those driving the English Revolution – law and conscience – were rooted to place, time, and even person: "what is law in one place, is not law in another; what is law here today, is not law even here tomorrow; and as for conscience, what is binding on one man's conscience is not binding on another's."[1]

Arnold's snapshot of this turbulent moment in English history pictures a provincial row made even more narrow in scope by its reliance on conscience.[2] To illustrate this point further, he continues, "The old woman who threw her stool at the head of the surpliced minister in St Giles's Church at Edinburgh obeyed an impulse to which millions of the human race may be permitted to remain strangers" (*Essays* 15). The "old woman" he mentions is the legendary Jenny Geddes, a Scottish vegetable dealer who is often credited with sparking the Bishops' Wars and, in turn, the English Revolution.[3] While Geddes's tale would certainly have been recognized in Victorian England considering its renown in Scotland, Arnold leaves this heroine of conscience unnamed.[4] In doing so, he reduces what is regarded as a foundational moment of the Revolution down to the impulsive action of an old woman. "When it went furthest," then, the English Revolution was not just provincial but limited to a province of one.

Yet, as this study has demonstrated, conscience in revolutionary England was by no means merely individual, private, or impulsive. Rather, for many writers and thinkers of the mid-seventeenth century, conscience emerged as a means *to know with* others rather than simply themselves. More specifically, they use conscience to reimagine England, forging dynamic connections between the self and nation and revolutionizing through writing the role conscience might play on the national stage, as well as what the nation might now come to mean. We have seen that 1642's asking of a thing, *Is it according to conscience?*, in fact inspired many to envision new ways for the idea of conscience to transcend time, place, and even person: *Eikon Basilike* sought to unite the nation in conscientious obedience to its late King; Cromwell's letters and speeches reveal an embattled leader hoping to use liberty of conscience to transform England into the nation of God; the Quakers believed the light within conscience to be a network connecting all believers, and thus a tool through which they might reach Cromwell and the nation; Hobbes shapes conscience into a civilizing force, capable of sustaining the nation from within; Lucy Hutchinson revises her husband's conscience to imagine a republican future for England; and in his writings, Milton founds a nation of conscience whose borders are finally determined by dissent.

These writings explore the full etymological potential of conscience, imagining new ways of *knowing with* at the national level. In the process, each writer also revolutionizes the very idea of nation and its boundaries. Far from provincial, these works exhibit an expansiveness mimicked unwittingly by Arnold himself. Indeed, in trying to rewrite Revolutionary history, he instead recreates it. While Arnold hopes to cast Geddes – a woman believed to have moved nations to war against their King – as singular, many seemed and still seem *to know with* this old woman of popular lore, celebrating her act of conscience.

Yet what is perhaps most ironic about Arnold's critique of conscience during the Revolution is the fact that he too turns to conscience in order to reimagine the English nation. Writing a year earlier about the importance of the French Academy, Arnold maintains that "a Frenchman has, to a considerable degree, what one may call a conscience in intellectual matters; he has an active belief that there is a right and wrong in them" (*Essays* 39). Rather than encouraging the English to emulate this French institution, Arnold concludes by exhorting his readers to internalize the intellectual conscience upon which it operates for the betterment of their nation.[5] In doing so, "every one amongst us with any turn for literature" will seek "steadily to widen his culture, [and] severely to check in himself the provincial spirit" (*Essays* 59). This cultivation of an intellectual conscience in "every one amongst us," Arnold believed, would help the English come *to know with* each other a new national identity.

Over 200 years after Charles I raised his standard at Nottingham Castle, conscience remained a potent tool for national reimaginings, even for one of the Revolution's greatest critics. While Arnold reduces Geddes to an old woman who threw a stool, he yearns for the English nation to know with him in the intellectual sphere as they knew with her in the religious sphere. Setting out to critique the English Revolution, Arnold instead evinces its continuing cultural importance. Hence, while Arnold may seem to have little in common with Milton, Cromwell, the Quakers, or Hutchinson, who in turn seem to have little in common with Charles I or Thomas Hobbes, they share a powerful and ongoing query that resonates in the nineteenth century and even today: *Is it according to conscience?*

Notes

Introduction: Revolutions of Conscience

1 "Letters to Mrs. Anne Sadleir of Standon," Wren Library, Trinity College Cambridge, Cent. xvii, R.5.5, 31–36v.
2 See, for example, Camille Wells Slights, *The Casuistical Tradition in Shakespeare, Donne, Herbert, and Milton* (Princeton, NJ: Princeton University Press, 1981); Lowell Gallagher, *Medusa's Gaze: Casuistry and Conscience in the Renaissance* (Stanford, CA: Stanford University Press, 1991); Meg Lota Brown, *Donne and the Politics of Conscience in Early Modern England* (Leiden: E.J. Brill, 1995); and, most recently, Ceri Sullivan, *The Rhetoric of Conscience in Donne, Herbert, and Vaughan* (Oxford: Oxford University Press, 2008). These literary studies are complemented by the work of historians, such as Edmund Leites, ed., *Conscience and Casuistry in Early Modern Europe* (Cambridge: Cambridge University Press, 1988); John Morrill, Paul Slack, and Daniel Woolf, eds., *Public Duty and Private Conscience in Seventeenth-Century England* (Oxford: Clarendon Press, 1993); Harald Braun and Edward Vallance, eds., *Contexts of Conscience in Early Modern Europe, 1500–1700* (Basingstoke: Palgrave Macmillan, 2004) and *The Renaissance Conscience* (Oxford: Wiley-Blackwell, 2011).
3 Edward G. Andrew, *Conscience and Its Critics: Protestant Conscience, Enlightenment Reason, and Modern Subjectivity* (Toronto: University of Toronto Press, 2001), 4.
4 For example, Richard Helgerson, *Forms of Nationhood: The Elizabethan Writing of England* (Chicago: University of Chicago Press, 1992); Andrew Hadfield, *Literature, Politics, and National Identity: Reformation to Renaissance* (Cambridge: Cambridge University Press, 1994); Claire McEachern, *The Poetics of English Nationhood, 1590–1612* (Cambridge: Cambridge University

Press, 1996); David Norbrook, *Writing the English Republic: Poetry, Rhetoric, and Politics 1627–1660* (Cambridge: Cambridge University Press, 1999); Willy Maley, *Nation, State and Empire in English Renaissance Literature: Shakespeare to Milton* (Basingstoke: Palgrave Macmillan, 2003); and Andrew Escobedo, *Nationalism and Historical Loss in Renaissance England: Foxe, Dee, Spenser, Milton* (Ithaca, NY: Cornell University Press, 2004).

5 Benedict Anderson, *Imagined Communities: Reflections on the Origin and Spread of Nationalism* (London: Verso, 1983).

6 David Loewenstein and Paul Stevens, eds., *Early Modern Nationalism and Milton's England* (Toronto: University of Toronto Press, 2008), 9; see also Elizabeth Sauer's *Milton, Toleration, and Nationhood* (Cambridge: Cambridge University Press, 2014).

7 Anderson, *Imagined Communities*, 7.

8 See note 4 above, as well as, for example, Adrian Hastings, *The Construction of Nationhood: Ethnicity, Religion and Nationalism* (Cambridge: Cambridge University Press, 1997); David J. Baker, *Between Nations: Shakespeare, Spenser, Marvell, and the Question of Britain* (Stanford, CA: Stanford University Press, 1997); Andrew Hadfield, "The English and Other Peoples," in *A Companion to Milton*, ed. Thomas N. Corns (Oxford: Blackwell, 2001), 174–90; and Patrick Schwyzer, *Literature, Nationalism, and Memory in Early Modern England and Wales* (Cambridge: Cambridge University Press, 2004).

9 Recently, scholars have expanded the concept of "revolution" during this period to include print culture and literature. See, for example, Nigel Smith, *Literature and Revolution in England* (New Haven, CT: Yale University Press, 1997); Joad Raymond, *Pamphlets and Pamphleteering in Early Modern Britain* (Cambridge: Cambridge University Press, 2003); Ann Hughes, *Gangraena and the Struggle for the English Revolution* (Oxford: Oxford University Press, 2004); and Laura Lunger Knoppers, ed., *The Oxford Handbook of Literature and the English Revolution* (Oxford: Oxford University Press, 2012).

10 Michael G. Baylor, *Action and Person: Conscience in Late Scholasticism and the Young Luther* (Leiden: Brill, 1977), 22–3; and Andrew, *Conscience and Its Critics*, 13, 8.

11 Martin Luther, *Luther's Works*, ed. Jaroslav Pelikan (St Louis, MO: Concordia Publishing House, 1963), 18:277.

12 Baylor, *Action and Person*, 23. See also C.A. Pierce, *Conscience in the New Testament* (London: SCM Press, 1955), 21–8, 108–9.

13 V.P. Furnish, quoted in Leon Morris, *The Epistle to the Romans* (Grand Rapids, MI: W.B. Eerdmans, 1988), 126–7.

14 Pierce, *Conscience in the New Testament*, 118.

15 Ibid.

16 Charlton T. Lewis, *An Elementary Latin Dictionary* (Oxford: Oxford University Press, 1969).

17 Pierce, *Conscience in the New Testament*, 107 (emphasis in the original).

18 Pierce notes that Jerome's choice of *conscientia* is problematic because it fails "completely to exclude the modern notion of conscience." Moreover, when the church "permit[s] her children to suppose that conscience is a sufficient guide in all things," "without clearly defining conscience" first, "she subscribes, in effect to the popular 'wresting from its proper sense' of the word, and countenances the interpretation of the word that men are only too ready to put upon it" (*Conscience in the New Testament*, 124–5). See also 129–30.

19 Timothy C. Potts, *Conscience in Medieval Philosophy* (Cambridge: Cambridge University Press, 1980).

20 See ibid., 41; and Dennis R. Klinck, *Conscience, Equity and the Court of Chancery in Early Modern England* (Aldershot: Ashgate, 2010), 3–4. Potts also notes that there is a "surprising lack of attention which [medieval philosophers] pay, when we consider that they were professional theologians as well as philosophers, to biblical material on conscience" (61). This lack of attention amplifies further the nature and scope of Luther's revolution of conscience, one based entirely on the treatment of conscience in the New Testament.

21 Paul Strohm, *Conscience: A Very Short Introduction* (Oxford: Oxford University Press, 2011), 11, 13–17; see also Strohm, "Conscience," in *Cultural Reformations: Medieval and Renaissance in Literary History*, ed. Brian Cummings and James Simpson (Oxford: Oxford University Press, 2010), 209–11.

22 Quoted in Baylor, *Action and Person*, 7–8.

23 Luther, *Luther's Works*, 26:386, 349–50, 152, 120.

24 Ibid., 32:112, 130.

25 Strohm, *Conscience*, 24.

26 Andrew, *Conscience and Its Critics*, 17.

27 Luther, *Luther's Works*, 21:236–7.

28 C.H. Williams, ed., *English Historical Documents*, vol. 5, *1485–1558* (Oxford: Oxford University Press, 1967), 708.

29 Ibid.

30 Henry VIII, *The Letters of King Henry VIII: A Selection with a few other Documents*, ed. M. St. Clare Byrne (London: Cassell & Company, 1968), 132.

31 Sir Thomas More, *The Correspondence of Sir Thomas More*, ed. Elizabeth Frances Rogers (Princeton, NJ: Princeton University Press, 1947), 502.

32 Ibid., 506.

33 Sensing a "shift in the meaning of conscience in the English language between the 1520s and the 1550s," Brian Cummings finds that More "stands on both sides rather than on one, and this divergence of meaning begins to infect More's lexis and praxis." See Cummings, "Conscience and the Law in Thomas More," in *The Renaissance Conscience*, ed. Harald E. Braun and Edward Vallance (Oxford: Wiley-Blackwell, 2011), 46.

34 Henry VIII, *The Letters*, 124.

35 For a more detailed description of this title page, see Rev. W.F. Moulton, *The History of the English Bible* (London: Cassell, Petter and Galpin, 1878), 138–9.

36 Alfred W. Pollard, ed., *Records of the English Bible: The Documents Related to the Translation and Publication of the Bible in English, 1525–1611* (London: Oxford University Press, 1911), 266.

37 Lacey Baldwin Smith, "A Matter of Conscience," in *Action and Conviction in Early Modern Europe: Essays in Honor of E.H. Harbison*, ed. Theodore K. Rabb and Jerrold E. Seigel (Princeton, NJ: Princeton University Press, 1969), 38.

38 According to Edward Coke in *The Reports*, vol. 4, parts 7–8, ed. John Henry Thomas and John Farquhar Fraser (London: Joseph Butterworth and Son, 1826), the text of the medieval oath reads as follows: "You shall swear, that from this day forward, you shall be true and faithfull to our Sovereign Lord King _______, and his heires, and truth and faith shall bear of life and member, and terrene honour, and you shall neither know nor hear of any ill or damage intended unto him, that you shall not defend. So help you Almighty God" (589).

39 Jonathan Michael Gray, *Oaths and the English Reformation* (Cambridge: Cambridge University Press, 2012), 114.

40 John King, *Foxe's "Book of Martyrs" and Early Modern Print Culture* (Cambridge: Cambridge University Press, 2006), 2.

41 John Foxe, *The Unabridged Acts and Monuments Online* (Sheffield, UK: HRI Online Publications, 2011), (1563 ed.) 1255, 1115.

42 King, *Foxe's "Book of Martyrs,"* 1.

43 Foxe, *Acts and Monuments* (1583 ed.), 575, 1285.

44 King, *Foxe's "Book of Martyrs,"* 150–1.

45 Foxe, *Acts and Monuments* (1563 ed.), 1788.

46 Quoted in Patrick Collinson, *The Elizabethan Puritan Movement* (Berkeley: University of California Press, 1967), 25.

47 For an extensive treatment of this event, see Stephen Hamrick, *The Catholic Imaginary and the Cults of Elizabeth, 1558–1582* (Aldershot: Ashgate,

2009), where he argues that Elizabeth's departure from the mass was premeditated for political impact (17–25).

48 Collinson argues that "further reformation" is "a phrase which can be associated with the Elizabethan puritan movement in two ways. In that they were organized to secure reform in the whole body of the Church, and by means of public authority, the puritans intended to complete the English Reformation" (*Elizabethan Puritan Movement*, 13).

49 Patrick Collinson, *Archbishop Grindal, 1519–1583: The Struggle for a Reformed Church* (Berkeley: University of California Press, 1979), 238, 239.

50 Robert Zaller, *The Discourse of Legitimacy in Early Modern England* (Stanford, CA: Stanford University Press, 2007), 74.

51 Kevin Sharpe, "Private Conscience and Public Duty in the Writings of James VI and I," in *Public Duty and Private Conscience in Seventeenth-Century England*, ed. John Morrill, Paul Slack, and Daniel Woolf (Oxford: Clarendon Press, 1993), 83–4.

52 James VI and I, *The Letters of King James VI and I*, ed. G.P.V. Akrigg (Berkeley: University of California Press, 1984), 166–7.

53 These are James's words, describing the Gunpowder Plot. See James VI and I, *King James VI and I: Political Writings*, ed. Johann P. Sommerville (Cambridge: Cambridge University Press, 1994), 85. The oath begins with, "I A.B. doe trewly and sincerely acknowledge, professe, testifie and declare in my conscience before God and the world, That our Soueraigne Lord King IAMES, is lawfull King of this Realme"; and it ends with a similar declaration: "I doe beleeue, and in conscience am resolued, that neither the *Pope* nor any person whatsoeuer, hath power to absolue me of this Oath, or any part thereof" (*Political Writings*, 88–9).

54 Quoted in full in James's *Triplici Nodo*. See James VI and I, *Political Writings*, 97.

55 Ibid., 94, 86.

56 Ibid., 18.

57 Gordon Campbell, *Bible: The Story of the King James Version 1611–2011* (Oxford: Oxford University Press, 2010), 26–7.

58 Pollard, *Records of the English Bible*, 46.

59 Ibid., 54.

60 William Laud, *The Works of the Most Reverend Father in God, William Laud*, vol. 4, *History of the Troubles and Trial*, ed. James Bliss and William Scott (Oxford: John Henry Parker, 1854), part 1, 262.

61 Christopher Hill, *The English Bible and the Seventeenth-Century Revolution* (New York: Penguin, 1995), 64–5.

62 See Victoria E. Burke, "Sadleir, Anne (1585–1671/2)," in *Oxford Dictionary of National Biography* (Oxford University Press, 2004–), accessed 24 June 2016, doi:10.1093/ref:odnb/68095.

63 See Francis J. Bremer, "Williams, Roger (c.1606–1683)," in *Oxford Dictionary of National Biography* (Oxford University Press, 2004–), accessed 24 June 2016, doi:10.1093/ref:odnb/29544.

1. Charles I, *Eikon Basilike*, and the Pulpit-Work of the King's Conscience

1 James Duport, *Three sermons preached in St. Maries Church in Cambridg, upon the three anniversaries of the martyrdom of Charles I, Jan. 30* (London, 1676), 41, 39, 42, 44, 45.

2 Jason McElligott, *Royalism, Print and Censorship in Revolutionary England* (Woodbridge, UK: Boydell Press, 2007), 14, 5.

3 *Eikon Basilike: The Portraiture of His Sacred Majesty in His Solitudes and Sufferings*, ed. Jim Daems and Holly Faith Nelson (Ontario: Broadview Editions, 2006), 25, 24.

4 Andrew Lacey, *The Cult of King Charles the Martyr* (Woodbridge, UK: Boydell Press, 2003), deems *Eikon Basilike*'s famous frontispiece in particular a drawing upon "a body of emblems and typologies which, as we have seen, were already established by the time of the king's death" (78).

5 Lacey, "Charles I and the *Eikon Basilike*," *Prose Studies* 29, no. 1 (2007): 5.

6 Kevin Sharpe, "Private Conscience and Public Duty in the Writings of Charles I," *Historical Journal* 40, no. 3 (1997): 643–65; and Lacey, "Charles I" and *The Cult*.

7 Lacey, *The Cult*, 83.

8 Elizabeth I, *Elizabeth I: Collected Works*, ed. Leah S. Marcus, Janel Mueller, and Mary Beth Rose (Chicago: University of Chicago Press, 2000), 173.

9 For the connection between conscience, obedience, and sermons during Charles's reign prior to the outbreak of the civil wars, see Laura Perille, "Harnessing Conscience for the King: Charles I, the Forced Loan Sermons, and Matters of Conscience," *Exemplaria* 24, nos. 1–2 (2012): 161–77.

10 Susan Wabuda, *Preaching during the English Reformation* (Cambridge: Cambridge University Press, 2002), points out that "Cromwell emphasized preaching as a political act," and "at the beginning of June 1535, Cromwell ordered the bishops to preach the sincere word of God and the king's title of supreme head of the Church of England on every Sunday and feast day throughout the year" (94).

11 John Donne, *The Sermons of John Donne*, vol. 7, ed. Evelyn Simpson and George R. Potter (Berkeley: University of California Press, 1954), 396, 408.

12 Nicholas Tyacke, *Anti-Calvinists: The Rise of English Arminianism c. 1590–1640* (Oxford: Clarendon Press, 1987), notes that the preachers chosen to speak at Paul's Cross were selected by the bishop of London himself (248).

13 Tyacke identifies less than a third of the printed Paul's Cross sermons from Elizabeth's, James's, and Charles's (pre-1627) reigns as mentioning the "predestinarian question." He also points out that not until 1632 "did an Arminian sermon preached at Paul's Cross appear in print" (*Anti-Calvinists*, 249).

14 Millar MacLure, *The Paul's Cross Sermons, 1534–1642* (Toronto: University of Toronto Press, 1958), 107–15.

15 Ibid., 107.

16 John Rushworth, *Historical Collections of Private Passages of State*, 8 vols. (London, 1721–2), 4:550.

17 *An exact collection of all remonstrances, declarations, votes, orders, … betweene the Kings most excellent Majesty, and his high court of Parliament* (London, 1642), 550.

18 Ibid., 556.

19 William Haller, *Liberty and Reformation in the Puritan Revolution* (New York: Columbia University Press, 1955), 66.

20 W. Dunn Macray, ed., *The History of the Rebellion and Civil Wars in England*, vol. 2 (Oxford: Clarendon Press, 1888), 319–20.

21 Susan Doran and Christopher Durston, *Princes, Pastors and People: The Church and Religion in England, 1500–1700* (London: Routledge, 2003), 175–77.

22 He wrote, "This is call'd the best Edition of yˢ Book in 'Wagstaffe's Vindication,' p. 139 being yᵉ 5th Impression with the Prayers."

23 This copy of *Eikon Basilike* is in Pennsylvania State University's Special Collections holdings, shelf mark DA400.C488 1649b. As PSU's catalogue entry states, it was part of an eighteenth-century library in Williamscote House near Banbury, England. The library was put together by John Loveday (1711–89), who was both a philologist and antiquarian. The library was moved to Williamscote House in 1799 by John Loveday II (1742–89).

24 David Scott, "Counsel and Cabal in the King's Party, 1642–1646," in *Royalists and Royalism during the English Civil Wars*, ed. Jason McElligot and David L. Smith (Cambridge: Cambridge University Press, 2007), 125–6.

25 Charles I, *The Letters, Speeches and Proclamations of King Charles I*, ed. Sir Charles Petrie (New York: Funk & Wagnalls, 1935), 176. All subsequent references to this text will be cited parenthetically according to page number.

26 These two letters to Sir Henry Vane the Younger were sent by the
command of Charles. In them, the author tells Vane to "prevail that the
King may come to London upon the terms he hath offered: where, if
Presbytery shall be so strongly insisted upon, as that there can be no peace
without it, you shall certainly have all the power my Master can make,
to join with you rooting out of this Kingdom that tyrannical government;
with this condition, that my Master may not have his conscience disturbed
(your's being free) when that work is finished." See Edward Hyde, Earl of
Clarendon, *State Papers Collected by Edward, earl of Clarendon, commencing
from the year 1621*, 3 vols., edited by Richard Scrope (Oxford: Clarendon
Press, 1767–86), 2:226–7. All subsequent references to this text will be cited
parenthetically according to volume and page number.

27 Scott, "Counsel and Cabal," 125–7.

28 Though Charles continues to address Jermyn, Culpepper, and
Ashburnham in this series of letters, Ashburnham does not seem to be
writing in league with Jermyn and Culpepper at this point.

29 Sharpe, "Private Conscience and Public Duty in the Writings of Charles I,"
649.

30 Richard Cust, *Charles I: A Political Life* (London: Pearson Longman, 2005),
427–8.

31 Cust similarly points out that Charles "was more flexible then he claimed.
There are several occasions during this period when he deliberately set
aside his conscientious scruples in pursuit of immediate advantage" (ibid.,
356).

32 Ibid., 426.

33 *Mercurius Elencticus*, no. 47, 11–18 October 1648, 385; *Mercurius
Pragmaticus*, no. 16, 28 December 1647–4 January 1648, 4v.

34 Elizabeth Skerpan-Wheeler, "Rhetorical Genres and the *Eikon Basilike*,"
Explorations in Renaissance Culture 2 (1985): 101.

35 As Skerpan-Wheeler points out, *Eikon Basilike* in fact attempts to justify
not the king's actions but his character, to refute the charge that Charles
Stuart was a "Man of Blood." Royalist defenders clearly recognized that
the popular appeal of *Eikon Basilike* lay not in any supposed justification of
action, but in the depiction of Charles's character." See Elizabeth Skerpan-
Wheeler, "*Eikon Basilike* and the Rhetoric of Self-Representation," in *The
Royal Image: Representations of Charles I*, ed. Thomas N. Corns (Cambridge:
Cambridge University Press, 1999), 127.

36 Richard Helgerson, "Milton Reads the King's Book: Print, Performance,
and the Making of a Bourgeois Idol," *Criticism* 29, no. 1 (1987): 7–9.

37 Most of the subsequent editions were printed as duodecimos, except for the fifteenth, twenty-first, twenty-second, twenty-fourth, twenty-fifth, and twenty-seventh editions. See Francis F. Madan, *A New Bibliography of the Eikon Basilike of King Charles I* (Oxford: Oxford University Press, 1950), for a catalogue of all thirty-five English editions printed in 1649.

38 Ian Green, *Print and Protestantism in Early Modern England* (Oxford: Oxford University Press, 2000), points out that the early seventeenth century marks the "appearance of the duodecimo bible, a size which proved increasingly popular in the 1640s and 1650s and after the Restoration when, though precision is not possible, it appears that twice as many duodecimos were published as of any other format" (57).

39 This particular title was featured on the eighty-fourth edition. See Madan, *New Bibliography of the Eikon Basilike*, 89.

40 Elizabeth Skerpan-Wheeler, "The First 'Royal': Charles I as Celebrity," *PMLA* 126, no. 4 (2011): 912–34, discusses the *Apophthegmata* as a "commonplace book" which "dignifies the entries as expressions of wisdom that readers can apply to their own writings or review for insight into their own thoughts and experiences" (927).

41 Green discusses the increase in simpler commentaries, paraphrases, expository notes, and so forth in Bibles during the middle of the seventeenth century in addition to abridgement (*Print and Protestantism in Early Modern England*, 101–44).

42 Both the Folger Shakespeare Library's duodecimo copy (shelf mark E287.8) and PSU's duodecimo (shelf mark DA400.C488 1648) are falling apart at the binding, and their leather covers (if original) also betray similar signs of regular use.

43 Madan quotes Mrs Gauden's narrative of Royston's experience: "'when [*Eikon*] was about half printed they that were in power found the press where it was printing, and likewise a letter of my husband, with a sheet which he sent up to the press, whereupon they destroyed all that they found then printed: but they could not find out from whence the letter came in regard it had no name to it: now notwithstanding all this yet my husband did attempt the printing of it again, but could by no means get the book finished till some few days after his Majesty was destroyed'" (*New Bibliography of the Eikon Basilike*, 164–5).

44 Henri-Jean Martin, *The History and Power of Writing*, trans. Lydia G. Cochrane (Chicago: University of Chicago Press, 1995), 313.

45 Skerpan-Wheeler, "*Eikon Basilike* and the Rhetoric of Self-Representation," 124.

46 Madan, *New Bibliography of the Eikon Basilike*, 128.

47 Quoted in Robert Wilcher, "What Was the King's Book For? The Evolution of 'Eikon Basilike,'" *Yearbook of English Studies* 21 (1991): 222.

48 Madan, *New Bibliography of the Eikon Basilike*, 153.

49 Wilcher, "What Was the King's Book For?" 222.

50 Lacey, "Charles I," 5.

51 Skerpan-Wheeler, "*Eikon Basilike* and the Rhetoric of Self-Representation," 127.

52 Ibid., 122.

53 This idea, of course, was a renaissance commonplace. Both Lacey in *The Cult* and Sharpe also point out Charles's use of this construction.

54 Daems and Nelson, *Eikon Basilike*, 54. All subsequent references to *Eikon Basilike* are from this edition unless otherwise noted, and will be cited parenthetically.

55 Madan, *New Bibliography of the Eikon Basilike*, 33–4.

56 Ibid., 28.

57 John Milton, *Complete Prose Works of John Milton*, ed. Don M. Wolfe et al., 8 vols. (New Haven: Yale University Press, 1953–82), 3:601. All subsequent references to Milton's prose are from this edition and cited parenthetically as *CPW* and by volume (sometimes volume and part) and page number.

58 Sharon Achinstein, "Milton Catches the Conscience of the King: *Eikonoklastes* and the Engagement Controversy," *Milton Studies* 29 (1992): 155.

59 See, for example, Bruce Boehrer, "Elementary Structures of Kingship: Milton, Regicide, and the Family," *Milton Studies* 23 (1987): 97–117; and Jane Hiles, "Milton's Royalist Reflex: The Failure of Argument and the Role of Dialogics in *Eikonoklastes*," in *Spokesperson Milton: Voices in Contemporary Criticism*, ed. Charles W. Durham and Kristin Pruitt McColgan (Selinsgrove, PA: Susquehanna University Press, 1994), 87–100. I borrow the quoted phrase from Achinstein, "Milton Catches the Conscience of the King," 154.

60 "Letters to Mrs. Anne Sadleir of Standon," Wren Library, Trinity College Cambridge, Cent. xvii, R.5.5, 80–80v.

61 Duport, *Three Sermons*, 11, 9.

2. Oliver Cromwell and the Duties of Conscience

1 "Newsletter from London," Bodleian Library, Clarendon MS 45, folio 292v (April 1653); *A Hue and Crie after Cromwell: Or, The Cities Lamentation for the losse of their Coyne and Conscience* (London, 1649), 1.

2 See, for example, *A Dialogue Betwixt the Ghosts of Charls the I, Late King of England: and Oliver, The late Usurping Protector* (1659), where Cromwell

laments, "oh the Sting of Conscience that troubles me, now too late I find the horridness of my Crimes, by oppressing the righteous, and spilling the blood of the innocent; Oh Sir little do you think what I feel for now I find the reward of all my evill doings" (7).

3 *A New Conference between the Ghosts of King Charles and Oliver Cromwell* (London, 1659), 3.

4 Christopher Hill, *God's Englishman: Oliver Cromwell and the English Revolution* (New York: Harper Torchbooks, 1970). For revisions of Hill's argument, see for example Patrick Little, ed., *The Cromwellian Protectorate* (Woodbridge, UK: Boydell Press, 2007) and *Oliver Cromwell: New Perspectives* (Basingstoke: Palgrave Macmillan, 2008); David L. Smith, ed., *Cromwell and the Interregnum: The Essential Readings* (Oxford: Blackwell, 2003); Patrick Little and David L. Smith, *Parliaments and Politics during the Cromwellian Protectorate* (Cambridge: Cambridge University Press, 2007); Barry Coward, *The Cromwellian Protectorate* (Manchester: Manchester University Press, 2002); and Laura Lunger Knoppers, *Constructing Cromwell: Ceremony, Portrait, and Print, 1645–1661* (Cambridge: Cambridge University Press, 2000).

5 Blair Worden, *The Rump Parliament 1648–1653* (Cambridge: Cambridge University Press, 1974), 69; Little and Smith, *Parliaments and Politics*, 135.

6 S.C. Lomas, ed., *The Letters and Speeches of Oliver Cromwell with Elucidations by Thomas Carlyle*, 3 vols. (London: Methuen & Co., 1904), 2:298. All subsequent references to this text will be cited parenthetically by volume and page number.

7 This phrase can be found in Bulstrode Whitlocke's *Memorials of the English Affairs*, vol. 4 (Oxford: Oxford University Press, 1853), 182.

8 John Morrill, "Cromwell, Oliver (1599–1658)," in *Oxford Dictionary of National Biography* (Oxford University Press, 2004–), accessed 7 July 2014, doi:10.1093/ref:odnb/6765.

9 Ibid.

10 David Masson, *The Quarrel Between the Earl of Manchester and Oliver Cromwell* (London, 1875), 72.

11 Wilbur Cortez Abbott, ed., *The Writings and Speeches of Oliver Cromwell*, 4 vols. (Cambridge, MA: Harvard University Press, 1939), claims that, in this case, Cromwell's defence of Packer "had little to do with those abstract principles of toleration and democracy." Instead, Cromwell's reasoning was "preeminently practical" because "there was a war to be won … and any instrument which would assist in the accomplishment of this great task was to be seized upon and used. That this involved toleration and democracy – if it did – was incidental to the immediate design" (1:278).

More recently, Andrew R. Murphy, *Conscience and Community: Revisiting Toleration and Religious Dissent in Early Modern England and America* (University Park: Pennsylvania State University Press, 2001), seconded Abbot's argument, asserting that "this much-quoted letter does not constitute an argument for toleration, but rather a statement of military necessity" (118n).

12 The wording of the Covenant is ambiguous where Presbyterianism was concerned. The first clause in *A Solemn League and Covenant* (London, November 16, 1643) states, "we shall sincerely, really, and constantly through the grace of God, endeavour in our severall places and callings, the preservation of the Reformed Religion in the Church of *Scotland* in Doctrine, Worship, Discipline and Government, against our common Enemies, The Reformation of Religion in the Kingdoms of *England* and *Ireland*, in Doctrine, Worship, Discipline, and Government, according to the Word of God, and the example of the best Reformed Churches" (1). The key phrase in this passage is "according to the Word of God," which left the "Reformation of Religion" up for interpretation.

13 *The Conclusion of Lieuten: General Cromwells Letter to the House of Commons* (London, 1645). On his copy, George Thomason penned, "September 22. This was printed by ye Independent Party and scattered up and downe ye streets last night. But expressly omitted by order of ye house" (British Library, 669.f.10/38).

14 For an exhaustive discussion of Cromwell's anti-formalism, see J.C. Davis, "Cromwell's Religion," in *Oliver Cromwell and the English Revolution*, ed. John Morrill (London: Longman, 1990), 181–208.

15 Austin Woolrych, *Britain in Revolution* (Oxford: Oxford University Press, 2004); Peter Gaunt, *Oliver Cromwell* (New York: New York University Press, 2004).

16 John Morrill, *Oliver Cromwell* (Oxford: Oxford University Press, 2007), 80.

17 J.C. Davis, "Oliver Cromwell," in *The Oxford Handbook of the English Revolution*, ed. Michael J. Braddick (Oxford: Oxford University Press, 2015), 233.

18 Ibid. For more on the limits and terms of Cromwell's toleration, see Bernard Capp, "Cromwell and Religion in a Multi-Faith Society," in *Cromwell's Legacy*, ed. Jane A. Mills (Manchester: Manchester University Press, 2012), 93–112; Blair Worden, "Toleration and the Cromwellian Protectorate," in *Persecution and Toleration*, Studies in Church History 21, ed. W.J. Sheils (Oxford: Basil Blackwell for the Ecclesiastical History Society, 1984), 199–233; and Worden, "Oliver Cromwell and the Sin of Achan," in Smith, *Cromwell and the Interregnum*, 37–60.

19 See Murphy, *Conscience and Community*, 120–1.

20 Peter Gaunt, "'To Create a Little World Out of Chaos': The Protectoral Ordinances of 1653–1654 Reconsidered," in *The Cromwellian Protectorate*, ed. Patrick Little (Woodbridge, UK: Boydell Press, 2007), 105–26, points out that during this period, Cromwell and the council "completed a substantial body of legislation, most of it respectable and worthy, some of it important and innovatory, responding to the needs and demands of the state and the three nations as well as to the requests and aspirations of localities and individuals. They may not have created a 'new world' out of 'chaos,' but the ordinances of protector and council of 1653–4 did go a long way towards bringing form out of confusion and, in the words of article thirty of the constitution, they did in various ways and to differing degrees promote 'the peace and welfare of these nations'" (126). See also Coward, *Cromwellian Protectorate*, where he claims that "in contrast to the Rump Parliament, the Protector and Council had made an efficient and energetic start towards reformation" (41).

21 Coward, *Cromwellian Protectorate*, 41.

22 John Thurloe, *A Collection of the State Papers of John Thurloe, Esq.*, ed. Thomas Birch, vol. 2 (London, 1742), 588.

23 From 5 to 11 September, parliamentary proceedings were dominated by those MPs like Sir Arthur Heselrige and Thomas Scot who were dissatisfied with the Instrument of Government, and particularly the principle of government by a single person. Guibon Goddard, the MP for King's Lynne, recorded these fiery debates in his journal. See "Guibon Goddard's Journal: September 1654," in *The Diary of Thomas Burton Esq*, vol. 1, *July 1653–April 1657*, ed. J.T. Rutt (London: H. Colburn, 1828), xvii–xliv, accessed 6 September 2009, http://www.british-history.ac.uk/report.aspx?compid=36727.

24 Ibid.

25 The indenture, instead, simply states, "*I do hereby freely promise, and engage myself, to be true and faithful to the Lord Protector and the Commonwealth of England, Scotland and Ireland; and shall not (according to the tenor of the Indenture whereby I am returned to serve in this present Parliament) propose, or give my consent, to alter the Government as it is settled in a Single Person and a Parliament*" (2:391).

26 Samuel Rawson Gardiner, *History of the Commonwealth and Protectorate, 1649–1656*, vol. 3 (New York: AMS Press, 1965), 242.

27 Burton, *Diary of Thomas Burton, Esq*, 79. Coward also discusses this passage from Goddard's journal, *Cromwellian Protectorate*, 45–6.

28 Burton, *Diary of Thomas Burton*, 114, 116.

29 Little and Smith, *Parliaments and Politics*, 200–1.
30 See "The Constitutional Bill of the First Parliament of the Protectorate" in Samuel Rawson Gardiner's *The Constitutional Documents of the Puritan Revolution, 1625–1660* (Oxford: Clarendon Press, 1889), 427–59, and especially 454–5.
31 Before dissolving this parliament, Cromwell states, "As I may not take notice what you have been doing, so I think I have very great liberty to tell you that I do not know what you have been doing!" (2:407), a perception shared by Carlyle. Peter Gaunt, "Law-Making in the First Protectorate Parliament," in *Politics and People in Revolutionary England*, ed. Colin Jones, Malyn Newitt, and Stephen Roberts (Oxford: Basil Blackwell, 1985), challenges this assessment (163–86).
32 Christopher Durston, *Cromwell's Major-Generals: Godly Government during the English Revolution* (Manchester: Manchester University Press, 2001), 16–21. See also Blair Worden, *God's Instruments: Political Conduct in the England of Oliver Cromwell* (Oxford: Oxford University Press, 2012), 22–3.
33 John Biddle, *Two Letters of Mr. John Biddle* (London, 1655), 2.
34 Stephen D. Snobelen, "Biddle, John (1615/16–1662)," in *Oxford Dictionary of National Biography* (Oxford University Press, 2004–), accessed 2 May 2016, doi:10.1093/ref:odnb/2361.
35 Cromwell, *A Declaration of His Highness with the advice of his Council inviting the people of this Commonwealth to a Day of Solemn Fasting and Humiliation* (London, 1655) and *A Declaration of His Highness inviting the People of England and Wales to a Solemn Day of Fasting and Humiliation* (London, 1656).
36 Durston, *Cromwell's Major-Generals*, 21.
37 Durston argues that "these positive contemporary assessments greatly exaggerated the success of the major-generals' campaign to bring about moral reform" (ibid., 179).
38 See Ronald Hutton, *The British Republic 1649–60* (Basingstoke: Palgrave Macmillan, 1990), 67. See also Abbott, *Writings and Speeches of Oliver Cromwell*, 3:627.
39 For a more detailed account of the Protectorate's deficit, see C.H. Firth, *The Last Years of the Protectorate*, 2 vols. (New York: Russell & Russell, 1909), 2:265–9.
40 Durston, *Cromwell's Major-Generals*, 187. The elections also yielded about one hundred MPs who were not allowed to sit because of their hostility towards the regime and another forty-one who refused to sit in protest of their dismissal.

41 Leo Damrosch, "Nayler, James (1618–1660)," in *Oxford Dictionary of National Biography* (Oxford University Press, 2004–), accessed 27 July 2015, doi:10.1093/ref:odnb/19814. For an in-depth study of the Nayler case, see also Damrosch, *The Sorrows of the Quaker Jesus: James Naylor and the Puritan Crackdown on the Free Spirit* (Cambridge, MA: Harvard University Press, 1996).

42 "The Diary of Thomas Burton: 5 December 1656," in *Diary of Thomas Burton Esq*, 20–37, accessed 17 August 2014, http://www.british-history.ac.uk/report.aspx?compid=36740.

43 Damrosch, "Nayler, James (1618–1660)," 219.

44 In his letter to the Speaker, Cromwell writes that "We detest and abhor the giving or occasioning the least countenance to persons of such opinions and practices, or who are under the guilt of such crimes as are commonly imputed to the said person" (3:20). Derek Hirst, *Authority and Conflict: England, 1603–1658* (Cambridge, MA: Harvard University Press, 1986), argues that Cromwell probably "believed Nayler had blasphemed appallingly" (344). Similarly, Damrosch maintains that Cromwell most likely "believed that Nayler really had blasphemed, even if the punishment was excessive" ("Nayler, James (1618–1660)," 221).

45 C.H. Firth, *Oliver Cromwell and the Rule of the Puritans in England* (London: Putnam Covent Garden, 1901), 425.

46 Barry Coward, *Cromwellian Protectorate*, after stating that a "major personal reason for this decision was his providential world-view," goes on to identify the political reasons that Cromwell refused the crown, such as pressure from the army and other "radical Cromwellians" (89–90). Similarly, Little and Smith, *Parliaments and Politics*, mention the "importance of providence" yet posit that it was equally possible that "Cromwell realised that he was perhaps more powerful as Lord Protector than he would have been as king." For Little and Smith, the most "crucial considerations" in Cromwell's mind were "a desire not to antagonise the army" and "a fear that to accept the Crown might indicate sinful ambition and greed" (137). Gaunt, *Oliver Cromwell*, also names providence as influential in Cromwell decision, but ultimately argues that "opposition from the army, God's chosen instrument, and from good and godly individuals, swayed Cromwell" (119). One exception is Martyn Bennett, *Oliver Cromwell* (London: Routledge, 2006), who holds that "Cromwell rejected the crown because it was a tainted title for God 'hath not only dealt so with the persons and the family, but he hath blasted the title' […] It is a mark of Cromwell's political consistency, rather than an indecisive

reaction to conflicting pressures that ensured that Oliver remained a protector to the people not a king over them, the greatest pause in history was simply not a pause at all: it was a period of negotiation aimed at getting what Oliver wanted from the *Humble Petition and Advice* without having to adopt the royal title" (252).

47 This phrase comes from Gaunt, *Oliver Cromwell*, 119.
48 Burton, *Diary of Thomas Burton*, 421–3.
49 *The English Devil: Or, Cromwell and his Monstrous Witch* (London, 1660), 3, 5.
50 Ibid., 4–5.
51 Ibid., 5, 4.
52 Little and Smith, *Parliaments and Politics*, 197.

3. Early Quaker Writing and the Unifying Light of Conscience

1 Anthony Pearson, Letter to George Fox, Library of the Society of Friends, Swarthmore MS, 354/34 (1654).
2 See, for example, A.R. Barclay, ed., *Letters of Early Friends* (London: Harvey and Darton, 1841); William Braithwaite, *The Beginnings of Quakerism*, 2nd ed. (Cambridge: Cambridge University Press, 1970); J.F. Maclear, "Quakerism and the End of the Interregnum," *Church History* 19 (1950): 240–70; Alan Cole, "Quakers and the English Revolution," *Past & Present* 10 (1956): 39–54; Hugh Barbour and Arthur Roberts, eds., *Early Quaker Writings 1650–1700* (Grand Rapids, MI: William B. Eerdmans, 1973); J.F. McGregor and Barry Reay, *Radical Religion in the English Revolution* (Oxford: Oxford University Press, 1984); Barry Reay, *The Quakers and the English Revolution* (New York: St. Martin's Press, 1985); T.L. Underwood, *Primitivism, Radicalism, and the Lamb's War: The Baptist-Quaker Conflict in Seventeenth-Century England* (Oxford: Oxford University Press, 1997); Adrian Davies, *The Quakers in English Society, 1655–1725* (Oxford: Clarendon Press, 2000); Rosemary Moore, *The Light in Their Consciences: Early Quakers in Britain, 1646–1666* (University Park: Pennsylvania State University Press, 2000); Meredith Baldwin Weddle, *Walking in the Way of Peace: Quaker Pacifism in the Seventeenth Century* (Oxford: Oxford University Press, 2001).
3 Thomas N. Corns and David Loewenstein, eds., "The Emergence of Quaker Writing: Dissenting Literature in Seventeenth-Century England," special issue, *Prose Studies* 17, no. 3 (1994), which was reissued as its own book a year later: Thomas N. Corns and David Loewenstein, eds., *The Emergence of Quaker Writing: Dissenting Literature in Seventeenth-Century England* (London: Frank Cass & Co., 1995). See also Nigel Smith, *Perfection Proclaimed: Language and Literature in English Radical Religion*

1640–1660 (Oxford: Clarendon University Press, 1989), 21–105; and David Loewenstein, *Representing Revolution in Milton and His Contemporaries* (Cambridge: Cambridge University Press, 2001), 125–42. For a focus more specifically on Quaker women's writings, see Margaret J.M. Ezell, "Breaking the Seventh Seal: Writings by Early Quaker Women," in *Writing Women's Literary History* (Baltimore: Johns Hopkins University Press, 1992), 132–60; Phyllis Mack, *Visionary Women: Ecstatic Prophecy in Seventeenth-Century England* (Berkeley: University of California Press, 1992); Marilyn S. Luecke, "'God Hath Made No Difference Such As Men Would': Margaret Fell and the Politics of Women's Speech," *Bunyan Studies* 7 (1997): 73–95; David Booy, *Autobiographical Writings by Early Quaker Women* (Aldershot: Ashgate, 2004); Catie Gill, *Women in the Seventeenth-Century Quaker Community: A Literary Study of Political Identities, 1650–1700* (Aldershot: Ashgate, 2005); Teresa Feroli, "Margaret Fell's *Womens Speaking Justified* and Quaker Ideas of Female Subjectivity," in *Political Speaking Justified: Women Prophets and the English Revolution* (Newark: University of Delaware Press, 2006), 148–95.

4 Despite the title of Moore's study (*The Light in Their Consciences*), neither the idea nor the language of conscience as it was used by Quakers during this period is central to her analysis.

5 Two exceptions here would be Cole and Reay. Both mention other figures in addition to Fox, like Edward Burrough and even George Bishop, in their discussions of Cromwell, yet they do not focus closely on the correspondences themselves.

6 Worden, "Toleration and the Cromwellian Protectorate, 199–233; Davis, "Cromwell's Religion," 181–208; Barry Coward, *Oliver Cromwell* (London: Longman, 1991) and *Cromwellian Protectorate*; and John Coffey, "The Toleration Controversy during the English Revolution," in *Religion in Revolutionary England*, ed. Christopher Durston and Judith Maltby (Manchester: Manchester University Press, 2005), 42–68.

7 Godfrey Davis, *The Early Stuarts 1603–1660* (Oxford: Clarendon Press, 1937), 195. See also Braithwaite, *Beginnings of Quakerism*, who similarly made little distinction between the early Quaker movement and their less politically involved successors.

8 Reprinted in Margaret Fell, *A Brief Collection of Remarkable Passages and Occurrences Relating to the Birth, Education, Life, Conversion, Travel, Services, and Deep Sufferings of that Ancient, Eminent, and Faithful Servant of the Lord, Margaret Fell* (London: J. Sowle, 1710), 75.

9 George Fox, *The Great Mystery of the Great Whore Unfolded* (London, 1659; repr., Philadelphia: Marcus T. Gould, and New York: Isaac T. Hopper, 1831),

518. Quakers were often at pains to make this distinction between their ideas of the "light within" and the "conscience." Moore points out that "Quakers were not consistent in the ways they used the word 'light.' They very rarely equated 'the light' with the Holy Spirit, and were often unclear about its relation to Christ. Their commonest phrases were 'the light of Christ' or simply 'the light,' and they often used the word in a way difficult to distinguish from 'conscience.' Opponents agreed that everybody had a conscience, but not that it was divine. Most writers who argued with Quakers, like Thomas Weld, wrote of two lights, a 'natural' light of conscience, which was part of the human make-up, and a 'divine' light that was the Holy Spirit" (*Light in Their Consciences*, 102–3). Even modern-day Quakers strive to make this distinction between the conscience and the Light: In *Friends for 350 Years* (Wallingford, PA: Pendle Hill, 2002), Howard H. Brinton points out that "the Light Within is not to be identified with conscience. Conscience is not the Light in its fullness but 'the measure of Light given us.' The Light illumines conscience and seeks to transform an impure conscience into its own pure likeness. Conscience is partly a product of the Light which shines into it and partly a product of social environment. Therefore conscience is fallible" (43).

10 James Nayler, *A Discovery of the Man of Sin* (London, 1654), A2.

11 "Convincement" referred to one who had become convinced of Quaker truth. It was generally thought to be the first step towards full conversion.

12 Barbour and Roberts, *Early Quaker Writings*, 159, 156.

13 Naylor, *A Vindication of Truth, As held forth in a Book* (London, 1656), 47. See also Moore regarding historical versus spiritual atonement: *Light in Their Consciences*, 107.

14 Naylor, *A Vindication*, 47; and Margaret Fell, *Undaunted Zeal: The Letters of Margaret Fell*, ed. Elsa F. Glines (Richmond, IN: Friends United Press, 2003), 61. All subsequent references to Fell's letters are from this edition unless otherwise indicated and are cited parenthetically.

15 Naylor, *Several Papers; Some of them given forth by George Fox; others by James Nayler* (London, 1654), 13.

16 Edward Burrough, *A Discovery of Divine Mysteries; Wherein is Unfoulded Secret Things of the Kingdom of God* (London, 1661), 26, 27. The next chapter, entitled "Concerning the Diversity of Judgments in Religion," similarly asserts that "The Cause of your Divisions, and of the Diversities of Judgements and Opinions that are amongst you concerning the things and matters of God's Kingdom, is, *Because you want the Spirit of God to guide you, and it is not the Rule of your Knowledge and Judgment*; and you [are] wanting the *Spirit of God*, in which is Unity among Saints" (29).

17 John Punshon, *Portrait in Grey: A Short History of the Quakers* (London: Quaker Home Services, 1984), points out that "it would be a mistake to regard [the Light] as a part of human nature, a personal possession, a fragment of divinity, our bit of God. The light is in all, but it is the same light that is in all, not sparks from the eternal flame. There are not many lights, but only one [...] Because it is common to all of us, the light calls us into unity with one another, into the community, into what we have seen George Fox call 'the Church in God, the general assembly written in heaven'" (50). See also Booy, *Autobiographical Writings by Early Quaker Women*, 9.

18 William Dewsbury, *Several Letters Written to the Saints of the Most High* (London, 1654), 3.

19 Edmund Skipp, *The Worlds Wonder, or the Quakers Blazing Starr* (London, 1654), 7, 8.

20 Humphrey Smith, *Something in reply to Edmund Skipps Book, which he calles the Worlds Wonder* (London, 1655), 17.

21 Fox, *The Great Mystery*, 491–2.

22 Fell, *A Brief Collection*, 75.

23 Davies, *Quakers in English Society*, 108; Corns and Loewenstein, *Emergence of Quaker Writing*, 1.

24 Kate Peters, "Patterns of Quaker Authorship, 1652–1656," in "The Emergence of Quaker Writing: Dissenting Literature in Seventeenth-Century England," ed. Thomas N. Corns and David Loewenstein, special issue, *Prose Studies* 17, no. 3 (1994): 8. For a more extensive treatment of this topic, see Peters's *Print Culture and the Early Quakers* (Cambridge: Cambridge University Press, 2005).

25 John Gaskin, *A Just Defence and Vindication of Gospel Ministers and Gospel Ordinances against the Quakers* (London, 1660), "To the Reader."

26 William Thomas, *Rayling Rebuked: Or, a Defence of the Ministers of this Nation* (London, 1656), "Epistle."

27 Davies, *Quakers in English Society*, 109–10.

28 William Dewsbury, *A True Prophecy of the Mighty Day of the Lord* (London, 1655), 1, 11, 3.

29 Ibid., 3.

30 Ibid., 3, 5.

31 George Fox, *To the Protector and Parliament of England* (London, 1657), 7–8.

32 The Library of the Religious Society of Friends, Spence MS 3/90 only indicates the year that this letter was written, "1653." Cromwell was installed as Lord Protector on 16 December, so it is possible that she wrote this letter after he was sworn in, especially since in this letter she writes "Not for any favour or protection from thee as thou art A governour."

33 See Barry Reay, "Quaker Opposition to Tithes 1652–1660," *Past & Present* 86 (1980): 98–120.

34 Barry Reay, "Quakerism and Society," in McGregor and Reay, *Radical Religion in the English Revolution*, 157–8; Davies, *Quakers in English Society*, 169–90.

35 *The Cry of the Oppressed from under their Oppressions* (London, 1656); "The Great Book of Sufferings," 44 vols. (1650–1856), is held in the Library of the Religious Society of Friends.

36 *The Cry of the Oppressed from under their Oppressions*, 32.

37 Elizabeth Hooten, Letter to Oliver Cromwell, Library of the Religious Society of Friends, Port MS 3/3 (1653).

38 Thomas Aldam, Letters to Oliver Cromwell, Library of the Religious Society of Friends, Port MS 36/117 (1654); Port MS 1/5a (1654); Port MS 1/9 (1654).

39 Aldam to Cromwell, Port MS 36/117.

40 Quoted in Geoffrey F. Nuttall, *Studies in Christian Enthusiasm: Illustrated from Early Quakerism* (Wallingford, PA: Pendle Hill, 1948), 33.

41 The date of Fell's second letter is also an estimate. The date in the Library of the Religious Society of Friends, Spence MS 3/93–4 appears as 1657; yet, as Glines points out in *Undaunted Zeal*, this date cannot be correct according to the topical events that Fell refers to in the letter, which occurred on 2 February 1654.

42 Barbour and Roberts, *Early Quaker Writings*, 384–5.

43 John Camm and Francis Howgill, *This was the Word of the Lord which John Camm and Francis Howgill Was moved to declare and write to Oliver Cromwell* (London, 1654), A2–A3.

44 Ibid., A4–A4v.

45 William Dewsbury, Letter to Oliver Cromwell, Library of the Religious Society of Friends, Caton MS 1:1–7, formerly the Barclay Box/3/1–3,1 (1655).

46 Ibid., 2, 5.

47 Ibid., 4–5.

48 William Dewsbury, Letter to Thomas Aldam, Library of the Religious Society of Friends, Port MS 15/26 (1655). This letter (a handwritten transcription of the original) is dated "The 14 day of the 2 Mo 1547," which clearly cannot be correct.

49 John Stubbs, Letter to Oliver Cromwell, Library of the Religious Society of Friends, Port MS 33/142–45, 142 (1654/5).

50 David Underdown, *Royalist Conspiracy in England, 1649–1660* (New Haven: Yale University Press, 1960), 163.

51 Ibid., 163. It is not clear whether or not this Hannam is the same man as the notorious thief executed in 1656.

52 See Gardiner, *History of the Commonwealth and Protectorate*, 368; and Worden, "Oliver Cromwell and the Sin of Achan."

53 This letter was later printed in George Bishop, *The Warnings of the Lord to the Men of this Generation* (London, 1660), 1–17, 1–2.

54 Ibid., 3.

55 Ibid., 7.

56 Ibid., 9.

57 Durston, *Cromwell's Major-Generals*.

58 Ibid., 139.

59 Edward Burrough and George Fox, *Good Counsel and Advice Rejected by Disobedient Men* (London, 1659), 21, 26, 3.

60 Ibid., 15, 7.

61 Ibid., 29–30.

62 Reflecting on Cromwell's failures, Fox and Burrough later published these letters as part of *Counsel and Advice* to reveal that *"the downfalls of these men* [Oliver and Richard Cromwell] *were not before sufficient warning"* (2).

63 Edward Burrough, *To the Rulers and to such as are in Authority* (London, 1659), 2–3.

64 Ibid., 9–10.

65 Ibid., 9.

66 Moore, *Light in Their Consciences*, 219–20.

67 Henry J. Cadbury, ed., *The Swarthmore Documents in America* (London: Friends' Historical Society, 1940), a supplement to *Journal of the Friends' Historical Society* 20 (1940): 49.

68 Burrough, *A Discovery of Divine Mysteries*, 27; Margaret Fell, *A Touch-Stone: Or, A Tryal by the Scriptures, of the Priests, Bishops, and Ministers* (London, 1666), reprinted in Fell, *A Brief Collection of Remarkable Passages*, 419.

4. Thomas Hobbes's *Leviathan* and the Civilizing Force of Conscience

1 Samuel Parker, *A Discourse of Ecclesiastical Politie* (London, 1670), 4. All subsequent references to this book are cited parenthetically as "*A Discourse.*"

2 J.A.I. Champion, "*An Historical Narration Concerning Heresie*: Thomas Hobbes, Thomas Barlow, and the Restoration Debate over 'Heresy,'" in *Heresy, Literature, and Politics in Early Modern English Culture*, ed. David Loewenstein and John Marshall (Cambridge: Cambridge University Press, 2006), 223.

3 Christopher N. Warren, "When Self-Preservation Bids: Approaching
 Milton, Hobbes, and Dissent," *English Literary Renaissance* 37 (2007): 124.

4 The first quotation is from Norberto Bobbio, *Thomas Hobbes and the Natural
 Law Tradition*, trans. Daniela Gobetti (Chicago: University of Chicago Press,
 1993), 70; and is quoted by R.S. White, *Natural Law in English Renaissance
 Literature* (Cambridge: Cambridge University Press, 1996), 244; the second
 appears in Catherine Gimelli Martin, "The Phoenix and the Crocodile:
 Milton's Natural Law Debate with Hobbes Retried in the Tragic Forum
 of *Samson Agonistes*," in *The English Civil Wars in the Literary Imagination*,
 ed. Claude J. Summers and Ted-Larry Pebworth (Columbia: University of
 Missouri Press, 1999), 257. Along similar lines, Keith Pepperell, "Religious
 Conscience and Civic Conscience in Thomas Hobbes's Civic Philosophy,"
 Educational Theory 39, no. 1 (1989): 17–25, argues that the "private
 conscience" "ought to have been properly subjugated to the public
 (civic) conscience of the sovereign as embodied in the civil law" (22); and
 Edward G. Andrew, "Hobbes on Conscience within the Law and Without,"
 Canadian Journal of Political Science 32, no. 2 (1999): 203–25, pits Hobbes
 against Locke, arguing, "Hobbes was skeptical about claims of conscience,
 except for the rights of defendants and jurors, conscience institutionalized
 within the law. For the Hobbesian point of view, Lockeian rights of
 conscience are both intolerant and revolutionary, antinomianism unyoked
 to law" (225).

5 Karsten Fischer, "Hobbes, Schmitt, and the Paradox of Religious
 Liberality," *Critical Review of International Social and Political Philosophy*
 13, nos. 2–3 (2010): 400. Lucien Jaume, "Hobbes and the Philosophical
 Sources of Liberalism," in *The Cambridge Companion to Hobbes's Leviathan*,
 ed. Patricia Springborg (Cambridge: Cambridge University Press, 2007),
 199–216, similarly argues that Hobbes "inspired liberalism" (201). See also
 Carl Schmitt, *The Leviathan in the State Theory of Thomas Hobbes: Meaning
 and Failure of a Political Symbol*, trans. George Schwab and Erna Hilfstein
 (Chicago: University of Chicago Press, 2008), who spearheaded this thesis
 in 1938. J. Judd Owen, "The Tolerant Leviathan: Hobbes and the Paradox
 of Liberalism," *Polity* 37, no. 1 (2005): 130–48, takes this idea one step
 further by arguing that Hobbes's liberalism is paradoxical, which reflects
 the paradoxical nature of liberalism itself (130).

6 See Quentin Skinner's *Hobbes and Republican Liberty* (Cambridge:
 Cambridge University Press, 2008), 169. See also Warren's "When Self-
 Preservation Bids," for a similar argument regarding Hobbes's views on
 the freedom of conscience.

7 Gabriella Slomp, "The Liberal Slip of Thomas Hobbes's Authoritarian Pen," *Critical Review of International Social and Political Philosophy* 13, nos. 2–3 (Spring 2010): 357–69.

8 Alan Ryan, "A More Tolerant Hobbes?" in *Justifying Toleration: Conceptual and Historical Perspectives*, ed. Susan Mendus (Cambridge: Cambridge University Press, 1988), 51. See also Alan Ryan, "Hobbes, Toleration, and the Inner Life," in *The Nature of Political Theory*, ed. David Miller and Larry Seidentop (Oxford: Clarendon Press, 1983), 197–218.

9 Richard Tuck, "Hobbes and Locke on Toleration," in *Thomas Hobbes and Political Theory*, ed. Mary G. Dietz (Lawrence: University Press of Kansas, 1990), 153–71. See also Edwin Curley, "Hobbes and the Cause of Religious Toleration," in Springborg, *Cambridge Companion to Hobbes's Leviathan*, 309–34.

10 Tralau, "Hobbes contra Liberty of Conscience," *Political Theory* 39, no. 1 (2011): 71.

11 Ibid., 77.

12 Thomas Hobbes, *Leviathan*, ed. Richard Tuck (Cambridge: Cambridge University Press, 1991), 48. All subsequent references to this text are from this edition and cited parenthetically.

13 C.S. Lewis, *Studies in Words* (Cambridge: Cambridge University Press, 1960), 190.

14 John Eachard, *Some Opinions of Mr Hobbes Considered in a Second Dialogue Between Philautus and Timothy* (London, 1673), 269–70.

15 Richard Sibbes, *A Learned Commentary or Exposition: Upon the First Chapter of the Second Epistle of S. Paul to the Corinthians* (London, 1655), 224. Lewis traces the origin of this proverb to Quintilian, "conscientia mille testes."

16 Ibid., 223.

17 Karen S. Feldman, *Binding Words: Conscience and Rhetoric in Hobbes, Hegel, and Heidegger* (Evanston, IL: Northwestern University Press, 2006), 30–1.

18 See also 73–4, where Hobbes argues that the "doctrine of Right and Wrong, is perpetually disputed, both by the Pen and the Sword" because individuals "appeale from custome to reason, and from reason to custome, as it serves their turn; receding from custome when their interest requires it, and setting themselves against reason, as oft as reason is against them."

19 Kinch Hoekstra argues that "we clamour for liberty, for equality, or for rights without realizing that we are demanding misery and destruction. We naturally prefer felicity and self-preservation, so if Hobbes makes us realize this, he will bring us to obey, and save us from ourselves." "Hobbes on the Natural Condition of Mankind," in Springborg, *Cambridge Companion to Hobbes's Leviathan*, 122.

20 Horst Bredekamp, "Thomas Hobbes's Visual Strategies," in Springborg, *Cambridge Companion to Hobbes's Leviathan*, 38.

21 Thomas Elyot, *The Boke Named the Gouernour* (London, 1534), 3r.

22 One exception is Gabriel Harvey's mention of a "publique Conscience" in *Pierces Supererogation or A new prayse of the old asse* (London, 1593), 117.

23 John Saltmarsh, *The Smoke in the Temple Wherein is a Designe for Peace and Reconciliation of Believers* (London, 1646), 17; Stephen Marshall, *An Expedient to Preserve Peace and Amity, Among Dissenting Brethren* (London, 1647), 34–5.

24 Jon Parkin, *Taming the Leviathan: The Reception of the Political and Religious Ideas of Thomas Hobbes in England 1640–1700* (Cambridge: Cambridge University Press, 2007), 177.

25 Jonathan Scott, "The Rapture of Motion: James Harrington's Republicanism," in *Political Discourse in Early Modern Britain*, ed. Nicholas Phillipson and Quentin Skinner (Cambridge: Cambridge University Press, 1993), 162. Luc Borot similarly argues that "there is a Hobbist in Harrington," in "Religion in Harrington's Political System: The Central Concepts and Methods of Harrington's Religious Solutions," in *Perspectives on English Revolutionary Republicanism*, ed. Dirk Wiemann and Gaby Mahlberg (Farnham: Ashgate, 2014), 149.

26 Matthew Wren, *Considerations on Mr. Harrington's Common-wealth of Oceana* (London, 1657), 44.

27 James Harrington, *The Prerogative of Popular Government* (London, 1657), 36.

28 Scott, "The Rapture of Motion," 160.

29 James Harrington, *The Commonwealth of Oceana and A System of Politics*, ed. J.G.A. Pocock (Cambridge: Cambridge University Press, 1992), 244. All subsequent references to this text are from this edition and cited parenthetically.

30 See, for instance, his description of the parliament as the heart of this body (174).

31 Jonathan Scott, *Commonwealth Principles: Republican Writing of the English Revolution* (Cambridge: Cambridge University Press, 2004), 53; see also Mark Goldie, "The Civil Religion of James Harrington," in *The Languages of Political Theory in Early-Modern Europe*, ed. Anthony Pagden (Cambridge: Cambridge University Press, 1987), 197–222.

32 Goldie, "Civil Religion of James Harrington," 207.

33 Harrington does use the phrase "public conscience" several years later in *The Art of Lawgiving in Three Books* (1659). See *The Political Works of James Harrington*, ed. J.G.A. Pocock (Cambridge: Cambridge University Press, 1977), 681.

34 Scott, *Commonwealth Principles*, 284.
35 H.M. Höpfl, "Harrington, James (1611–1677)," in *Oxford Dictionary of National Biography* (Oxford University Press, 2004–), accessed 1 June 2015, doi:10.1093/ref:odnb/12375.
36 Goldie, "Civil Religion of James Harrington." 207.
37 For more on *Oceana* as a form of counsel to Cromwell, see Scott, *Commonwealth Principles*, 284–93; Norbrook, *Writing the English Republic*, 363–74; and Benjamin Woodford, *Perceptions of a Monarchy without a King: Reactions to Oliver Cromwell's Power* (Montreal: McGill-Queen's University Press, 2013), 164–79.
38 Scott, *Commonwealth Principles*, 291.
39 John Toland, "The Life of James Harrington," in *The Oceana of James Harrington … with An Exact Account of his Life* (London, 1700), xx.
40 Although dated 1670, the actual publication date must have been 1669 since several responses appeared that year. See Jon Parkin, "Hobbism in the Later 1660s: Daniel Scargill and Samuel Parker," *Historical Journal* 42, no. 1 (1999): 97n.
41 Jon Parkin, "Parker, Samuel (1640–1688)," in *Oxford Dictionary of National Biography* (Oxford University Press, 2004–), accessed 4 June 2015, doi:10.1093/ref:odnb/21336.
42 Gary De Krey coined this terminology in "The First Restoration Crisis: Conscience and Coercion in London, 1667–73," *Albion* 25 (1993): 565–80. See also De Krey, "Rethinking the Restoration: Dissenting Cases for Conscience, 1667–1672," *Historical Journal* 38 (1995): 53–83.
43 De Krey, "The First Restoration Crisis," 566.
44 Benjamin Laney, *A Sermon Preached Before His Majesty* (London, 1665), 26–7.
45 I borrow this phrase from Parkin's "Hobbism in the Later 1660s," 108.
46 Parkin points out that "calling Parker a Hobbist was a popular tactic" after the publication of *A Discourse*. See "Liberty Transpros'd: Andrew Marvell and Samuel Parker," in *Marvell and Liberty*, ed. Warren Chernaik and Martin Dzelzainis (Houndmills, Basingstoke: Macmillan Press, 1999), 273.
47 John Humfrey, *A Case of Conscience* (London, 1669), 12.
48 Andrew Marvell, *The Rehearsal Transpros'd: The Second Part*, ed. D.I.B. Smith (Oxford: Clarendon Press, 1971), 214.
49 *Insolence and Impudence Triumphant* (London, 1669), 5–6.
50 Marvell, *The Rehearsal Transpros'd: The Second Part*, 289; Marvell, *The Rehearsal Transpros'd: The First Part*, ed. D.I.B. Smith (Oxford: Clarendon Press, 1971), 52.
51 Marvell, *The Rehearsal Transpros'd: The Second Part*, 256–7, 243, 257.
52 John Owen, *Truth and Innocence Vindicated* (London, 1669), 373, 374.

53 Samuel Parker, *A Defence and Continuation of the Ecclesiastical Politie* (London, 1671), 279, 280. Parker accuses Owen of coupling his passage about the public conscience "with another sentence above two hundred Pages distance, that speaks *of the most important parts* of Religion [as] if they had been spoken upon the same occasion, and related to the same matter" (280). It is unclear as to which passage he is referring. Owen does cite a passage several pages earlier which he does relate to the public conscience passage, but that passage appears about one hundred pages prior to the passage under question (211–13).
54 Samuel Parker, *A Reproof to the Rehearsal Transposed* (London, 1673), 36.
55 Owen, *Truth and Innocence Vindicated*, 377.
56 Ibid., 408, 389.
57 *Insolence and Impudence*, 20.

5. Lucy Hutchinson's Revisions of Conscience

1 Lucy Hutchinson, *Memoirs of the Life of Colonel Hutchinson*, ed. James Sutherland (London: Oxford University Press, 1973), 229. All subsequent references to the *Memoirs* will be to this edition unless otherwise noted and will be cited parenthetically.
2 See ibid., xviii; Lucy Hutchinson, *Memoirs of the Life of Colonel Hutchinson*, ed. N.H. Keeble (London: J.M. Dent, 1995), xxvii. This is with the exception of Lucy Hutchinson, *Memoirs of the Life of Colonel Hutchinson*, 2 vols., ed. C.H. Firth (London, 1885); and Derek Hirst, "Remembering a Hero: Lucy Hutchinson's *Memoirs* of Her Husband," in *Ashgate Critical Essays on Women Writers in England, 1550–1700*, vol. 5, *Anne Clifford and Lucy Hutchinson*, ed. Mihoko Suzuki (Aldershot: Ashgate, 2009), 263–72, whose close attention to Firth's argument has brought to light – once again – the discrepancy in Lucy Hutchinson's account.
3 *Memoirs of the Life of Colonel Hutchinson* (Firth), 1:xix, xxi.
4 Hirst, "Remembering a Hero," 265; David Norbrook, "Memoirs and Oblivion: Lucy Hutchinson and the Restoration," *Huntington Library Quarterly* 75, no. 2 (2012): 260.
5 Norbrook, "Memoirs and Oblivion."
6 Christopher Hill, "Colonel John Hutchinson, 1615–1664: A Tercentenary Tribute," *Transactions of the Thoroton Society of Nottinghamshire* 69 (1965): 86; N.H. Keeble, "'The Colonel's Shadow': Lucy Hutchinson, Women's Writing and the Civil War," in *Literature and the English Civil War*, ed. Thomas Healy and Jonathan Sawday (Cambridge: Cambridge University Press, 1990), 229; David Norbrook, "Margaret Cavendish and Lucy

Hutchinson: Identity, Ideology, and Politics," *In-between* 9 (2000): 192. See also Susan Cook, "'The Story I Most Particularly Intend': The Narrative Style of Lucy Hutchinson," *Critical Survey* 5, no. 3 (1993): 271–7; Devoney Looser, *British Women Writers and the Writing of History, 1670–1820* (Baltimore: Johns Hopkins University Press, 2000); Paul Salzman, *Reading Early Modern Women's Writing* (Oxford: Oxford University Press, 2006); Robert Mayer, "Lucy Hutchinson: A Life of Writing," in Suzuki, *Ashgate Critical Essays on Women Writers*, 469–500.

7 Keeble, "'The Colonel's Shadow,'" 228.

8 See Norbrook, "Memoirs and Oblivion."

9 Both Firth and Sutherland have included the letter, while N.H. Keeble's recent edition does not include it.

10 *Oxford English Dictionary*, s.v. "conviction," 1, 3, 6, http://www.oed.com.

11 Francis Bloomefield, *An Essay towards a Topographical History of the County of Norfolk*, vol. 3, *The History of the City and County of Norwich, part I* (London, 1806), 399–403, accessed 1 July 2010, http://www.britishhistory.ac.uk/report.aspx?compid=78000Q1.

12 William Bankes, Diary of the Convention Parliament, Lancashire Record Office, DD/Ba, Bankes Family Papers, *sub* 11 May. Hirst also notes the diarist's report, "Remembering a Hero," 268–9.

13 Because another diarist's account, Sir Edward Dering, does not mention Hutchinson's comment about working for the Restoration, Norbrook concludes that it "was not emphasized very strongly" ("Memoirs and Oblivion," 248). Yet he would certainly not have had to emphasize such a point very strongly for his wife to recall it.

14 Quoted in Firth, *Last Years of the Protectorate*, 1:xxi; and Hirst, "Remembering a Hero," 266. Hirst identifies the original source as R.W. Blencowe, ed., *The Sydney Papers* (London, 1825), 196.

15 Edmund Ludlow, *A Voyce from the Watch Tower, Part Five: 1660–1662*, ed. A.B. Worden (London: University College London, 1978), 175.

16 See Hirst, "Remembering a Hero," 267–8.

17 "House of Commons Journal Volume 8: 9 June 1660," in *Journal of the House of Commons*, vol. 8, *1660–1667* (London, 1802), 59–61, accessed September 2015, http://www.british-history.ac.uk/commons-jrnl/vol8/pp59-61.

18 Firth, *Last Years of the Protectorate*, 1:xx.

19 The surviving parts of the manuscript, fragmented in the nineteenth century, are now British Library Additional MSS 25,901, 39,779, and 46,172N. The most in-depth discussion of this manuscript to date is Sydney Race's "The British Museum MS of the Life of Colonel Hutchinson and Its Relation to the Published Memoirs," *Transactions of the Thoroton*

Society 18 (1914): 35–66. For a more detailed account of John Hutchinson's role as governor of both the castle and town, see P.R. Seddon, "Colonel Hutchison and the Disputes between Nottinghamshire Parliaments, 1643–45," *Transactions of the Thoroton Society of Nottinghamshire* 98 (1994): 71–81.

20 Norbrook, "'But a Copie': Textual Authority and Gender in Editions of *The Life of John Hutchinson*," in Suzuki, *Ashgate Critical Essays*, 275. Following Norbrook's lead, as well as the forthcoming Oxford edition, I will refer to this manuscript throughout as the "Defense of John Hutchinson," though Hutchinson herself did not assign a title to the document.

21 Norbrook, "'But a Copie,'" also makes this point (275).

22 Lucy Hutchinson, "Defense of John Hutchinson," British Library Additional MS 25901, 68.

23 Ibid., 60v.

24 Race also notes Lucy Hutchinson's deliberate choice not to include this episode in the *Memoirs* ("British Museum MS," 50–2).

25 P.R. Seddon, "Hutchinson, John (*bap.* 1615, *d.* 1664)," in *Oxford Dictionary of National Biography* (Oxford University Press, 2004–), accessed 8 July 2010, doi:10.1093/ref:odnb/14283.

26 Hutchinson, "Defense of John Hutchinson," British Library Additional MS 25901, 73.

27 Ibid., 86.

28 Ibid., 70–70v.

29 Norbrook, "'But a Copie,'" 276.

30 Hutchinson, "Defense of John Hutchinson," British Library Additional MS 25901, 34.

31 Commenting on this episode, Firth quotes Ludlow, who wrote that "some of us expressing our dissatisfaction, desired that our protestation might be entered but that being denied as against the orders of the House, I contented myself to declare publicly that being convinced that they had deserted the common cause and interest of the nation, I could no longer join with them." He also notes that "if Colonel Hutchinson actually entered a protest, it must have been erased," a sentiment that Lucy Hutchinson herself includes in the *Memoirs* (*Last Years of the Protectorate*, 2:147n).

32 Keeble, "'The Colonel's Shadow,'" 236. Norbrook, "'But a Copie,'" similarly points out that "if the text remained largely within her family, it was because it would have been politically dangerous to circulate it further" (275).

33 Hutchinson, *Memoirs*, 36, 72, 146, 167.

34 This MS is held in the Nottinghamshire Archives, ref. DD/HU/4, and this index can be found at the end of the MS.

35 Norbrook, "'But a Copie,'" 277.

36 Unfortunately, the last line of the *Memoirs* has been scratched out and is mostly illegible. We cannot know if this was Hutchinson's editorial choice or that of one of her descendants.

37 *Oxford English Dictionary*, s.v. "preserve," 1.a, http://www.oed.com.

38 The first five books of *Order and Disorder* were published in 1679; but since much of the text was too radical for publication, it was published for the first time in full in 2001 and edited by Norbrook.

39 Lucy Hutchinson, *Order and Disorder*, ed. David Norbrook (Oxford: Blackwell, 2001), 17:330–42.

40 David Norbrook, "A Devine Originall: Lucy Hutchinson and the 'Woman's Version,'" *TLS*, March 19, 1999: 14.

6. Milton's Nation of Conscience

1 Milton, *Complete Prose Works*, 7:458, 433–4, 445. All subsequent references to Milton's prose are from this edition and cited parenthetically as *CPW* and by volume and page number.

2 See especially Loewenstein and Stevens, *Early Modern Nationalism and Milton's England*; and Sauer, *Milton, Toleration, and Nationhood*. See also Linda Gregerson, "Milton and the Tragedy of Nations," *PMLA* 129, no. 4 (2014): 672–87.

3 Conscience in Milton has been traditionally viewed through a theological lens. See, for example, Lee Jacobus, "Self-Knowledge in *Paradise Lost*: Conscience and Contemplation," *Milton Studies* 3 (1971): 103–18; Camille Wells Slights, "A Hero of Conscience: Samson Agonistes and Casuistry," *PMLA* 90, no. 3 (1975): 395–413; Alinda Sumers, "Milton's 'Umpire Conscience,' the 'Two-Handed Engine,' and the English Protestant Tradition of the Divine Similitude," in *A Fine Tuning: Studies of the Religious Poetry of Herbert and Milton*, ed. Mary A. Maleski (Binghamton, NY: Center for Medieval and Early Renaissance Studies, 1989), 221–48; Anthony Low, "'Umpire Conscience': Freedom, Obedience, and the Cartesian Flight from Calvin in *Paradise Lost*," *Studies in Philology* 96 (1999): 348–65; Diana Treviño Benet, "Adam's Evil Conscience and Satan's Surrogate Fall," *Milton Quarterly* 39, no. 1 (2005): 2–15. For other (especially more recent) studies that do include some political aspects, albeit not nationalism, see Achinstein, "Milton Catches the Conscience of the King," 143–63; Lana

Cable, "Secularizing Conscience in Milton's Republican Community," in *Milton and Toleration*, ed. Sharon Achinstein and Elizabeth Sauer (Oxford: Oxford University Press, 2007), 268–83; Jessica C. Beckman, "Milton's Evolving Faculty of Conscience: 'On the New Forcers of Conscience,' *A Treatise of Civil Power*, and *Paradise Lost*," *Exemplaria* 24, nos. 1–2 (2012): 46–61; David R. Schmitt, "Heroic Deeds of Conscience: Milton's Stand against Religious Conformity in *Paradise Regained*," *Huntington Library Quarterly* 76, no. 1 (2013): 105–35.

4 Achinstein, "Milton Catches the Conscience of the King," 159, 158.

5 Sauer sees this image as "indebted to the figure of the widowed Judah after the fall of the sinful Jerusalem in the Lamentations (of Jeremiah)" (*Milton, Toleration, and Nationhood*, 27).

6 Robert Greville, *A Discourse Opening the Natvre of that Episcopacie, which is Exercised in England* (London, 1641), 62.

7 Numbers 6:8.

8 The eagle's ability to renew its youth is mentioned in Psalms 103:5. In *Myrrour of the World or Thymage of the Same* (London, 1481), William Caxton maintains that "whan the Egle is moche aged he fleeth so hye that he passeth the clowdes / And holdeth there his syght so long ayenst the sonne / that he hath all loste it and brente alle his fethers / Thenne he falleth doun on a montayn in the water that he hath to fore chosen / and in this manere he reneweth his lyf" ("Of the maner of byrdes of thyse forsayd contrees Capitulo").

9 Sharon Achinstein notes that "conscience is central to Milton's argument" in *Areopagitica* in her *Milton and the Revolutionary Reader* (Princeton, NJ: Princeton University Press, 1994), 63.

10 Milton explicitly excludes Catholics and those engaging in "open superstition" from his national vision (*CPW* 2:565).

11 *John Milton: Complete Shorter Poems*, ed. Stella Revard (Oxford: Blackwell, 2009), 314–15. All subsequent references to Milton's sonnets are from this edition and are cited parenthetically by line number.

12 Ann Hughes, "'Popular' Presbyterianism in the 1640s and 1650s: The Cases of Thomas Edwards and Thomas Hall," in *England's Long Reformation: 1500–1800*, ed. Nicholas Tyacke (London: University College London Press, 1998), 239.

13 Thomas Edwards, *Gangraena* (London, 1646), A4v. For a detailed study of this important text, see Hughes, *Gangraena and the Struggle for the English Revolution*.

14 Edwards argues, "God accounts all those errours, heresies, and schismes, &c. committed in a land, but let alone, and suffered without punishment

by those who have power, and he will proceed against them as if they were the authors of them. A man comes to be a partaker of other mens sins, by countenancing, consenting and suffering without punishment, as well as by formally committing them" (*Gangraena*, A6r).

15 Bernard Capp, *England's Culture Wars: Puritan Reformation and Its Enemies in the Interregnum, 1649–1660* (Oxford: Oxford University Press, 2012), 42.

16 Cornelius Burges, *A Vindication of the Ministers of the Gospel in and about London* (London, 1649). See, for example, *The Humble Advice and Earnest Desires of Certain Well-Affected Ministers* (London, 1649), 8; and *To the Right Honorable, Thomas Lo: Fairfax, General of the Army, and the Councel of Officers under His Command: A Sincere and Respective Manifestation of the Judgments of Ministers of the Gospel within the County of Essex* (London, 1648), 3.

17 *Humble Advice and Earnest Desires*, 4, 10. The 47 signatories to *A Serious and Faithfull Representation of the Judgments of Ministers of the Gospell Within the Province of London* (Thomas Gataker; London, 1649), similarly appeal directly to Fairfax and the army's own consciences (7).

18 "House of Commons Journal Volume 6: 3 February 1649," in *Journal of the House of Commons*, vol. 6, *1648–1651* (London, 1802), 130–1, accessed 28 January 2015, http://www.british-history.ac.uk/commons-jrnl/vol6/pp130-131.

19 Capp, *England's Culture Wars*, 41–4.

20 Barbara Lewalski, *The Life of John Milton* (Oxford: Blackwell, 2000), 231.

21 Ibid., 266–7.

22 Daems and Nelson, *Eikon Basilike*, 88, 68.

23 Knoppers, *Constructing Cromwell*.

24 Worden, *The Rump*, 292–8.

25 Stephen B. Dobranski, "Licensing Milton's Heresy," in *Milton and Heresy*, ed. Stephen B. Dobranski and John P. Rumrich (Cambridge: Cambridge University Press, 1998), 148. See also Martin Dzelzainis, "Milton and Antitrinitarianism," in Achinstein and Sauer, *Milton and Toleration*, 177n16.

26 "House of Commons Journal Volume 7: 10 February 1652," in *Journal of the House of Commons*, vol. 7, *1651–1660* (London, 1802), 85–6, accessed 22 July 2012, http://www.british-history.ac.uk/commons-jrnl/vol7/pp85-86.

27 John Owen, *The Humble Proposals of Mr. Owen, Mr. Tho. Goodwin, Mr. Nye, Mr. Sympson, and other Ministers, who presented the Petition to Parliament* (London, 1652), 5.

28 According to Roger Williams, *The Fourth Paper, Presented by Maior Butler* (London, 1652), "*many have earnestly desired a sight of the* Ministers Proposals," while others petitioned committee members with their own proposals (20). Over the course of the next several months, the committee

"freely (and with abundance of Christian Civility *and gentleness) received many and several* Papers *from many and several sorts of* Men *and* Consciences" ("Preface"). Parliamentarian Army officer Robert Norwood, despite being convicted of heresy the year before, supposes in *Proposals for the propagation of the Gospel, Offered to Parliament* (London, 1652) that he has "equally with others the liberty of throwing in my mite," hoping that "whatever is proposed shall not finde the less or more acceptance in respect of to the Proposers thereof" (2). The anonymous author of *Of Severall Queries Now Published and Propounded* (London, 1652) frames his proposals as queries *"to be considered of by all, especially, of those which assume a power of Propagating the GOSPELL, and Settling the Ministers and Ministry thereof in this Nation."*

29 Williams, *Fourth Paper*, 2 and 3.

30 Ibid., 23.

31 Williams wrote to a friend in 1652 that "The Secretarie of the Councell, (Mr. Milton) for my Dutch I read him, read me many more languages." See Roger Williams, *The Correspondence of Roger Williams*, ed. Glenn La Fantasie, 2 vols. (Providence: Brown University Press, 1988), 2:389, 383. See also David Masson, *The Life of Milton*, 7 vols. (New York: Peter Smith, 1946), 4:529–33; and Lewalski, *Life of John Milton*, who supposes, "It is easy to imagine these three [Milton, Williams, and Henry Vane] discussing their common repugnance for the proposals under debate and how to oppose them" (285).

32 *Several Proceedings*, 29 April 29–6 May, p. 2124.

33 Lewalski, *Life of John Milton*, 286.

34 Stevens argues, "It becomes clear that neither antipathy to the rule of a single person nor any other republican imperative can compete with the desire for liberty of individual conscience that stands at the heart of Milton's Protestant nationalism" (Paul Stevens, "Milton's 'Renunciation' of Cromwell: The Problem of Raleigh's *Cabinet-Council*," *Modern Philology* 98, no. 3 (2001): 392).

35 Regarding the dissolution of the Rump, Milton remarks, "When you saw delays being contrived and every man more attentive to his private interest than to that of the state, when you saw the people complaining that they had been deluded of their hopes and circumvented by the power of the few, you put an end to the domination of these few men, since they, although so often warned, had refused to do so" (*CPW* 4.1:671). Ten months earlier, Cromwell had characterized himself prior to the dissolution as "finding the people dissatisfied in every corner of the nation" for the "non-performance of those things, which had been

promised," and a parliament concerned only with how to "perpetuate *themselves*" (2:278, 279–80).

36 Worden finds Cromwell "the violator of liberty" in *Defensio Secunda*, yet Milton's language seems to suggest the exact opposite. See *Literature and Politics in Cromwellian England: John Milton, Andrew Marvell, Marchamont Nedham* (Oxford: Oxford University Press, 2009), 295.

37 Jeffrey R. Collins, "The Church Settlement of Oliver Cromwell," *History* 87 (2002): 18–40.

38 Woolrych and others suppose these requests one in the same. See Austin Woolrych, "Milton & Cromwell: 'A Short but Scandalous Night of Interruption,'" in *Achievements of the Left Hand: Essays on Milton's Prose*, ed. Michael Lieb and John Shawcross (Amherst: University of Massachusetts Press, 1974), 196–7.

39 Little and Smith, *Parliaments and Politics*, 197.

40 Gary De Krey, *London and the Restoration, 1659–1683* (Cambridge: Cambridge University Press, 2005), 101.

41 See, for example, Mary Ann Radzinowicz, "The Politics of *Paradise Lost*," in *Politics of Discourse: The Literature and History of Seventeenth-Century England*, ed. Kevin Sharpe and S.N. Zwicker (Berkeley: University of California Press, 1987), 204–29; David Quint, *Epic and Empire: Politics and Generic Form from Virgil to Milton* (Princeton, NJ: Princeton University Press, 1993); Achinstein, *Milton and the Revolutionary Reader*; Thomas Corns, *Regaining "Paradise Lost"* (London: Longman, 1994); Laura Lunger Knoppers, *Historicizing Milton: Spectacle, Power, and Poetry in Restoration England* (Athens: University of Georgia Press, 1994); Norbrook, *Writing the English Republic*; and Barbara Lewalski, "*Paradise Lost* and Milton's Politics," *Milton Studies* 38 (2000): 141–68.

42 See note 2 above.

43 Sharon Achinstein, *Literature and Dissent in Milton's England* (Cambridge: Cambridge University Press, 2003), 124. Achinstein makes a related argument in "Toleration in Milton's Epics: A Chimera?" in *Milton and Toleration*, ed. Sharon Achinstein and Elizabeth Sauer (Oxford: Oxford University Press, 2007), where she claims that "while Milton's major epics are vivid in their denunciations of those who would force consciences, they are not good places to look for explicit representations of toleration of varying faiths" (228). William Walker, on the other hand, suggests that in book 12, Michael "implicitly recommends the limited religious toleration Milton urges in the *Treatise* [*of Civil Power*]." See Walker's "Milton's Dualistic Theory of Religious Toleration in *A Treatise of Civil Power*, *Of Christian Doctrine*, and *Paradise Lost*," *Modern Philology* 99 (2001): 226.

44 John Milton, *Paradise Lost*, edited by Barbara Lewalski (Oxford: Blackwell, 2007). All subsequent references will be parenthetical.

45 Charles II, *King Charls II: His Declaration To all His Loving Subjects of The Kingdome of England* (London, 1660), 5.

46 In *A Declaration and an Information from us the People of God Called Quakers* (London, 1660), Margaret Fell directly addressed the King and Parliament to claim such "liberty of conscience" for the much-feared Quakers: "we *desire* and also *expect* to have *the liberty of our Consciences* and *just Rights*, and *outward Liberties* as other people of the Nation, which we have promise of *from the word of a King*" (7). Religious controversialist Theophilus Brabourne defended the royal Declaration and argued against the intervention of the civil magistrate in religion in his tract *God save the King, And Prosper Him and His Parliament: Or, A justification by the Word of God, of the Kings gracious proffer for Liberty of Conscience, Made to His Parliament and Subjects*, before he came into England (London, 1660).

47 John Spurr, *The Restoration Church of England, 1646–1689* (New Haven: Yale University Press, 1991), 42; De Krey, *London and the Restoration*, 87.

48 W.M. Spellman, *The Latitudinarians and the Church of England, 1660–1700* (Athens: University of Georgia Press, 1993), 34. For more on Charles II's willingness to compromise early on, see Ian Green's *The Re-Establishment of the Church of England 1660–1663* (Oxford: Oxford University Press, 1978). On the Church of England's ministers and their attempt to use persecution as a means of getting dissenters back into the church, see Donald A. Spaeth, *The Church in an Age of Danger: Parsons and Parishioners, 1660–1740* (Cambridge: Cambridge University Press, 2000), especially 157–72.

49 Quoted in Spaeth, *The Church*, 159.

50 Roger L'Estrange, *Considerations and Proposals in order to the Regulation of the Press* (London, 1663), sig. A3.

51 Edmund Calamy, *An Exact Collection of Farewel Sermons, Preached by the late London-Ministers* (London, 1662), 5.

52 Ibid., 7–8.

53 Ibid., 55, 79, 273.

54 George Whitehead, *An Epistle of Consolation* (London, 1664), 3.

55 S.J. Guscott, "Cawdrey, Zachary (1618–1684)," in *Oxford Dictionary of National Biography* (Oxford University Press, 2004–), accessed 3 September 2015, doi:10.1093/ref:odnb/4956.

56 Zachary Cawdrey, *The Christians Prize and Race, Or, A Plain Discourse on the Good Things Promised to Us in Christ* (London, 1680), 20.

57 Benjamin Myers, "Prevenient Grace and Conversion in *Paradise Lost*," *Milton Quarterly* 40, no. 1 (2006): 20–36, stresses the importance of

prevenient grace in Arminian thought whereby "the fallen will [is able] to cooperated with grace, and so to be converted." In this way, prevenient grace is "only a necessary condition for conversion," though it does not guarantee salvation without the wilful cooperation of the individual (23).

58 *Oxford English Dictionary*, s.v. "umpire, n," http://www.oed.com, accessed 14 April 2015. See the etymology for "umpire" as well as the definitions and etymologies offered for the noun "noumpere," which was current in English for "arbiter" as late as 1613.

59 Parker, *Discourse of Ecclesiastical Politie*, 7.

60 This copy of *Paradise Lost* is in the British Library's holdings, shelfmark C.69.ff.5.

61 Louis Schwartz, *Milton and Maternal Mortality* (Cambridge: Cambridge University Press, 2009), discusses Sin's odd self-awareness at length, similarly commenting on the circularity of this passage: "This self-consciousness in an allegorical figure produces a circular process of reference, like a serpent with its stinging tail in its mouth. Sin is an allegory of a particular theological condition, but we are invited to view her, to some extent, as a self-aware subject, one who is immersed in the very condition she represents as an allegory. When she looks at her lower half, she sees not that she is changing into something she recognizes as not herself, but that she is changing into what she actually *is*, and she is overwhelmed in the process by the pain and fear that are her own attributes. In other words, she sees from within the distorting condition that she herself represents. In this way, 'subjectivity' is, in effect, accommodated to allegorical figuration, and the subjectivity is that of a suffering mother" (228–9).

62 John Hollander, *Vision and Resonance: Two Senses of Poetic Form* (New York: Oxford University Press, 1975), points out that the "perfect schematic chiasmus of line 20 swirls up as a momentary picture in an agitated phantasmagoria, until our attention moves on, dragged by the force of continuing syntax and its tugging toward completion (we must have the verb, however inverted, for which "Hell" is an object, as well as a symmetrical tessera in a mosaic pattern)" (95).

63 Benet, "Adam's Evil Conscience," comparing Satan's soliloquy in book 4 to Adam's in book 10, points out that "the text identifies the oppositional voice that interrogates Satan and Adam, and it does not belong to them" (4).

64 Richard Arnold, *Logic of the Fall: Right Reason and [Im]pure Reason in Milton's "Paradise Lost"* (New York: Peter Lang, 2006), defines "right reason" as a "form of reasoning that simultaneously unites the intellectual

or ratiocinative faculty *and* the moral or spiritual sense; it is animated and sustained by (and operates according to) one's higher conscience, moral sense, or, in theological terms – and certainly in the case of *Paradise Lost* – the holy spirit or religious conscience" (ix). Milton also draws together conscience and right reason early on in *De Doctrina Christiana* when he argues, "No one would try to be virtuous, no one would refrain from sin because he felt ashamed of it or feared the law, if the voice of Conscience or right reason did not speak from time to time in the heart of every man" (*CPW* 6:132).

65 *CPW* 6:653.

66 Corns, *Regaining "Paradise Lost,"* 133.

67 Calamy, *Farewel Sermons*, 1.

68 All subsequent quotations from *Paradise Regain'd* and *Samson Agonistes* will be cited parenthetically by line number and, where relevant, book and line number and are from *The Complete Works of John Milton*, vol. 2, *Paradise Regain'd and Samson Agonistes*, ed. Laura Lunger Knoppers (Oxford: Oxford University Press, 2008). This particular quotation is from *Paradise Regain'd*, 1:4.

69 Loewenstein, *Representing Revolution in Milton*, 273.

70 *Oxford English Dictionary*, "Nazirite, n. and adj.," http://www.oed.com, accessed 14 April 2015.

Afterword

1 Matthew Arnold, *Matthew Arnold's Essays in Criticism: First and Second Series*, intr. G.K. Chesterton (London: J.M. Dent, 1964), 15. All subsequent references will be cited parenthetically as *Essays*.

2 Arnold characterizes Victorian England as plagued by a *"note of provinciality"* in "The Literary Influence of Academies" (1864) because of its lack of an "intellectual metropolis like an academy" (*Essays* 47). A year later in "The Function of Criticism," he seems to read this same provinciality back into the English Revolution.

3 Arnold cites an incident that took place on 23 July 1637, a riot in the church of St Giles following the first reading of King Charles I's loathed prayer book. According to popular tradition, this uprising was ignited when Geddes shouted, "Dost thou say the mass at my lug [ear]?" before flinging her stool at James Hannay, the dean of St Giles.

4 Though a woman by this name may not have actually existed, the tradition celebrating her rebellion strikes through the centuries. She enjoys mention in an early-eighteenth-century satirical poem, "The History of the Most

Famous and Most Renowned Janny Geddes," John Stuart Blackie's "The Song of Mrs. Jenny Geddes" (1842), and Sir Walter Scott's *Tale of a Grandfather* (1830). So familiar was her legend that Robert Burns named his mare after Geddes and wrote several comical accounts of her in his letters of 1787–8. Moreover, in 1886, Lord Glencorse, Lord Justice General of Scotland, penned the inscription for a plaque commemorating the spot from which Geddes allegedly launched her stool, citing hers as the *"first blow in the great struggle for freedom of conscience, which, after a conflict of half a century, ended in the establishment of civil and religious liberty."* And as recently as 23 August 1992, the Cutty Stool, a bronze rendering of Geddes's projectile by artist Merilyn Smith, was unveiled in St Giles's and now has a permanent place beside the celebratory plaque. See Murdoch Lothian, *The Cutty Stool* (Glasgow: Hughson Gallery, 1995), and David Stevenson, "Geddes, Jenny (*fl.* 1637)," in *Oxford Dictionary of National Biography* (Oxford University Press, 2004–), accessed 6 June 2016, doi:10.1093/ ref:odnb/10488.

5 Clinton Machann, in "Matthew Arnold (1822–1888)," similarly points out that "Arnold is ultimately interested in the articulation of a common culture, not a formal institution. The real authority will emerge from a social bond developed collectively by individuals who transcend their provincialism." In *The Cambridge History of Literary Criticism*, vol. 6, *The Nineteenth Century*, ed. M.A.R. Habib (Cambridge: Cambridge University Press, 2013), 425.

Bibliography

Manuscript Sources

Aldam, Thomas. Letter to Oliver Cromwell. Library of the Religious Society of Friends. Port MS 1/5a. 1654.
– Letter to Oliver Cromwell. Library of the Religious Society of Friends. Port MS 1/9. 1654.
– Letter to Oliver Cromwell. Library of the Religious Society of Friends. Port MS 36/117. 1654.
Bankes, William. Diary of the Convention Parliament. Lancashire Record Office. Ref. DD/Ba. 11 May 1660.
Dewsbury, William. Letter to Oliver Cromwell. Library of the Religious Society of Friends. Caton MS, 1:1–7, formerly Barclay Box/3/1–3,1. 1655.
– Letter to Thomas Aldam. Library of the Religious Society of Friends. Port MS 15/26. 1655.
"The Great Book of Sufferings." 17 vols. The Library of the Religious Society of Friends. 1650–1725.
Hooten, Elizabeth. Letter to Oliver Cromwell. Library of the Religious Society of Friends. Port MS 3/3. 1653.
Hutchinson, Lucy. "The Defense of John Hutchinson." British Library. Additional MSS 25,901, 39,779, and 46,172N.
– "The Life of Colonel Hutchinson." Nottinghamshire Archives. Ref. DD/HU/4.
"Letters to Mrs. Anne Sadleir of Standon." Trinity College Cambridge, Wren Library. Cent. xvii, R.5.5.
"Newsletter from London." Bodleian Library. Clarendon MS 45, folio 292v. April 1653.
Pearson, Anthony. Letter to George Fox. Library of the Religious Society of Friends. Swarthmore MS, 354/34. 1654.

Stubbs, John. Letter to Oliver Cromwell. Library of the Religious Society of Friends. Port MS 33/142–45. 1654/5.

Primary Print Sources

Abbott, Wilbur Cortez, ed. *The Writings and Speeches of Oliver Cromwell*. 4 vols. Cambridge, MA: Harvard University Press, 1939–47.

Arnold, Matthew. *Matthew Arnold's Essays in Criticism: First and Second Series*. Introduction by G.K. Chesterton. London: J.M. Dent, 1964.

Barbour, Hugh, and Arthur Roberts, eds. *Early Quaker Writings 1650–1700*. Grand Rapids, MI: William B. Eerdmans, 1973.

Barclay, A.R., ed. *Letters of Early Friends*. London: Harvey and Darton, 1841.

Biddle, John. *Two Letters of Mr. John Biddle*. London, 1655.

Bishop, George. *The Warnings of the Lord to the Men of this Generation*. London, 1660.

Bloomefield, Francis. *An Essay towards a Topographical History of the County of Norfolk*, vol. 3, *The History of the City and County of Norwich, part I*. London, 1806. Accessed 1 July 2010, http://www.britishhistory.ac.uk/report. aspx?compid=78000Q2.

Brabourne, Theophilus. *God save the King, And Prosper Him and His Parliament: Or, A justification by the Word of God, of the Kings gracious proffer for Liberty of Conscience, Made to His Parliament and Subjects, before he came into England*. London, 1660.

Burges, Cornelius. *A Vindication of the Ministers of the Gospel in and about London*. London, 1649.

Burrough, Edward. *A Discovery of Divine Mysteries; Wherein is Unfoulded Secret Things of the Kingdom of God*. London, 1661.

– *To the Rulers and to such as are in Authority*. London, 1659.

Burrough, Edward, and George Fox. *Counsel and Advice Rejeced by Disobedient Men*. London, 1659.

Burton, Thomas. *The Diary of Thomas Burton Esq*, vol. 1, *July 1653–April 1657*. Edited by J.T. Rutt. London: H. Colburn, 1828. http://www.british-history. ac.uk/burton-diaries/vol1/.

Cadbury, Henry J., ed. *The Swarthmore Documents in America*. London: Friends' Historical Society, 1940.

Calamy, Edmund. *An Exact Collection of Farewel Sermons, Preached by the late London-Ministers*. London, 1662.

Camm, John, and Francis Howgill. *This was the Word of the Lord which John Camm and Francis Howgill Was moved to declare and write to Oliver Cromwell*. London, 1654.

Cawdrey, Zachary. *The Christians Prize and Race, Or, A Plain Discourse on the Good Things Promised to Us in Christ*. London, 1680.

Caxton, William. *Myrrour of the World or Thymage of the Same*. London, 1481.

Charles I. *The Letters, Speeches and Proclamations of King Charles I*. Edited by Sir Charles Petrie. New York: Funk & Wagnalls, 1935.

Charles II. *King Charls II: His Declaration To all His Loving Subjects of The Kingdome of England*. London, 1660.

Clarendon, Earl of (Edward Hyde). *State Papers Collected by Edward, earl of Clarendon, commencing from the year 1621*. 3 vols. Edited by Richard Scrope. Oxford: Clarendon Press, 1767–86.

Coke, Sir Edward. *The Reports*. Vol. 4, parts 7–8. Edited by John Henry Thomas and John Farquhar Fraser. London: Joseph Butterworth and Son, 1826.

The Conclusion of Lieuten: General Cromwells Letter to the House of Commons. London, 1645.

Cromwell, Oliver. *A Declaration of His Highness, inviting the people of England and Wales to a day of Solemn Fasting and Humiliation*. London, 1656.

– *A Declaration of His Highness with the advice of his Council inviting the people of this Commonwealth to a Day of Solemn Fasting and Humiliation*. London, 1655.

The Cry of the Oppressed from under their Oppressions. London, 1656.

Dewsbury, William. *Several Letters Written to the Saints of the Most High*. London, 1654.

– *A True Prophecy of the Mighty Day of the Lord*. London, 1655.

A Dialogue Betwixt the Ghosts of Charls the I, Late King of England: and Oliver, The late Usurping Protector. London, 1659.

Donne, John. *The Sermons of John Donne*. Vol. 7. Edited by Evelyn Simpson and George R. Potter. Berkeley: University of California Press, 1954.

Duport, James. *Three sermons preached in St. Maries Church in Cambridg, upon the three anniversaries of the martyrdom of Charles I, Jan. 30*. London, 1676.

Eachard, John. *Some Opinions of Mr Hobbes Considered in a Second Dialogue Between Philautus and Timothy*. London, 1673.

Edwards, Thomas. *Gangraena*. London, 1646.

Eikon Basilike: The Portraiture of His Sacred Majesty in His Solitudes and Sufferings. Edited by Jim Daems and Holly Faith Nelson. Ontario: Broadview Editions, 2006.

Eikon Basilike: The Portraiture of His Sacred Majesty in His Solitudes and Sufferings. The Folger Shakespeare Library. E287.8. London, 1649.

Eikon Basilike: The Portraiture of His Sacred Majesty in His Solitudes and Sufferings. The Pennsylvania State University Special Collections. DA400. C488 1648 and DA400.C488 1649b. London, 1649.

Elizabeth I. *Elizabeth I: Collected Works.* Edited by Leah S. Marcus, Janel Mueller, and Mary Beth Rose. Chicago: University of Chicago Press, 2000.

Elyot, Thomas. *The Boke Named the Gouernour.* London, 1534.

The English Devil: Or, Cromwell and his Monstrous Witch. London, 1660.

An exact collection of all remonstrances, declarations, votes, orders, … betweene the Kings most excellent Majesty, and his high court of Parliament. London, 1642.

Fell, Margaret. *A Brief Collection of Remarkable Passages and Occurrences Relating to the Birth, Education, Life, Conversion, Travel, Services, and Deep Sufferings of that Ancient, Eminent, and Faithful Servant of the Lord, Margaret Fell.* London: J. Sowle, 1710.

– *A Declaration and an Information from us the People of God Called Quakers.* London, 1660.

– *A Touch-Stone: Or, A Tryal by the Scriptures, of the Priests, Bishops, and Ministers.* London, 1666.

– *Undaunted Zeal: The Letters of Margaret Fell.* Edited by Elsa F. Glines. Richmond, IN: Friends United Press, 2003.

Fox, George. *The Great Mystery of the Great Whore Unfolded.* London, 1659. Reprint, Philadelphia: Marcus T. Gould; and New York: Isaac T. Hopper, 1831.

– *To the Protector and Parliament of England.* London, 1657.

Foxe, John. *The Unabridged Acts and Monuments Online.* Sheffield: HRI Online Publications, 2011. https://www.johnfoxe.org.

Gaskin, John. *A Just Defence and Vindication of Gospel Ministers and Gospel Ordinances against the Quakers.* London, 1660.

Gataker, Thomas. *A Serious and Faithfull Representation of the Judgments of Ministers of the Gospell Within the Province of London.* London, 1649.

Greville, Robert. *A Discourse Opening the Natvre of that Episcopacie, which is Exercised in England.* London, 1641.

Harrington, James. *The Commonwealth of Oceana and A System of Politics.* Edited by J.G.A. Pocock. Cambridge: Cambridge University Press, 1992.

– *The Political Works of James Harrington.* Edited by J.G.A. Pocock. Cambridge: Cambridge University Press, 1977.

– *The Prerogative of Popular Government.* London, 1657.

Harvey, Gabriel. *Pierces Supererogation or A new prayse of the old asse.* London, 1593.

Henry VIII. *The Letters of King Henry VIII: A Selection with a Few Other Documents.* Edited by M. St. Clare Byrne. London: Cassell & Company, 1968.

Hobbes, Thomas. *Leviathan.* Edited by Richard Tuck. Cambridge: Cambridge University Press, 1991.

"House of Commons Journal Volume 6: 3 February 1649." In *Journal of the House of Commons*, vol. 6, *1648–1651*. London, 1802. Accessed 28 January 2015, http://www.british-history.ac.uk/commons-jrnl/vol6/pp130-131.

"House of Commons Journal Volume 7: 10 February 1652." In *Journal of the House of Commons*, vol. 7, *1651–1660*. London, 1802. Accessed 22 July 2012, http://www.british-history.ac.uk/commons-jrnl/vol7/pp85-86.

"House of Commons Journal Volume 8: 9 June 1660." In *Journal of the House of Commons*, vol. 8, *1660–1667*. London, 1802. Accessed 3 September 2015, http://www.british-history.ac.uk/commons-jrnl/vol8/pp59-61.

A Hue and Crie after Cromwell: Or, The Cities Lamentation for the losse of their Coyne and Conscience. London, 1649.

The Humble Advice and Earnest Desires of Certain Well-Affected Ministers. London, 1649.

Humfrey, John. *A Case of Conscience*. London, 1669.

Hutchinson, Lucy. *Memoirs of the Life of Colonel Hutchinson*. 2 vols. Edited by C.H. Firth. London, 1885.

– *Memoirs of the Life of Colonel Hutchinson*. Edited by James Sutherland. London: Oxford University Press, 1973.

– *Memoirs of the Life of Colonel Hutchinson*. Edited by N.H. Keeble. London: J.M. Dent, 1995.

– *Order and Disorder*. Edited by David Norbrook. Oxford: Blackwell, 2001.

Insolence and Impudence Triumphant. London, 1669.

James VI and I. *King James VI and I: Political Writings*. Edited by Johann P. Sommerville. Cambridge: Cambridge University Press, 1994.

– *The Letters of King James VI and I*. Edited by G.P.V. Akrigg. Berkeley: University of California Press, 1984.

Laney, Benjamin. *A Sermon Preached Before His Majesty*. London, 1665.

Laud, William. *The Works of the Most Reverend Father in God, William Laud*, vol. 4, History of the Troubles and Trial. Edited by James Bliss and William Scott. Oxford: John Henry Parker, 1854.

L'Estrange, Roger. *Considerations and Proposals in order to the Regulation of the Press*. London, 1663.

Lomas, S.C., ed. *The Letters and Speeches of Oliver Cromwell with Elucidations by Thomas Carlyle*. 3 vols. London: Methuen & Co., 1904.

Ludlow, Edmund. *A Voyce from the Watch Tower, Part Five: 1660–1662*. Edited by A.B. Worden. London: University College London, 1978.

Luther, Martin. *Luther's Works*. Vols. 21, 26, and 32. Edited by Jaroslav Pelikan. St Louis, MO: Concordia Publishing House, 1963.

Marshall, Stephen. *An Expedient to Preserve Peace and Amity, Among Dissenting Brethren*. London, 1647.

Marvell, Andrew. *The Rehearsal Transpros'd: The First Part*. Edited by D.I.B. Smith. Oxford: Clarendon Press, 1971.

– *The Rehearsal Transpros'd: The Second Part*. Edited by D.I.B. Smith. Oxford: Clarendon Press, 1971.

Milton, John. *Complete Prose Works of John Milton*. 8 vols. Edited by Don M. Wolfe et al. New Haven: Yale University Press, 1953–82.

– *The Complete Works of John Milton*, vol. 2, *Paradise Regain'd and Samson Agonistes*. Edited by Laura Lunger Knoppers. Oxford: Oxford University Press, 2008.

– *John Milton: Complete Shorter Poems*. Edited by Stella Revard. Oxford: Blackwell, 2009.

– *Paradise Lost*. The British Library. C.69.ff.5. London, 1674.

– *Paradise Lost*. Edited by Barbara Lewalski. Oxford: Blackwell, 2007.

More, Sir Thomas. *The Correspondence of Sir Thomas More*. Edited by Elizabeth Frances Rogers. Princeton, NJ: Princeton University Press, 1947.

Nayler, James. *A Discovery of the Man of Sin*. London, 1654.

– *Several Papers; Some of them given forth by George Fox; others by James Nayler*. London, 1654.

– *A Vindication of Truth, As held forth in a Book*. London, 1656.

A New Conference between the Ghosts of King Charles and Oliver Cromwell. London, 1659.

Norwood, Robert. *Proposals for the propagation of the Gospel, Offered to Parliament*. London, 1652.

Owen, John. *The Humble Proposals of Mr. Owen, Mr. Tho. Goodwin, Mr. Nye, Mr. Sympson, and other Ministers, who presented the Petition to Parliament*. London, 1652.

– *Truth and Innocence Vindicated*. London, 1669.

Parker, Samuel. *A Defence and Continuation of the Ecclesiastical Politie*. London, 1671.

– *A Discourse of Ecclesiastical Politie*. London, 1670.

– *A Reproof to the Rehearsal Transposed*. London, 1673.

To the Right Honorable, Thomas Lo: Fairfax, General of the Army, and the Councel of Officers under His Command: A Sincere and Respective Manifestation of the Judgments of Ministers of the Gospel within the County of Essex. London, 1648.

Saltmarsh, John. *The Smoke in the Temple Wherein is a Designe for Peace and Reconciliation of Believers*. London, 1646.

Of Severall Queries Now Published and Propounded. London, 1652.

Sibbes, Richard. *A Learned Commentary or Exposition: Upon the First Chapter of the Second Epistle of S. Paul to the Corinthians*. London, 1655.

Skipp, Edmund. *The Worlds Wonder, or the Quakers Blazing Starr*. London, 1654.

Smith, Humphrey. *Something in reply to Edmund Skipps Book, which he calles the Worlds Wonder*. London, 1655.

A Solemn League and Covenant. London, 1643.

Thomas, William. *Rayling Rebuked: Or, a Defence of the Ministers of this Nation*. London, 1656.

Thurloe, John. *A Collection of the State Papers of John Thurloe, Esq*. Vol. 2. Edited by Thomas Birch. London, 1742.

Whitehead, George. *An Epistle of Consolation*. London, 1664.

Williams, C.H., ed. *English Historical Documents*, vol. 5, 1485–1558. Oxford: Oxford University Press, 1967.

Williams, Roger. *The Correspondence of Roger Williams*. Edited by Glenn La Fantasie. 2 vols. Providence: Brown University Press, 1988.

– *The Fourth Paper, Presented by Maior Butler*. London, 1652.

Wren, Matthew. *Considerations on Mr. Harrington's Common-wealth of Oceana*. London, 1657.

Secondary Sources

Achinstein, Sharon. *Literature and Dissent in Milton's England*. Cambridge: Cambridge University Press, 2003.

– *Milton and the Revolutionary Reader*. Princeton, NJ: Princeton University Press, 1994.

– "Milton Catches the Conscience of the King: *Eikonoklastes* and the Engagement Controversy." *Milton Studies* 29 (1992): 143–63.

– "Toleration in Milton's Epics: A Chimera?" In *Milton and Toleration*, edited by Sharon Achinstein and Elizabeth Sauer, 224–42. Oxford: Oxford University Press, 2007.

Anderson, Benedict. *Imagined Communities: Reflections on the Origin and Spread of Nationalism*. London: Verso, 1983.

Andrew, Edward G. *Conscience and Its Critics: Protestant Conscience, Enlightenment Reason, and Modern Subjectivity*. Toronto: University of Toronto Press, 2001.

– "Hobbes on Conscience within the Law and Without." *Canadian Journal of Political Science* 32, no. 2 (1999): 203–25.

Arnold, Richard. *Logic of the Fall: Right Reason and [Im]pure Reason in Milton's "Paradise Lost."* New York: Peter Lang, 2006.

Baker, David J. *Between Nations: Shakespeare, Spenser, Marvell, and the Question of Britain*. Stanford, CA: Stanford University Press, 1997.

Baylor, Michael G. *Action and Person: Conscience in Late Scholasticism and the Young Luther*. Leiden: Brill, 1977.

Beckman, Jessica C. "Milton's Evolving Faculty of Conscience: 'On the New Forcers of Conscience,' *A Treatise of Civil Power*, and *Paradise Lost*." *Exemplaria* 24, nos. 1–2 (2012): 46–61.

Benet, Diana Treviño. "Adam's Evil Conscience and Satan's Surrogate Fall." *Milton Quarterly* 39, no. 1 (2005): 2–15.

Bennett, Martyn. *Oliver Cromwell*. London: Routledge, 2006.

Bobbio, Norberto. *Thomas Hobbes and the Natural Law Tradition*. Translated by Daniela Gobetti. Chicago: University of Chicago Press, 1993.

Boehrer, Bruce. "Elementary Structures of Kingship: Milton, Regicide, and the Family." *Milton Studies* 23 (1987): 97–117.

Booy, David. *Autobiographical Writings by Early Quaker Women*. Aldershot: Ashgate, 2004.

Borot, Luc. "Religion in Harrington's Political System: The Central Concepts and Methods of Harrington's Religious Solutions." In *Perspectives on English Revolutionary Republicanism*, edited by Dirk Wiemann and Gaby Mahlberg, 149–64. Farnham: Ashgate, 2014.

Braithwaite, William. *The Beginnings of Quakerism*. 2nd ed. Cambridge: Cambridge University Press, 1970.

Braun, Harald, and Edward Vallance, eds. *Contexts of Conscience in Early Modern Europe, 1500–1700*. Basingstoke: Palgrave Macmillan, 2004.

– *The Renaissance Conscience*. Oxford: Wiley-Blackwell, 2011.

Bredekamp, Horst. "Thomas Hobbes's Visual Strategies." In *The Cambridge Companion to Hobbes's Leviathan*, edited by Patricia Springborg, 29–60. Cambridge: Cambridge University Press, 2007.

Bremer, Francis J. "Williams, Roger (*c*.1606–1683)." In *Oxford Dictionary of National Biography*. Oxford University Press, 2004–. Accessed 24 June 2016. doi:10.1093/ref:odnb/29544.

Brinton, Howard H. *Friends for 350 Years*. Wallingford, PA: Pendle Hill, 2002.

Brown, Meg Lota. *Donne and the Politics of Conscience in Early Modern England*. Leiden: E.J. Brill, 1995.

Burke, Victoria E. "Sadleir, Anne (1585–1671/2)." In *Oxford Dictionary of National Biography*. Oxford University Press, 2004–. Accessed 24 June 2016. doi:10.1093/ref:odnb/68095.

Cable, Lana. "Secularizing Conscience in Milton's Republican Community." In *Milton and Toleration*, edited by Sharon Achinstein and Elizabeth Sauer, 268–83. Oxford: Oxford University Press, 2007.

Campbell, Gordon. *Bible: The Story of the King James Version 1611–2011*. Oxford: Oxford University Press, 2010.

Capp, Bernard. "Cromwell and Religion in a Multi-Faith Society." In *Cromwell's Legacy*, edited by Jane A. Mills, 93–112. Manchester: Manchester University Press, 2012.

– *England's Culture Wars: Puritan Reformation and Its Enemies in the Interregnum, 1649–1660*. Oxford: Oxford University Press, 2012.

Champion, J.A.I. *"An Historical Narration Concerning Heresie*: Thomas Hobbes, Thomas Barlow, and the Restoration Debate over 'Heresy.'" In *Heresy, Literature, and Politics in Early Modern English Culture*, edited by David Loewenstein and John Marshall, 221–53. Cambridge: Cambridge University Press, 2006.

Coffey, John. "The Toleration Controversy during the English Revolution." In *Religion in Revolutionary England*, edited by Christopher Durston and Judith Maltby, 42–68. Manchester: Manchester University Press, 2005.

Cole, Alan. "Quakers and the English Revolution." *Past & Present* 10 (1956): 39–54.

Collins, Jeffrey R. "The Church Settlement of Oliver Cromwell." *History* 87 (2002): 18–40.

Collinson, Patrick. *Archbishop Grindal, 1519–1583: The Struggle for a Reformed Church*. Berkeley: University of California Press, 1979.

– *The Elizabethan Puritan Movement*. Berkeley: University of California Press, 1967.

Cook, Susan. "'The Story I Most Particularly Intend': The Narrative Style of Lucy Hutchinson." *Critical Survey* 5, no. 3 (1993): 271–7.

Corns, Thomas N. *Regaining "Paradise Lost."* London: Longman, 1994.

Corns, Thomas N., and David Loewenstein, eds. "The Emergence of Quaker Writing: Dissenting Literature in Seventeenth-Century England." Special issue, *Prose Studies* 17, no. 3 (1994).

Coward, Barry. *The Cromwellian Protectorate*. Manchester: Manchester University Press, 2002.

– *Oliver Cromwell*. London: Longman, 1991.

Cummings, Brian. "Conscience and the Law in Thomas More." In *The Renaissance Conscience*, edited by Harald E. Braun and Edward Vallance, 29–51. Oxford: Wiley-Blackwell, 2011.

Curley, Edwin. "Hobbes and the Cause of Religious Toleration." In *The Cambridge Companion to Hobbes's Leviathan*, edited by Patricia Springborg, 309–34. Cambridge: Cambridge University Press, 2007.

Cust, Richard. *Charles I: A Political Life*. London: Pearson Longman, 2005.

Damrosch, Leo. "Nayler, James (1618–1660)." In *Oxford Dictionary of National Biography*. Oxford University Press, 2004–. Accessed 27 July 2015. doi:10.1093/ref:odnb/19814.

– *The Sorrows of the Quaker Jesus: James Naylor and the Puritan Crackdown on the Free Spirit*. Cambridge, MA: Harvard University Press, 1996.

Davies, Adrian. *The Quakers in English Society, 1655–1725*. Oxford: Clarendon Press, 2000.

Davis, Godfrey. *The Early Stuarts 1603–1660*. Oxford: Clarendon Press, 1937.

Davis, J.C. "Cromwell's Religion." In *Oliver Cromwell and the English Revolution*, edited by John Morrill, 181–208. London: Longman, 1990.

– "Oliver Cromwell." In *The Oxford Handbook of the English Revolution*, edited by Michael J. Braddick, 223–42. Oxford: Oxford University Press, 2015.

De Krey, Gary. "The First Restoration Crisis: Conscience and Coercion in London, 1667–73." *Albion* 25 (1993): 565–80.

– *London and the Restoration, 1659–1683*. Cambridge: Cambridge University Press, 2005.

– "Rethinking the Restoration: Dissenting Cases for Conscience, 1667–1672." *Historical Journal* 38 (1995): 53–83.

Dobranski, Stephen B. "Licensing Milton's Heresy." In *Milton and Heresy*, edited by Stephen B. Dobranski and John P. Rumrich, 139–58. Cambridge: Cambridge University Press, 1998.

Doran, Susan, and Christopher Durston. *Princes, Pastors and People: The Church and Religion in England, 1500–1700*. London: Routledge, 2003.

Durston, Christopher. *Cromwell's Major-Generals: Godly Government during the English Revolution*. Manchester: Manchester University Press, 2001.

Dzelzainis, Martin. "Milton and Antitrinitarianism." In *Milton and Toleration*, edited by Sharon Achinstein and Elizabeth Sauer, 171–85. Oxford: Oxford University Press, 2007.

Escobedo, Andrew. *Nationalism and Historical Loss in Renaissance England: Foxe, Dee, Spenser, Milton*. Ithaca, NY: Cornell University Press, 2004.

Ezell, Margaret J.M. *Writing Women's Literary History*. Baltimore: Johns Hopkins University Press, 1992.

Feldman, Karen S. *Binding Words: Conscience and Rhetoric in Hobbes, Hegel, and Heidegger*. Evanston, IL: Northwestern University Press, 2006.

Feroli, Teresa. *Political Speaking Justified: Women Prophets and the English Revolution*. Newark: University of Delaware Press, 2006.

Firth, C.H. *The Last Years of the Protectorate*. 2 vols. New York: Russell & Russell, 1909.

– *Oliver Cromwell and the Rule of the Puritans in England*. London: Putnam Covent Garden, 1901.

Fischer, Karsten. "Hobbes, Schmitt, and the Paradox of Religious Liberality." *Critical Review of International Social and Political Philosophy* 13, nos. 2–3 (2010): 399–416.

Gallagher, Lowell. *Medusa's Gaze: Casuistry and Conscience in the Renaissance*. Stanford, CA: Stanford University Press, 1991.

Gardiner, Samuel Rawson. *The Constitutional Documents of the Puritan Revolution, 1625–1660*. Oxford: Clarendon Press, 1889.

– *History of the Commonwealth and Protectorate, 1649–1656.* Vol. 3. New York: AMS Press, 1965.

Gaunt, Peter. "'To Create a Little World out of Chaos': The Protectoral Ordinances of 1653–1654 Reconsidered." In *The Cromwellian Protectorate*, edited by Patrick Little, 105–26. Woodbridge, UK: Boydell Press, 2007.

– "Law-Making in the First Protectorate Parliament." In *Politics and People in Revolutionary England*, edited by Colin Jones, Malyn Newitt, and Stephen Roberts, 163–86. Oxford: Basil Blackwell, 1985.

– *Oliver Cromwell.* London: British Library, 2004.

– *Oliver Cromwell.* New York: New York University Press, 2004.

Gill, Catie. *Women in the Seventeenth-Century Quaker Community: A Literary Study of Political Identities, 1650–1700.* Aldershot: Ashgate, 2005.

Goldie, Mark. "The Civil Religion of James Harrington." In *The Languages of Political Theory in Early-Modern Europe*, edited by Anthony Pagden, 197–222. Cambridge: Cambridge University Press, 1987.

Gray, Jonathan Michael. *Oaths and the English Reformation.* Cambridge: Cambridge University Press, 2012.

Green, Ian. *Print and Protestantism in Early Modern England.* Oxford: Oxford University Press, 2000.

– *The Re-Establishment of the Church of England 1660–1663.* Oxford: Oxford University Press, 1978.

Gregerson, Linda. "Milton and the Tragedy of Nations." *PMLA* 129, no. 4 (2014): 672–87.

Guscott, S.J. "Cawdrey, Zachary (1618–1684)." In *Oxford Dictionary of National Biography.* Oxford University Press, 2004–. Accessed 3 September 2015. doi:10.1093/ref:odnb/4956.

Hadfield, Andrew. "The English and Other Peoples." In *A Companion to Milton*, edited by Thomas N. Corns, 174–90. Oxford: Blackwell, 2001.

– *Literature, Politics, and National Identity: Reformation to Renaissance.* Cambridge: Cambridge University Press, 1994.

Haller, William. *Liberty and Reformation in the Puritan Revolution.* New York: Columbia University Press, 1955.

Hamrick, Stephen. *The Catholic Imaginary and the Cults of Elizabeth, 1558–1582.* Farnham: Ashgate, 2009.

Hastings, Adrian. *The Construction of Nationhood: Ethnicity, Religion and Nationalism.* Cambridge: Cambridge University Press, 1997.

Helgerson, Richard. *Forms of Nationhood: The Elizabethan Writing of England.* Chicago: University of Chicago Press, 1992.

– "Milton Reads the King's Book: Print, Performance, and the Making of a Bourgeois Idol." *Criticism* 29, no. 1 (1987): 1–25.

Hiles, Jane. "Milton's Royalist Reflex: The Failure of Argument and the Role of Dialogics in *Eikonoklastes*." In *Spokesperson Milton: Voices in Contemporary Criticism*, edited by Charles W. Durham and Kristin Pruitt McColgan, 87–100. Selinsgrove, PA: Susquehanna University Press, 1994.

Hill, Christopher. "Colonel John Hutchinson, 1615–1664: A Tercentenary Tribute." *Transactions of the Thoroton Society of Nottinghamshire* 69 (1965): 79–87.

– *The English Bible and the Seventeenth-Century Revolution*. New York: Penguin, 1995.

– *God's Englishman: Oliver Cromwell and the English Revolution*. New York: Harper Torchbooks, 1970.

Hirst, Derek. *Authority and Conflict: England, 1603–1658*. Cambridge, MA: Harvard University Press, 1986.

– "Remembering a Hero: Lucy Hutchinson's *Memoirs* of Her Husband." In *Ashgate Critical Essays on Women Writers in England, 1550–1700*, vol. 5, *Anne Clifford and Lucy Hutchinson*, edited by Mihoko Suzuki, 263–72. Aldershot: Ashgate, 2009.

Hoekstra, Kinch. "Hobbes on the Natural Condition of Mankind." In *The Cambridge Companion to Hobbes's Leviathan*, edited by Patricia Springborg, 109–27. Cambridge: Cambridge University Press, 2007.

Hollander, John. *Vision and Resonance: Two Senses of Poetic Form*. New York: Oxford University Press, 1975.

Höpfl, H.M. "Harrington, James (1611–1677)." In *Oxford Dictionary of National Biography*. Oxford University Press, 2004–. Accessed 1 June 2015. doi:10.1093/ref:odnb/12375.

Hughes, Ann. *Gangraena and the Struggle for the English Revolution*. Oxford: Oxford University Press, 2004.

– "'Popular' Presbyterianism in the 1640s and 1650s: The Cases of Thomas Edwards and Thomas Hall." In *England's Long Reformation: 1500–1800*, edited by Nicholas Tyacke, 235–59. London: University College London Press, 1998.

Hutton, Ronald. *The British Republic 1649–60*. Basingstoke: Palgrave Macmillan, 1990.

Jacobus, Lee. "Self-Knowledge in *Paradise Lost*: Conscience and Contemplation." *Milton Studies* 3 (1971): 103–18.

Jaume, Lucien. "Hobbes and the Philosophical Sources of Liberalism." In *Cambridge Companion to Hobbes's Leviathan*, edited by Patricia Springborg, 199–216. Cambridge: Cambridge University Press, 2007.

Keeble, N.H. "'The Colonel's Shadow': Lucy Hutchinson, Women's Writing and the Civil War." In *Literature and the English Civil War*, edited by Thomas

Healy and Jonathan Sawday, 227–47. Cambridge: Cambridge University Press, 1990.

King, John. *Foxe's "Book of Martyrs" and Early Modern Print Culture.* Cambridge: Cambridge University Press, 2006.

Klinck, Dennis R. *Conscience, Equity and the Court of Chancery in Early Modern England.* Aldershot: Ashgate, 2010.

Knoppers, Laura Lunger. *Constructing Cromwell: Ceremony, Portrait, and Print, 1645–1661.* Cambridge: Cambridge University Press, 2000.

– *Historicizing Milton: Spectacle, Power, and Poetry in Restoration England.* Athens: University of Georgia Press, 1994.

–, ed. *The Oxford Handbook of Literature and the English Revolution.* Oxford: Oxford University Press, 2012.

Lacey, Andrew. "Charles I and the *Eikon Basilike*." *Prose Studies* 29, no. 1 (2007): 4–18.

– *The Cult of King Charles the Martyr.* Woodbridge, UK: Boydell Press, 2003.

Leites, Edmund, ed. *Conscience and Casuistry in Early Modern Europe.* Cambridge: Cambridge University Press, 1988.

Lewalski, Barbara. *The Life of John Milton.* Oxford: Blackwell, 2000.

– "*Paradise Lost* and Milton's Politics." *Milton Studies* 38 (2000): 141–68.

Lewis, Charlton T. *An Elementary Latin Dictionary.* Oxford: Oxford University Press, 1969.

Lewis, C.S. *Studies in Words.* Cambridge: Cambridge University Press, 1960.

Little, Patrick, ed. *The Cromwellian Protectorate.* Woodbridge, UK: Boydell Press, 2007.

– *Oliver Cromwell: New Perspectives.* Basingstoke: Palgrave Macmillan, 2008.

Little, Patrick, and David L. Smith. *Parliaments and Politics during the Cromwellian Protectorate.* Cambridge: Cambridge University Press, 2007.

Loewenstein, David. *Representing Revolution in Milton and His Contemporaries.* Cambridge: Cambridge University Press, 2001.

Loewenstein, David, and Paul Stevens, eds. *Early Modern Nationalism and Milton's England.* Toronto: University of Toronto Press, 2008.

Looser, Devoney. *British Women Writers and the Writing of History, 1670–1820.* Baltimore: Johns Hopkins University Press, 2000.

Lothian, Murdoch. *The Cutty School.* Glasgow: Hughson Gallery, 1995.

Low, Anthony. "'Umpire Conscience': Freedom, Obedience, and the Cartesian Flight from Calvin in *Paradise Lost*." *Studies in Philology* 96 (1999): 348–65.

Luecke, Marilyn S. "'God Hath Made No Difference Such as Men Would': Margaret Fell and the Politics of Women's Speech." *Bunyan Studies* 7 (1997): 73–95.

Machann, Clinton. "Matthew Arnold (1822–1888)." In *The Cambridge History of Literary Criticism*, vol. 6, *The Nineteenth Century*, edited by M.A.R. Habib, 419–39. Cambridge: Cambridge University Press, 2013.

Mack, Phyllis. *Visionary Women: Ecstatic Prophecy in Seventeenth-Century England*. Berkeley: University of California Press, 1992.

Maclear, J.F. "Quakerism and the End of the Interregnum." *Church History* 19 (1950): 240–70.

MacLure, Millar. *The Paul's Cross Sermons, 1534–1642*. Toronto: University of Toronto Press, 1958.

Macray, W. Dunn, ed. *The History of the Rebellion and Civil Wars in England*. Vol. 2. Oxford: Clarendon Press, 1888.

Madan, Francis F. *A New Bibliography of the Eikon Basilike of King Charles I*. Oxford: Oxford University Press, 1950.

Maley, Willy. *Nation, State and Empire in English Renaissance Literature: Shakespeare to Milton*. Basingstoke: Palgrave Macmillan, 2003.

Martin, Catherine Gimelli. "The Phoenix and the Crocodile: Milton's Natural Law Debate with Hobbes Retried in the Tragic Forum of *Samson Agonistes*." In *The English Civil Wars in the Literary Imagination*, edited by Claude J. Summers and Ted-Larry Pebworth, 242–70. Columbia: University of Missouri Press, 1999.

Martin, Henri-Jean. *The History and Power of Writing*. Translated by Lydia G. Cochrane. Chicago: University of Chicago Press, 1995.

Masson, David. *The Life of Milton*. 7 vols. New York: Peter Smith, 1946.

– *The Quarrel Between the Earl of Manchester and Oliver Cromwell*. London, 1875.

Mayer, Robert. "Lucy Hutchinson: A Life of Writing." In *Ashgate Critical Essays on Women Writers in England, 1550–1700*, vol. 5, *Anne Clifford and Lucy Hutchinson*, edited by Mihoko Suzuki, 469–500. Aldershot: Ashgate, 2009.

McEachern, Claire. *The Poetics of English Nationhood, 1590–1612*. Cambridge: Cambridge University Press, 1996.

McElligott, Jason. *Royalism, Print and Censorship in Revolutionary England*. Woodbridge, UK: Boydell Press, 2007.

McGregor, J.F., and Barry Reay. *Radical Religion in the English Revolution*. Oxford: Oxford University Press, 1984.

Moore, Rosemary. *The Light in the Consciences: Early Quakers in Britain, 1646–1666*. University Park: Pennsylvania State University Press, 2000.

Morrill, John. "Cromwell, Oliver (1599–1658)." In *Oxford Dictionary of National Biography*. Oxford University Press, 2004–. Accessed 3 September 2015. doi:10.1093/ref:odnb/6765.

– *Oliver Cromwell*. Oxford: Oxford University Press, 2007.

Morrill, John, Paul Slack, and Daniel Woolf, eds. *Public Duty and Private Conscience in Seventeenth-Century England*. Oxford: Clarendon Press, 1993.

Morris, Leon. *The Epistle to the Romans*. Grand Rapids, MI: W.B. Eerdmans, 1988.

Moulton, Rev. W.F. *The History of the English Bible*. London: Cassell, Petter and Galpin, 1878.

Murphy, Andrew R. *Conscience and Community: Revisiting Toleration and Religious Dissent in Early Modern England and America*. University Park: Pennsylvania State University Press, 2001.

Myers, Benjamin. "Prevenient Grace and Conversion in *Paradise Lost*." *Milton Quarterly* 40, no. 1 (2006): 20–36.

Norbrook, David. "'But a Copie': Textual Authority and Gender in Editions of *The Life of John Hutchinson*." In *Ashgate Critical Essays on Women Writers in England, 1550–1700*, vol. 5, *Anne Clifford and Lucy Hutchinson*, edited by Mihoko Suzuki, 273–96. Aldershot: Ashgate, 2009.

– "A Devine Originall: Lucy Hutchinson and the 'Woman's Version.'" *TLS*, March 19, 1999: 13–15.

– "Margaret Cavendish and Lucy Hutchinson: Identity, Ideology, and Politics." *In-between* 9 (2000): 179–203.

– "Memoirs and Oblivion: Lucy Hutchinson and the Restoration." *Huntington Library Quarterly* 75, no. 2 (2012): 233–82.

– *Writing the English Republic: Poetry, Rhetoric, and Politics 1627–1660*. Cambridge: Cambridge University Press, 1999.

Nuttall, Geoffrey F. *Studies in Christian Enthusiasm: Illustrated from Early Quakerism*. Wallingford, PA: Pendle Hill, 1948.

Owen, J. Judd. "The Tolerant Leviathan: Hobbes and the Paradox of Liberalism." *Polity* 37, no. 1 (2005): 130–48.

Parkin, Jon. "Hobbism in the Later 1660s: Daniel Scargill and Samuel Parker." *Historical Journal* 42, no. 1 (1999): 85–108.

– "Liberty Transpros'd: Andrew Marvell and Samuel Parker." In *Marvell and Liberty*, edited by Warren Chernaik and Martin Dzelzainis, 269–89. Houndmills, Basingstoke: Macmillan Press, 1999.

– "Parker, Samuel (1640–1688)." In *Oxford Dictionary of National Biography*. Oxford University Press, 2004–. Accessed 4 June 2015. doi:10.1093/ref:odnb/21336.

– *Taming the Leviathan: The Reception of the Political and Religious Ideas of Thomas Hobbes in England 1640–1700*. Cambridge: Cambridge University Press, 2007.

Pepperell, Keith. "Religious Conscience and Civic Conscience in Thomas Hobbes's Civic Philosophy." *Educational Theory* 39, no. 1 (1989): 17–25.

Perille, Laura. "Harnessing Conscience for the King: Charles I, the Forced
   Loan Sermons, and Matters of Conscience." *Exemplaria* 24, nos. 1–2 (2012):
   161–77.
Peters, Kate. "Patterns of Quaker Authorship, 1652–1656." In "The Emergence
   of Quaker Writing: Dissenting Literature in Seventeenth-Century
   England," edited by Thomas N. Corns and David Loewenstein, special
   issue, *Prose Studies* 17, no. 3 (1994): 6–24.
– *Print Culture and the Early Quakers*. Cambridge: Cambridge University Press,
   2005.
Pierce, C.A. *Conscience in the New Testament*. London: SCM Press, 1955.
Pollard, Alfred W., ed. *Records of the English Bible: The Documents Related to the
   Translation and Publication of the Bible in English, 1525–1611*. London: Oxford
   University Press, 1911.
Potts, Timothy C. *Conscience in Medieval Philosophy*. Cambridge: Cambridge
   University Press, 1980.
Punshon, John. *Portrait in Grey: A Short History of the Quakers*. London: Quaker
   Home Services, 1984.
Quint, David. *Epic and Empire: Politics and Generic Form from Virgil to Milton*.
   Princeton, NJ: Princeton University Press, 1993.
Race, Sydney. "The British Museum MS of the Life of Colonel Hutchinson and
   Its Relation to the Published Memoirs." *Transactions of the Thoroton Society*
   18 (1914): 35–66.
Radzinowicz, Mary Ann. "The Politics of *Paradise Lost*." In *Politics of Discourse:
   The Literature and History of Seventeenth-Century England*, edited by Kevin
   Sharpe and S.N. Zwicker, 204–29. Berkeley: University of California Press, 1987.
Raymond, Joad. *Pamphlets and Pamphleteering in Early Modern Britain*.
   Cambridge: Cambridge University Press, 2003.
Reay, Barry. "Quakerism and Society." In *Radical Religion in the English
   Revolution*, edited by J.F. McGregor and Barry Reay, 141–64. Oxford: Oxford
   University Press, 1984.
– "Quaker Opposition to Tithes 1652–1660." *Past & Present* 86 (1980): 98-120.
– *The Quakers and the English Revolution*. New York: St. Martin's Press, 1985.
Rushworth, John. *Historical Collections of Private Passages of State*. 8 vols.
   London, 1721–2.
Ryan, Alan. "Hobbes, Toleration, and the Inner Life." In *The Nature of Political
   Theory*, edited by David Miller and Larry Seidentop, 197–218. Oxford:
   Clarendon Press, 1983.
– "A More Tolerant Hobbes?" In *Justifying Toleration: Conceptual and Historical
   Perspectives*, edited by Susan Mendus, 37–59. Cambridge: Cambridge
   University Press, 1988.

Salzman, Paul. *Reading Early Modern Women's Writing*. Oxford: Oxford University Press, 2006.

Sauer, Elizabeth. *Milton, Toleration, and Nationhood*. Cambridge: Cambridge University Press, 2014.

Schmitt, Carl. *The Leviathan in the State Theory of Thomas Hobbes: Meaning and Failure of a Political Symbol*. Translated by George Schwab and Erna Hilfstein. Chicago: University of Chicago Press, 2008.

Schmitt, David R. "Heroic Deeds of Conscience: Milton's Stand against Religious Conformity in *Paradise Regained*." *Huntington Library Quarterly* 76, no. 1 (2013): 105–35.

Schwartz, Louis. *Milton and Maternal Mortality*. Cambridge: Cambridge University Press, 2009.

Schwyzer, Patrick. *Literature, Nationalism, and Memory in Early Modern England and Wales*. Cambridge: Cambridge University Press, 2004.

Scott, David. "Counsel and Cabal in the King's Party, 1642–1646." In *Royalists and Royalism during the English Civil Wars*, edited by Jason McElligot and David L. Smith, 112–35. Cambridge: Cambridge University Press, 2007.

Scott, Jonathan. *Commonwealth Principles: Republican Writing of the English Revolution*. Cambridge: Cambridge University Press, 2004.

– "The Rapture of Motion: James Harrington's Republicanism." In *Political Discourse in Early Modern Britain*, edited by Nicholas Phillipson and Quentin Skinner, 139–63. Cambridge: Cambridge University Press, 1993.

Seddon, P.R. "Colonel Hutchinson and the Disputes between Nottinghamshire Parliaments, 1643–45." *Transactions of the Thoroton Society of Nottinghamshire* 98 (1994): 71–81.

– "Hutchinson, John (*bap.* 1615, *d.* 1664)." In *Oxford Dictionary of National Biography*. Oxford University Press, 2004–. Accessed 8 July 2010. doi:10.1093/ref:odnb/14283.

Sharpe, Kevin. "Private Conscience and Public Duty in the Writings of Charles I." *Historical Journal* 40, no. 3 (1997): 643–65.

– "Private Conscience and Public Duty in the Writings of James VI and I." In *Public Duty and Private Conscience in Seventeenth-Century England*, edited by John Morrill, Paul Slack, and Daniel Woolf, 77–100. Oxford: Clarendon Press, 1993.

Skerpan-Wheeler, Elizabeth. "*Eikon Basilike* and the Rhetoric of Self-Representation." In *The Royal Image: Representations of Charles I*, edited by Thomas N. Corns, 122–40. Cambridge: Cambridge University Press, 1999.

– "The First 'Royal': Charles I as Celebrity." *PMLA* 126, no. 4 (2011): 912–34.

– "Rhetorical Genres and the *Eikon Basilike*." *Explorations in Renaissance Culture* 2 (1985): 99–111.

Skinner, Quentin. *Hobbes and Republican Liberty.* Cambridge: Cambridge University Press, 2008.

Slights, Camille Wells. *The Casuistical Tradition in Shakespeare, Donne, Herbert, and Milton.* Princeton, NJ: Princeton University Press, 1981.

– "A Hero of Conscience: Samson Agonistes and Casuistry." *PMLA* 90, no. 3 (1975): 395–413.

Slomp, Gabriella. "The Liberal Slip of Thomas Hobbes's Authoritarian Pen." *Critical Review of International Social and Political Philosophy* 13, nos. 2–3 (Spring 2010): 357–69.

Smith, David L., ed. *Cromwell and the Interregnum: The Essential Readings.* Oxford: Blackwell, 2003.

Smith, Lacey Baldwin. "A Matter of Conscience." In *Action and Conviction in Early Modern Europe:* Essays in Honor of E.H. Harbison, edited by Theodore K. Rabb and Jerrold E. Seigel, 32–51. Princeton, NJ: Princeton University Press, 1969.

Smith, Nigel. *Literature and Revolution in England.* New Haven: Yale University Press, 1997.

– *Perfection Proclaimed: Language and Literature in English Radical Religion 1640– 1660.* Oxford: Clarendon University Press, 1989.

Snobelen, Stephen D. "Biddle, John (1615/16–1662)." In *Oxford Dictionary of National Biography.* Oxford University Press, 2004–. Accessed 2 May 2016. doi:10.1093/ref:odnb/2361.

Spaeth, Donald A. *The Church in an Age of Danger: Parsons and Parishioners, 1660–1740.* Cambridge: Cambridge University Press, 2000.

Spellman, W.M. *The Latitudinarians and the Church of England, 1660–1700.* Athens: University of Georgia Press, 1993.

Spurr, John. *The Restoration Church of England, 1646–1689.* New Haven: Yale University Press, 1991.

Stevens, Paul. "Milton's 'Renunciation' of Cromwell: The Problem of Raleigh's *Cabinet-Council.*" *Modern Philology* 98, no. 3 (2001): 363–92.

Stevenson, David. "Geddes, Jenny (*fl.* 1637)." In *Oxford Dictionary of National Biography.* Oxford University Press, 2004–. Accessed 6 June 2016. doi:10.1093/ref:odnb/10488.

Strohm, Paul. *Conscience: A Very Short Introduction.* Oxford: Oxford University Press, 2011.

– "Conscience." In *Cultural Reformations: Medieval and Renaissance in Literary History,* edited by Brian Cummings and James Simpson, 206–23. Oxford: Oxford University Press, 2010.

Sullivan, Ceri. *The Rhetoric of Conscience in Donne, Herbert, and Vaughan.* Oxford: Oxford University Press, 2008.

Sumers, Alinda. "Milton's 'Umpire Conscience,' the 'Two-Handed Engine,' and the English Protestant Tradition of the Divine Similitude." In *A Fine Tuning: Studies of the Religious Poetry of Herbert and Milton*, edited by Mary A. Maleski, 221–48. Binghamton, NY: Center for Medieval and Early Renaissance Studies, 1989.

Toland, John. "The Life of James Harrington." In *The Oceana of James Harrington … with An Exact Account of his Life*. London, 1700.

Tralau, Johan. "Hobbes contra Liberty of Conscience." *Political Theory* 39, no. 1 (2011): 58–84.

Tuck, Richard. "Hobbes and Locke on Toleration." In *Thomas Hobbes and Political Theory*, edited by Mary G. Dietz, 153–71. Lawrence: University Press of Kansas, 1990.

Tyacke, Nicholas. *Anti-Calvinists: The Rise of English Arminianism c.1590–1640*. Oxford: Clarendon Press, 1987.

Underdown, David. *Royalist Conspiracy in England, 1649–1660*. New Haven: Yale University Press, 1960.

Underwood, T.L. *Primitivism, Radicalism, and the Lamb's War: The Baptist-Quaker Conflict in Seventeenth-Century England*. Oxford: Oxford University Press, 1997.

Wabuda, Susan. *Preaching during the English Reformation*. Cambridge: Cambridge University Press, 2002.

Walker, William. "Milton's Dualistic Theory of Religious Toleration in *A Treatise of Civil Power, Of Christian Doctrine*, and *Paradise Lost*." *Modern Philology* 99 (2001): 201–30.

Warren, Christopher N. "When Self-Preservation Bids: Approaching Milton, Hobbes, and Dissent." *English Literary Renaissance* 37 (2007): 118–50.

Weddle, Meredith Baldwin. *Walking in the Way of Peace: Quaker Pacifism in the Seventeenth Century*. Oxford: Oxford University Press, 2001.

White, R.S. *Natural Law in English Renaissance Literature*. Cambridge: Cambridge University Press, 1996.

Whitlocke, Bulstrode. *Memorials of the English Affairs*. Vol. 4. Oxford: Oxford University Press, 1853.

Wilcher, Robert. "What Was the King's Book For? The Evolution of 'Eikon Basilike.'" *Yearbook of English Studies* 21 (1991): 218–28.

Woodford, Benjamin. *Perceptions of a Monarchy without a King: Reactions to Oliver Cromwell's Power*. Montreal: McGill-Queen's University Press, 2013.

Woolrych, Austin. *Britain in Revolution*. Oxford: Oxford University Press, 2004.

– "Milton & Cromwell: 'A Short but Scandalous Night of Interruption.'" In *Achievements of the Left Hand: Essays on Milton's Prose*, edited by Michael

Lieb and John Shawcross, 185–218. Amherst: University of Massachusetts Press, 1974.

Worden, Blair. *God's Instruments: Political Conduct in the England of Oliver Cromwell*. Oxford: Oxford University Press, 2012.

– *Literature and Politics in Cromwellian England: John Milton, Andrew Marvell, Marchamont Nedham*. Oxford: Oxford University Press, 2009.

– "Oliver Cromwell and the Sin of Achan." In *Cromwell and the Interregnum: The Essential Readings*, edited by David L. Smith, 37–60. Oxford: Blackwell, 2003.

– *The Rump Parliament 1648–1653*. Cambridge: Cambridge University Press, 1974.

– "Toleration and the Cromwellian Protectorate." In *Persecution and Toleration*, Studies in Church History 21, edited by W.J. Sheils, 199–233. Oxford: Basil Blackwell for the Ecclesiastical History Society, 1984.

Zaller, Robert. *The Discourse of Legitimacy in Early Modern England*. Stanford, CA: Stanford University Press, 2007.

Index